TEACHER'S GUIDE

WE ALL CAN READ:

A RESEARCH-BASED, MULTISENSORY,
STEP-BY-STEP PHONICS PROGRAM
FOR TEACHING ANYONE TO READ AND SPELL.

JAMES E. WILLIAMS

Illustrations by Joy Franklin
Cover photo by Carolyn Lake
Editing by Ellen Williams

Winding River Books

≈

P. O. BOX 8839 / ATLANTA, GEORGIA 31106-0839
404-310-2839
www.weallcanread.com

WE ALL CAN READ: THIRD GRADE THROUGH ADULT EDITION

TEACHER'S GUIDE

Table of Contents

Teacher's Guide
Getting Started In Section One

This program should be taught a *minimum* of thirty minutes a day each day of the school week. The pace at which a student will proceed through this program will be governed by many different variables. There is a tremendous developmental difference between a student in third grade and a student in high school. Even students in the same grade will have a wide and varying set of learning needs. Most students come to third grade already reading while other students in that same grade have not yet learned even the most fundamental aspects of the alphabet. **Proceed at the pace that is appropriate for the student.**

The goal for your student in this first section of the book is for him to learn the sounds of all of the single consonants and the short sounds for the five major vowels and to discover how all of these sounds may be blended smoothly together to form words. In addition consonant blends and consonant teams or digraphs are introduced.

The letters of the English alphabet are divided into two groups: vowels and consonants. The five major vowel letters are *a, e, i, o,* and *u*. All the remaining twenty-one letters of the English alphabet are consonants. The letter *y* can function as either a vowel or consonant, depending upon its position in a word. In *Section One* and *Section Two* the letter *y* will function only as a consonant. (Later in the program we will discover in what situations this letter functions as a vowel.)

On most pages in *Section One* the instructional procedure is identical. First students will read every word or letter combination in a lesson. Next the teacher will dictate every word or letter combination found in each lesson. Students should learn to listen to the individual sounds within each dictated word and associate a letter or group of letters to represent each of the sounds within the word in order to spell it correctly.

Most pages of *Sections One* and *Section Two* are divided into two parts: real words and nonsense words. Nonsense words are essential to use in teaching phonics to older students and adults. Many students have memorized hundreds or even thousands of words and yet have little or no knowledge of phonics. No purpose is served by having them call out or spell words they long ago have memorized; in fact, older students who are asked to read and spell one-syllable words they already know will often prematurely conclude that this phonics program is too easy for them. **For this reason it is strongly recommended that teachers use only the nonsense words from each page in *Sections One* and *Two* of the book to teach students in sixth grade through high school and also for adults no longer in school. The two exceptions to this recommendation for students in the sixth grade and beyond would be in the instance where students in these grades read and spell less than eighty percent of the real words from any given page correctly or in the instance where students are learning English as a second language. (See page 143 to view the exact sequence of lessons to use with students beyond fifth grade.)**

Teaching with nonsense words forces a student to look at the individual letters within words and to associate sounds with those letters. Since many older students and adults have already developed a sight reading vocabulary, the best way and in many instances the only way to teach them phonics is by presenting them with words they have never before seen. This rationale for using nonsense words to teach decoding for older students is equally compelling for teaching spelling. A student will often know how to spell a word without any knowledge of the phonetic relationship of the sounds and letters in a given word. When a student is asked to spell a nonsense word, he must rely upon his ability to isolate the individual sounds he hears within the pronounced word and his knowledge of the letters that represent those sounds.

It is vital to be precise when teaching the sounds of all letters but of particular importance when teaching the short sounds for each of the five major vowels. Take as long as is necessary in these initial exercises. These sounds presented in *Section One* are the building blocks for the pronunciation of the entire English language, and thus these pages constitute the heart of the phonics program for teaching reading and spelling.

What follows is a page-by-page *Teacher's Guide* for every lesson in the book *We All Can Read*. Each lesson in the *Teacher's Guide* is subdivided into three parts that are organized under the headings *Supplemental Materials*, *Information Teacher Presents or Reviews on this Page*, and *Student Exercises*.

The information under *Supplemental Materials* tells the teacher what materials correlated to the core book *We All Can Read* are to be used in conjunction with any given page in the book. The information under *Information Teacher Presents or Reviews on this Page* provides the teacher with new information to be presented or information to review with students on a given page. The information under *Student Exercises* provides the teacher with specific activities for students to perform in order for them to consolidate and review skills for that particular lesson.

It is important to stress that the core book is designed as a stand-alone program; teachers, parents, tutors, and students, however, often find additional support materials helpful to them in implementing or learning the program. The supplemental materials that are published as an aid to teachers, parents, tutors, and students working in the core book consist of the following items:

1. **VHS Video Edition / DVD Video Edition** accompanies the entire book lesson-by-lesson
2. **Video CD Edition (no Internet required)** accompanies the entire book lesson-by-lesson
3. **Online Program** combines video, audio, and text to make every lesson in the program available through the Internet and enables students to work independently
4. **Supplemental Reader** provides additional oral reading practice material using decodable text
5. **Flashcard Review Kit** contains three flashcard sets totaling 280 flashcards
6. **Wall Chart Set** contains sixteen posters correlated to specific units in the core book
7. **Blackline Masters** is a book that provides reproducible word lists for students to take home
8. **Phonics Game** provides review and practice of the skills developed in a way that is fun and interactive for students

Ordering information for these materials is found at **www.weallcanread.com**.

As mentioned in the above paragraph, the entire reading program is also published in a VHS Video Edition, DVD Video Edition, a CD Video Edition, and an Online Edition; these supplemental editions coupled with the core book make the program immediately accessible to both instructors and students. (See pages XIII-XIV from the core book for more information regarding the video and online editions.) Teachers who have never taught phonics before have used the online and video programs with great success. By watching and/or listening to these program editions, a teacher who has never taught phonics before can learn how to introduce the material to students. **Many teachers never learned phonics as young children because the subject was not taught**

to them in the schools they attended. Not only did many of these individuals fail to receive phonics instruction as young children, many of them did not receive phonics instruction at any point in their schooling up to and including the education courses taken in college to receive their teaching certification. Many teachers are reluctant to acknowledge the fact that they do not have an adequate background in phonics; instead they simply avoid teaching the subject. This behavior while understandable is unfortunate because research is very clear regarding the fact that anyone behind in reading must receive intensive, systematic phonics instruction if he is ever likely to have the opportunity to read at an independent level.

The video and online editions can be used as the primary instructional vehicle in the instance where a teacher does not have an adequate background in phonics and is unable to present the material on his own. Many teachers, parents, and tutors have successfully used these materials to teach themselves phonics while simultaneously presenting this information to their students. The video and online editions are also intended to allow mature students to work independently through the program or to provide makeup lessons or independent review from any lesson within the book.

The Supplemental Reader provides additional oral reading practice using decodable text. Decodable text primarily contains words made up of only the letters and letter teams taught up to any given point in the program. Students are not presented with words that contain phonic elements that have not yet been taught. Requiring students to read orally from text that contains only those phonetic principles already introduced is a critical element to help students become fluent readers. A student must be given the opportunity to practice word recognition skills using decodable text until he is able to read accurately and fluently. Accuracy and fluency are both critical factors in reading comprehension. *The Supplemental Reader* **is not intended to serve as a substitute for the core book.** *The Supplemental Reader* is intended to provide additional reading practice to augment instruction from the core book. **A complete audio edition of** *The Supplemental Reader* **is published in our online program. Students can follow along in the book and listen as every page from** *The Supplemental Reader* **is read aloud.**

The **Flashcard Review Kit** consists of three separate yet interrelated flashcard sets designed to provide a comprehensive and concise review of the course for use at the beginning of each instructional period. Begin each instructional period with a review of these three flashcard decks. Introduce the flashcards indicated in the *Teacher's Guide* when you reach the designated page in the core book *We All Can Read*. Continue to add new flashcards, and review previously introduced flashcards throughout the entire program. These flashcards provide a succinct and comprehensive way to review all the phonic elements already introduced up to any given point in the program.

The **Wall Chart Set** contains sixteen 16" by 22" posters and is designed to organize and summarize key information which students must learn. By visually displaying this information on classroom walls, students have ready access to key concepts on a need-to-know basis. Also because the program is cumulative in nature, the posters provide a visual organization of the information presented in the program in a sequential manner. **Visual aids help facilitate learning and retention.**

Blackline Masters is a book that provides a series of reproducible word lists that may be sent home so that parents may participate in their child's learning. These word lists also provide a way to document a student's progress in the program.

Teacher's Guide

The We All Can Read Phonics Game is designed to provide review and practice of the phonics skills developed in a fun and interactive way. Thirty-two individual card decks along with a game board and playing pieces compose the game set. Each game is correlated to a particular unit from the core book *We All Can Read*.

The **Informal Student Assessment Procedure and Chart,** located on pages 103-116 of this book, organizes all of the information presented in this program into a sequential checklist of skills teachers present as they proceed lesson-by-lesson through the entire program. This assessment chart also provides a teacher with a way to document a student's progress. In addition the **Formal Student Accuracy and Fluency Assessment Procedure and Chart** on page 101 presents a formal oral reading assessment procedure to use to measure a student's ability to read fluently and accurately.

Teaching Note – Dry-erase marker board is a wonderful tool to use with students when dictating words for spelling. Students love to write on marker board, and teachers find it much easier to monitor the spelling of an entire class using marker board. Students are taught to hold up their marker boards to show the teacher their spelling of the just dictated word. With one glance a teacher can check the spelling of an entire classroom rather than needing to walk to each student's desk individually. Students seem to find writing on a marker board to be less intimidating psychologically than writing on paper. A misspelled word can be easily erased, and the activity of spelling takes on the characteristics of a word game. Dry-erase marker boards may be purchased at office supply stores or many other kinds of retail outlets as well.

Pacing

Once students begin in the book, the pace of instruction is completely determined by the student's ability to assimilate the information being presented. Because this program is sequential in nature, it is crucial to spend as much time as is necessary on each lesson to be sure that students have learned the skills developed in that lesson. But it is as equally important not to spend more time than is necessary on a given lesson. Most students beyond the second grade know at least some of the information in the beginning portion of this book, and many students know a majority of the information that is presented in *Section One*. A critical element to the success of teaching this program is to calibrate the pace of instruction so as to meet the needs of the students. Pacing is by far the most difficult issue for many teachers to resolve as they proceed through their first instructional cycle. If a teacher goes too fast for the learning level of the students in the class, the students will gradually fall behind and eventually lose interest in the program. If a teacher goes too slowly for the learning level of the students in class, the students will become increasingly fidgety, frustrated, and bored.

In some instances high school teachers will begin this program only to conclude in a short period of time that the program is not advanced enough for their students' needs; this situation is virtually never the case when high school students are reading below an independent reading level. Often when high school students lose interest in the program, the difficulty is that the teacher has spent far too long in *Section One* asking students to read and spell both the real words and nonsense words in each lesson of *Section One*. Most high school students, even students reading several grade levels behind, will not be challenged by the real words contained in *Section One* and *Section Two* of the book. Therefore, as previously stated, students in sixth grade through high school and adults no longer in school should not use the real words found in *Section One* and *Section Two* of the book for oral reading practice. (See page 143 for the exact sequence of lessons to use with students beyond fifth grade.) For spelling practice have these same students spell only nonsense words until page 74. Starting on page 74 nonsense words are no longer used for dictation.

If students can read and spell both the nonsense and real words on any given page of this book with an eighty percent or higher degree of accuracy, then those students have demonstrated that they are ready to move on to the next lesson. Later in the program students will not only need to be able to read and spell the words with accuracy but also be able to mark the words in each lesson with an eighty percent or higher degree of accuracy. (This marking system will be explained in great detail as we proceed through the program.) As the teacher has an opportunity to work with students in this program, he will gradually develop a feel for the pace at which to deliver the instruction.

Divergence of Reading Skills Among Students in the Same Class

One common issue that classroom teachers often face is how to meet the needs of all students in a class when there is a large gap between reading skill levels of individual students within the same class. This issue of divergence in reading skills among students in the same class is a very common situation and one that unfortunately offers no easy solution. **Grouping students together in terms of their reading skills is almost always advantageous unless the chronological ages of the students becomes too diverse.**

If it is not possible to group students together into homogenous reading classes, then several other suggestions present themselves. Divide a class into smaller groups. One group can do oral reading practice while another group works in spelling dictation using the video or audio editions of the program that accompany the book. If some students are very far behind the majority of students in the class, they can work independently using the videos, video CDs, or online lessons with earphones. The teacher can monitor their work periodically while still providing instruction to the bulk of the class. Students who miss class can use the videos, video CDs or online lessons to review material missed due to absence. Also consider using some of the more advanced students in class to serve as reading tutors with other students in class who are struggling. These student-tutors can monitor their partner's responses during oral reading exercises and spelling dictation and provide feedback and instruction when appropriate. If the classroom teacher has access to a classroom aide or community volunteer, then that individual can be paired with students who require additional individual instruction and review.

Assessment

It is important to measure all students' progress in this program on a weekly basis if at all possible. (See pages 97-116.) Some evaluation can be administered to the entire class at the same time, but some individual monitoring with each student should also occur each week. **Weekly assessment is critical because it provides a teacher with vital feedback regarding how well each student is learning the material as it is being presented.** Weekly assessment enables the teacher to evaluate what adjustments need be made regarding the instructional process. Questions regarding whether or not the most recently introduced lessons have been learned by students are answered by the assessment procedure. Questions regarding whether or not previously introduced lessons need only be reviewed or retaught in their entirety are answered with the feedback from the assessments. Students who require additional practice or intensive remediation are identified. **The assessment feedback will also indicate whether the teacher should slow-down, maintain, or accelerate the current pace of instruction.**

Teacher's Guide
Page-by-Page Instructions for Section One
All lessons are presented in chronological/numerical order. Please do not skip steps!
Page 1
Supplemental Materials
Posters – Display poster titled *The Consonant and Vowel Sounds.*

Information Teacher Presents or Reviews on this Page

Begin on page one by teaching students the sounds of the consonant letters. Have students refer to page one. On this page is found each consonant letter with a picture above it. For instance the letter *b* is located directly under the picture of a bus. The first sound heard in the word *bus* is /b/. **In this book when either a letter or group of letters are located between slanted lines (virgules), the letter or letters located between the slanted lines represent the sound of the letter.** This /b/ sound is the sound which the letter *b* represents. Carefully go through each letter, and determine how well students know the consonant sounds. Explain to your students that if they have difficulty remembering any of the consonants' sounds, they should remember the key word pictured above each letter. The key word for *b*, for example, is *bus*; for *c* the key word is *cat*. After remembering the key word, students must then learn to isolate the first sound heard in the key word in order to determine the sound represented by the given letter.

When teaching the consonant sounds, avoid as much as possible adding the /uh/ sound after the consonant sounds. As an example the sound for *b* is not /buh/; the sound for *b* is /b/. The sound for *c* is not /cuh/; the sound for *c* is /c/. Two consonant letters, however, do require that a slight /uh/ sound be added at the end of their sounds in order to pronounce them correctly. Those two consonant letters are *w* /wuh/, and *y* /yuh/.

The letters *c* and *g* each represent a second sound. Later in the program (pages 132 - 138) students will learn in what situations these two letters will represent their second sounds. Until that point in the program is reached, when students encounter the letters *c* and *g*, the letters *c* and *g* will always represent their primary sounds as indicated on page one. The letter *y* as a vowel is not introduced in this program until page 139; until that page the letter *y* functions exclusively as a consonant. **For teachers who desire more detailed information regarding the formation of the basic consonant sounds, please see pages 92-96 in the *Teacher's Guide*.**

Student Exercises
Lesson 1

Call out the name of all of the letters from this page in an arbitrary order. Ask the student to think of a word that begins with that letter and to make the sound the letter represents. Reverse this process and make a sound representing one of the consonant letters on this page; students call out the name of the letter that represents the sound you have made.

Page 2
Supplemental Materials
Flash Cards – Introduce Card Set A #'s 1-23 / Card Set B # 1 / Card Set C #'s 1-18.

The flashcards are designed as a cumulative review element. Once a letter and its corresponding sound or sounds are taught, that information is then integrated into the flashcard set to be reviewed in an ongoing way. **It is suggested that approximately two-to-five minutes at the beginning of each instructional period be spent in the review of these three flashcard decks.** Students enter this program at all different levels of reading proficiency. Some students do not know any of the sounds of any of the letters in the alphabet. Other students know most if not all of the sounds represented by the various letters in the alphabet. **Some of the information presented on these flashcards is already very well known by the majority of students beyond the second grade.** As an example most students in third grade and beyond already know most of the common sounds represented by the consonant letters. In such an instance it is important not to review endlessly information students already have mastered. If it becomes obvious to you that certain flashcards in one of the three decks contain information that students already know, feel free to retire those cards. **Nothing is gained by reviewing material that students already know very well; in fact, unnecessary review can and will cause students to lose interest in the program and limit instructional momentum.**

Information Teacher Presents or Reviews on this Page

Please note that the following information must be presented to your students prior to having them read and spell from page two.

1. The letter *q* is always followed by the letter *u*. The letter team *qu* is classified as a consonant letter team and represents two sounds blended together. The letter *u* is not considered a vowel when it is part of the consonant team *qu*. **In English we use the consonant letter team *qu* to represent the sounds /kw/; the letters *k* and *w* are almost never used for this purpose in spelling words.** <u>qu</u> = /kw/ as in <u>qu</u>ilt

2. Students underline all consonant teams found in words during dictation.

3. The letter x represents two sounds blended together. x = /ks/ as in *box* (The letter x represents a different sound when it comes before the vowel. Only a small number of words contain the letter x where it comes before the vowel, and almost all of these words are uncommon words; thus this second sound for the letter *x* is not taught in this program.)

4. The letters *c* and *k* form a consonant team. **The letter team *ck* is never used at the beginning of a word and must come directly after a short vowel**: <u>ck</u> = /k/ as in ro<u>ck</u>

5. The letter *s* represents two sounds: *s* = /s/ as in sun and <u>s</u> = /z/ as in no<u>se</u>. Words which begin with the sound /z/ are always spelled with the letter *z*, never the letter *s*. **Students double underline a letter when it represents its second sound.**

Student Exercises
Lesson 2

Have students read page two in its entirety beginning from row one through row thirteen. Students should be able to make the sound represented by each letter/letter team in each row.

Lesson 3 (Quiz 1)

After students have gone through all thirteen rows, reverse the process. The teacher makes the consonant sounds represented by the letters found in all thirteen rows, and the students write the letters that represent those sounds. **Students use lower case only.** Repeat this procedure as many times as is necessary until it is obvious students have mastered the relationship of the consonant letters and their corresponding sounds. The quiz corresponding to its respective lesson is listed in parenthesis after the lesson number. **Administer the indicated quiz only after all other activities related to that lesson are completed first. Students should demonstrate mastery of the current lesson by scoring eighty percent or higher before proceeding to the next lesson.**

Supplemental Materials
Flash Cards – Introduce Card Set A # 24 / Card Set C # 19. Review all cards previously introduced.

Information Teacher Presents or Reviews on this Page
The short *a* sound is introduced. The key word for short *a* is the word *apple*. The short *a* sound is the first sound you must make to say the word *apple*.

Student Exercises
Lesson 4 / Lesson 6
Students read the letter combinations in these lessons. (See the discussion of *Guided Oral Reading Practice* that directly follows.)
Lesson 5 (Quiz 2) / Lesson 7 (Quiz 3)
The teacher dictates the sounds represented by the letter combinations from these lessons, and students write the letters that represent the sounds made by the teacher.

Guided and Repeated Oral Reading Practice
Use both nonsense words and real words for oral reading practice for students through the fifth grade. **Use only the nonsense words for oral reading practice for students in the sixth grade, middle school, high school, and beyond. The two exceptions to this recommendation for sixth grade students and beyond would be in the instance where students in these grades read and spell correctly less than eighty percent of the real words on any given page or in the instance where students are learning English as a second language.** Upon reaching *Section Three* on page 108 in the core book nonsense words are no longer used and all students read from the same word lists.

Reading rests upon a hierarchy of skill development. Students must become capable of reading words both accurately and fluently. *Guided and Repeated Oral Reading Practice*, therefore, consists of two distinct activities.

Students read the words in each lesson accurately. The teacher must carefully monitor each oral reading exercise to make sure students accurately read the words on the page. If a student misreads a word, the teacher should immediately intervene by telling the student to read the word again, and if necessary the teacher should provide step-by-step instructions to the student in sounding out the word. (See *Procedure to Follow When Sounding Out an Unknown Word* on pages 10 - 11.)

Students read the words in each lesson fluently. The ability to read words accurately is a necessary skill that must be mastered by all emerging readers and a skill whose acquisition is justifiably celebrated both by teacher and student alike. But reading words accurately is not enough; a student must also be able to read fluently. Fluency is an essential skill strand that has often been neglected in reading instruction; yet research overwhelmingly and consistently emphasizes the relationship between reading fluency and comprehension. All too often teachers conclude that once students are able to read with accuracy, they will be able to read fluently. Research on the other hand has established the fact that the transference between decoding accuracy and reading fluency is not automatic. Fluency is a skill that can and must be taught, and students who receive fluency training experience marked improvement in their ability to read with accuracy, fluency, and understanding. Students who read and then repeatedly reread text while receiving guidance and feedback become better readers. Explicit instruction in fluency aids struggling readers of all ages from elementary grades through the middle school and high school grades and adults as well. Without the ability to recognize text automatically, the student's primary focus while reading is on decoding words instead of comprehending the meaning that the flow of words on the page conveys. Fluency is the bridge that connects a student's ability to decode words accurately with the ability of that student to read with understanding. For this reason fluency activities are organically interwoven into virtually every page within this book.

The best way to develop reading fluency is to provide guidance and feedback to students as they read the same text repeatedly.

Guided and Repeated Oral Reading Practice consists of the following activities:

1. **The teacher models fluent reading for the students.** The teacher reads the words in the lesson row-by-row while students listen and silently follow along with the text in the book. The teacher reads each word two times. (For stories read each paragraph twice.)

2. **Students echo the teacher as he reads the words from each row of words in the lesson or each paragraph within a story.** The teacher reads out loud one row of words in the lesson or each paragraph within the story; the students then read out loud that row of words or paragraph. The teacher repeats this procedure twice with each row; for lessons with stories the teacher repeats this procedure with each paragraph within a story.

3. **The teacher and students do choral or unison reading.** The teacher along with the entire class reads together the words from each row of words in the lesson or each paragraph in the story.

4. (Optional) **Students read from the lesson while listening to the audio file that accompanies each fluency lesson.** The student listens to the audio file while silently following along with the text in the book. The student uses his finger and points at each word as he hears that word pronounced. The student then replays the audio file and reads aloud along with the audio file.

5. (Optional) **Students are paired together as partners.** Whenever possible pair strong readers with less fluent partners. The stronger partner models fluent reading in one row and then the other partner reads the same row. The stronger reader provides feedback and when necessary helps the other reader sound out and read the words correctly and with increasing fluency. It is also possible to have two readers of approximately equal skill levels partner together. These partner readers can practice rereading text after having received teacher-guided instruction with that same text.

Most students develop accuracy and fluency skills over time; it takes practice and exposure to print. Students perform repeated readings of the words in each fluency lesson until they are able to read the words effortlessly and without conscious effort spent in decoding or sounding out the words. The fluency activities listed above can be adjusted to meet the individual needs of students. Some students require more repetition in oral reading than do others. Adjust these fluency activities to the frequency rate that is appropriate for your students' needs. Please be aware that these activities are not necessarily all done on the same day and can instead be performed over several days duration.

Guided and Repeated Oral Reading Practice Using Decodable Text

Research shows that the single best instructional technique for developing reading fluency is to provide guided oral reading practice for students using *decodable text*. *Decodable text* is text that is composed of words that primarily contain only those phonetic elements that have been previously introduced. Words containing phonic elements not yet taught in this program are not included in the text. As an example if the consonant team *ch* has not yet been introduced in the program, then no word in the text will contain the *ch* team until that consonant team is formally presented in the program. All of the word lists and sentences and stories in this book have been carefully developed to include only those phonetic elements that have been taught up to the particular point currently reached in the program. Some common sight words are used on the pages with sentences and stories. In addition a supplemental companion book, *The Supplemental Reader*, has been published to provide additional oral reading practice activities using decodable text. The sentences and stories contained in *The Supplemental Reader* are carefully correlated to follow the order in which phonic elements are presented in this core book. The reading selections in *The Reader* have been carefully developed to insure that the student will encounter only those words that contain phonetic elements the student has already been taught. Ordering information is found at the back of this book for *The Supplemental Reader*. To hear guided oral reading exercises modeled, go to **www.weallcanread.com** and select the page titled *Online Instruction*.

Page 4
Supplemental Materials
Flash Cards – Review all cards previously introduced.
The Reader – Read pages 1-2 (1st Ed.) or pages 1-4 (2nd. Ed.) on completing page 4.

Information Teacher Presents or Reviews on this Page
Tell your students that for the first time on page four they encounter words under two headings: *Nonsense Words* and *Real Words*. Explain to them that a nonsense word as its name implies is a made-up word that has no meaning. Tell them that nonsense words are used in this book to teach phonics because many students have already memorized many if not most of the real words contained in the words listed under the heading *Real Words*. Nonsense words are used in the first two sections of the book to teach phonics because students cannot read and spell these nonsense words from memory. Students must know the sounds represented by the letters in these words in order to read them correctly, and they must also know how to associate the correct letters with the sounds heard in a nonsense word in order to spell the nonsense word correctly during spelling dictation. Teach students the procedure for sounding out words that is listed in the section that immediately follows. Present students with words on the board, and ask them to demonstrate the correct way to sound out the words letter by letter. Use nonsense words chosen from page four for students to demonstrate the correct procedure to use when sounding out unknown words.

Sounding Out Words
Beginning on this page, students encounter nonsense words and real words. If a student encounters a word that he does not know how to decode, he must sound out the word. Sounding out a word refers to the process of decoding a word by identifying the sounds of each individual letter in the word and then blending those sounds together. A student sounds out a word when he does not know the identity of the word. There is a specific sequence of steps to follow when using this sounding-out procedure. When a student is sounding out a word, have him perform the following steps, and insist that this sequence of activities be systematically followed.

Procedure To Follow When Sounding Out an Unknown Word:
Step One: Always begin by identifying the vowel sound. (See paragraph below box.)
Step Two: After accurately identifying the vowel sound, identify the consonant sound that immediately follows the vowel sound.
Step Three: Blend together the vowel sound with the following consonant sound.

Step Four:	If two consonants follow the vowel and do not join to together to form a consonant team, isolate the vowel sound and the first consonant that follows the vowel. Blend those two sounds together. Next isolate the sound of the second consonant following the vowel. Blend the sound of the vowel and the first consonant with the sound of the second consonant.
Step Five:	After the vowel sound and all consonant sounds found after the vowel have been blended together, have the student identify the sound of the consonant letter that comes immediately before the vowel.
Step Six:	Blend together the consonant sound with the sound of the vowel and the consonant letter or letters that come after the vowel.
Step Seven:	If two or three consonant letters come before the vowel and do not join together to form a team, start with the consonant closest to the vowel. Identify that consonant's sound and blend it with the sound of the vowel and the consonant letters that follow the vowel. Next isolate the sound of the next adjacent consonant letter. Blend that letter's sound with the sound of the rest of the word that has already been decoded. If a third consonant occurs before the vowel, isolate that letter's sound last and then blend its sound with the rest of the word.

Teach students always to begin sounding out one-syllable words by identifying the sound of the vowel within the syllable first. Researchers have discovered that syllables can be subdivided into two component parts. *Onsets* are that part of the syllable that consist of whatever consonants occur before the vowel; *rhymes* are that part of the syllable containing the vowel and whatever consonants follow the vowel. Researchers have further identified the fact that students are more easily able to decode a word by being taught to isolate the onsets and rhymes within words. Thus by teaching students to start the decoding process by isolating the sound of the vowel and any subsequent consonants which follow the vowel, you are in effect teaching students to subdivide a syllable into its most basic component parts.

When sounding out a word, your student is being asked to perform two tasks simultaneously: 1) to associate a specific sound with a specific letter and 2) to blend smoothly one sound to another. Either of these two skills can individually be difficult for some. Blending for someone to whom this concept is foreign can be particularly challenging. However with persistence your student will learn to perform both of these skills automatically.

Student Exercises
Lesson 8 / Lesson 10
Students read the words in these lessons. (See the discussion of *Guided Oral Reading Practice* on pages 8 - 10.)
Lesson 9 (Quiz 4) / Lesson 11 (Quiz 5)
The teacher dictates the words from these lessons. (See information under *Spelling Dictation* that immediately follows.)

Spelling Dictation
Until page 74 in the core book use both nonsense and real words for spelling dictation for students through the fifth grade. Until page 74 use only nonsense words for spelling dictation for students in the sixth grade, middle school, high school, and adults. The two exceptions to this recommendation for sixth grade students through adults would be in the instance where students in these grades read and spell

correctly less than eighty percent of the real words on this page or in the instance where students are learning English as a second language. Upon reaching page seventy-four in this book, nonsense words are no longer used for dictation for any students, regardless of their grade or age. This information will be explained in further detail in this *Teacher's Guide* when students reach page 74.

Decoding words accurately, reading words fluently, and spelling words correctly are the three key skill strands developed in this phonics program. English is a phonetic language because of the fact that our letters each represent a specific sound or in some instances more than one sound. The decoding process consists of associating sounds with the already-known letters in the word and blending those sounds together to identify a word. The activity of spelling reverses this process. The identity of the word is already known; it is the spelling of the word that must be discovered. **The student first identifies the number of sounds he hears in the dictated word and then tracks or represents those sounds by writing the letters of the alphabet which represent the various individual sounds he has identified within the dictated word.** Spelling dictation is an intrinsic part of this phonics program; half of the instructional activity in this program consists of dictating the words from each lesson in the book to students. **A major purpose in dictation is to establish for the student the direct and consistent relationship in English between letters and their sounds.**

Note for dictation: **If at all possible, have your weakest readers sit closest to you.** Students should be able to see clearly the teacher's lip movements as each word is pronounced. Dictate the words as clearly as is possible. Be sure the students in the back of the room are able to hear you. One cannot spell correctly what one has not heard accurately. When doing dictation, the teacher should not hesitate to exaggerate the individual sounds within the word when it seems helpful.

Be sure to insist from the beginning that students properly form their letters. (Refer to the letter formation charts *How to Form Lower and Upper Case Letters* found on pages 95 – 96 if students need help in correctly writing any of the lower or upper-case letters.) **When dictating words for spelling, insist that students use only lower-case letters unless there is a specific reason for them to use an upper-case letter.** Many students will arbitrarily use lower or upper case letters in the same word. This pattern indicates a lack of understanding of the difference between lower and upper case letters. Most individuals who have experienced a lifetime of difficulty in learning to read and write believe the language is not learnable because it is arbitrary. And the corollary to the belief that something is arbitrary is that it is also, therefore, unfair. **Stress from the very beginning that the English language is predictable, that there exists an underlying set of rules, and that by systematically learning and applying these rules, virtually anyone can learn to read and to spell successfully.**

Dictation Procedure for *Section One*

1. The teacher pronounces the word two times. **"The word is *jam, jam.*"** If necessary, the teacher should exaggerate the pronunciation of the individual sounds in the word in order for the more challenged students to be able to hear those individual sounds.
2. The teacher identifies the number of sounds contained in the word and makes those sounds. The teacher says, **"three sounds (and pronounces them slowly and clearly) - /j/, /a/** (short a sound), **/m/."**
3. Students write the letters in the word on dry-erase marker board or on practice paper as they hear each individual sound in the word pronounced by the teacher.

---

4. The teacher pronounces the word a final time. The teacher says, **"jam."**
5. Students hold up their marker boards for the teacher to see. If the teacher sees a student has misspelled the word, the teacher will say to the student, **"Think about it."** The teacher will not tell the student how to spell the word but will instead pronounce the word again and exaggerate whatever element in the word the student has misspelled. Even if the student continues to misspell the word, the teacher does not tell the student the correct spelling of the word at this point.
6. The teacher asks students to say the word. The teacher says, **"Say the word."**
7. Students say, *"jam."*
8. The teacher asks how many sounds are in the word. The teacher asks, **"How many sounds?"**
9. Students identify the number of sounds in the word. Students reply, **"three."**
10. The teacher asks for the first sound in the word *jam*. The teacher asks, **"first sound?"** Students do not say the name of the letter *j* but instead make the sound, **"/j/."** The teacher writes the letter *j* on the board.
11. The teacher asks for second sound in the word *jam*. "The teacher asks, **"second sound?"** Students do not call out the name of the letter *a* but instead make the sound, **"/a/"** (short *a* sound). The teacher writes the letter *a* on the board.
12. The teacher asks for the third sound in the word *jam*. "The teacher asks, **"third sound?"** Students do not call out the name of the letter *m* but instead make the sound, **"/m/."** The teacher writes the letter *m* on the board.
13. Students check to make sure they have spelled the word correctly and make any changes in their spelling of the word at this time. If a word contains the letter teams *qu* or *ck*, those letter teams are underlined at this point. (Beginning on page 74 additional consonant teams are introduced.) If a word contains the letter *s* where *s* represents its second sound, the letter *s* is double underlined at this time.

During dictation exercises students will often see how other students are spelling the dictated words. Some students will not always spell the dictated words correctly, and other students will make note of that fact. When this occurrence happens and when it is appropriate for a student to comment on the spelling of another student, teach your students to use a specific sentence to alert another student to the fact that he has misspelled a word. The sentence is, *Think about it.* By instructing your students to use this sentence, students are able to indicate to one another that an error has been made without hurting the other student's feelings. As indicated in step five in the box titled *Dictation Procedure* for *Section One*, the sentence, *Think about it*, is an excellent sentence for teachers to use to indicate to a student that he has misspelled a word.

Multisensory Phonics
Visual, Kinesthetic, and Auditory Activities Are Interwoven In the Dictation Process
In the *Dictation Procedure for Section One* listed above, the teacher asks students to spell the word *jam*. The teacher makes the sound /j/. The student writes the letter *j* on practice paper or on a marker board as he simultaneously hears the sound that the letter *j* represents pronounced by the teacher. The teacher makes the sound /a/ (short a sound). The student writes the letter *a* on practice paper or on a marker board as he simultaneously hears the sound that the letter *a* represents pronounced by the teacher. The teacher makes the sound /m/. The student writes the letter *m* on practice paper or on a marker board as he simultaneously hears the sound the letter *m* represents pronounced by the teacher. **Kinesthetic and auditory reinforcement occur when students form the individual letters as the sounds those letters represent are uttered by the teacher.**

Teacher's Guide

In the second half of the dictation process starting with step six, the reverse procedure is introduced to the dictation process. Students have already spelled the word; **now students will segment the individual sounds in the word.** The teacher asks the students to make the first sound in the word *jam*. As the students make the sound /j/, the teacher writes the letter *j* on the board. The teacher asks for the second sound in the word *jam*, and the students make the sound /a/ (short a sound). As the students make the sound /a/, the teacher writes the letter *a* on the board. The teacher asks for the third sound in the word *jam*, and the students make the sound /m/. As students make the sound /m/, the teacher writes the letter *m* on the board. **Visual and auditory reinforcement occur when students see the letters written on the board by the teacher as the students simultaneously make the sounds represented by those letters.**

Please Note the Following Additional Information Regarding Dictation

Most of the words contained in *Section One* of the book can be dictated without any special instructions from the teacher to the student; however, there are four elements within some of these words that require additional attention. Before dictating a word to students, the teacher must scan the word to determine if the word contains any one of the following four elements:

1. Does the word contain the letter team *qu* or *ck*?
2. Does the word contain the sound /k/ at the beginning of the word?
3. Does the word end in the letter *x*?
4. Does the letter *s* represent its second sound in the word?

If any one of these four elements are present within a word, then the teacher must somewhat modify the dictation procedure in order to accommodate these four specific elements. Please refer to the boxes that immediately follow in order to determine the correct procedure to follow in dictating words containing these elements.

Dictating Words Which Contain the Consonant Team *qu* or *ck*

In English we almost always use the consonant letter team *qu* to represent the sounds /kw/; the letters *k* and *w* are not used for this purpose. **Therefore in both real and nonsense words when students hear the sounds /kw/ within a word, they must use the consonant team *qu* to represent those two sounds.** Because the consonant team *qu* represents the two sounds /kw/ blended together, students must count two sounds when accounting for the number of sounds the *qu* team represents. As an example if you dictate the word *quit* and then ask your students how many sounds are in the word *quit*, the correct answer is that the word *quit* contains four separate sounds – /k/, /w/, /i/ (short i sound) and /t/. The consonant team *ck* always follows directly after a short vowel sound and represents a single sound. **When a nonsense word is dictated which ends in a short vowel sound followed by the sound /k/, tell students always to use the *ck* team to represent the sound /k/.**

Dictation Procedure for Words that Contain the Consonant Teams *qu* or *ck*

1. The teacher pronounces the word two times. **"The word is *quit, quit.*"** (This same principle applies with words that contain the consonant team *ck*.) **Students are not told that the word contains a consonant team.** Students have already been told to use the consonant team *qu* to represent the sounds /kw/ in both nonsense and real words. Students have also been told to use the team *ck* to represent the /k/ sound when that sound follows directly after a short vowel in all nonsense words. Students are never given information regarding the correct spelling of dictated words that they can deduce by applying the spelling rules they have thus far been taught.

---

2. The teacher identifies the number of sounds contained in the word and makes those sounds. The teacher says, **"four sounds (and pronounces them slowly and clearly) –first two sounds /kw/, /i/** (short i sound), **/t/."** (If a word contains the *ck* team, the two letter team *ck* represents only one sound.)

3. Students write the letters in the word on dry-erase marker board or on practice paper as they hear each sound within the word pronounced by the teacher.

4. The teacher pronounces the word a final time. The teacher says, **"quit."**

5. Students hold up their marker boards for the teacher to see. If the teacher sees a student has misspelled the word, the teacher will say to the student, **"Think about it."** The teacher will not tell the student how to spell the word but will instead pronounce the word again and exaggerate whatever element in the word the student has misspelled. Even if the student continues to misspell the word, the teacher does not tell the student the correct spelling of the word at this point.

6. The teacher asks students to say the word. The teacher says, **"Say the word."**

7. Students say, *"quit."*

8. The teacher asks how many sounds are in the word. The teacher asks, **"How many sounds?"**

9. Students identify the number of sounds in the word. Students reply, **"four."**

10. The teacher asks for the first two sounds in the word *quit*. The teacher asks, **"first two sounds?"** Students do not say the name of the letter team *qu* but instead make the sounds, **"/kw/."** The teacher writes the letter team *qu* on the board.

11. The teacher asks for third sound in the word *quit*. "The teacher asks, **"third sound?"** Students do not call out the name of the letter *i* but instead make the sound, **"/i/"** (short i sound). The teacher writes the letter *i* on the board.

12. The teacher asks for the fourth sound in the word *quit*. "The teacher asks, **"fourth sound?"** Students do not call out the name of the letter *t* but instead make the sound, **"/t/."** The teacher writes the letter *t* on the board.

13. Students check to make sure they have spelled the word correctly and make any changes in their spelling of the word at this time. Because the word contains the letter team *qu*, that letter team is underlined at this point. The letter team *ck* is also underlined at this point. (Beginning on page 74 additional consonant teams are introduced.) If a word contains the letter *s* where *s* represents its second sound, the letter *s* is double underlined at this time.

Dictating Words that Begin with the Sound /k/

The sound /k/ may be represented in three different ways, *c*, *k*, and *ck*. **The *ck* team is used to represent the /k/ sound when the sound /k/ immediately follows after a short vowel.** (All of the vowels in *Section One* of the book are short vowels.) **When dictating a nonsense word containing the sound /k/ as the first sound in the word, tell students which letter you want them to use.** As an example, if you dictate the word *cug*, tell students to use the letter *c* to represent the sound /k/. If you dictate the word *keb*, tell students to use the letter *k* to represent the sound /k/. It is usually not necessary to tell students whether to use *c* or *k* when spelling real words as most students are familiar with the spelling of these common words. Upon reaching page 27 in the core book, students learn the rule governing whether to use the letter *c* or the letter *k* in spelling a word beginning with the /k/ sound. Until page 27 you must tell your students which of those two letters to use when the /k/ sound is the first sound in a nonsense word; upon reaching page 27, the student is no longer told which letter to use and instead must learn to apply the rule taught on page 27 to determine whether to spell the word with *c* or *k*.

Teacher's Guide
Dictation Procedure for Words that Begin with the Sound /k/

1. The teacher pronounces the word two times. **"The word is *kiv, kiv*."**
2. The teacher identifies the number of sounds contained in the word and makes those sounds. The teacher says, **"This word begins with the letter *k* and has three sounds (and pronounces them slowly and clearly) – /k/, /i/** (short i sound), **/v/."**
3. Students write the letters in the word on dry-erase marker board or on practice paper as they hear each individual sound within the word pronounced by the teacher.
4. The teacher pronounces the word a final time. The teacher says, **"*kiv*."**
5. Students hold up their marker boards for the teacher to see. If the teacher sees a student has misspelled the word, the teacher will say to the student, **"Think about it."** The teacher will not tell the student how to spell the word but will instead pronounce the word again and exaggerate whatever element in the word the student has misspelled. Even if the student continues to misspell the word, the teacher does not tell the student the correct spelling of the word at this point.
6. The teacher asks students to say the word. The teacher says, **"Say the word."**
7. Students say, **"*kiv*."**
8. The teacher asks how many sounds are in the word. The teacher asks, **"How many sounds?"**
9. Students identify the number of sounds in the word. Students reply, **"three."**
10. The teacher asks for the first sound in the word *kiv*. The teacher asks, **"first sound?"** Students do not say the name of the letter *k* but instead make the sound, **"/k/."** The teacher writes the letter *k* on the board.
11. The teacher asks for second sound in the word *kiv*. "The teacher asks, **"second sound?"** Students do not call out the name of the letter *i* but instead make the sound, **"/i/"** (short i sound). The teacher writes the letter *i* on the board.
12. The teacher asks for the third sound in the word *kiv*. "The teacher asks, **"third sound?"** Students do not call out the name of the letter *v* but instead make the sound, **"/v/."** The teacher writes the letter *v* on the board.
13. Students check to make sure they have spelled the word correctly and make any changes in their spelling of the word at this time. If a word contains the letter teams *qu* or *ck*, those letter teams are underlined at this point. (Beginning on page 74 additional consonant teams are introduced.) If a word contains the letter *s* where *s* represents its second sound, the letter *s* is double underlined at this time.

Dictating Words that End In the Letter *x*

When dictating a three letter word which contains a short vowel sound immediately followed by the letter *x*, tell your students that the word which you are about to dictate contains three letters. Also note that the letter *x* represents two sounds blended together: /ks/. Therefore when you ask your students to count the number of sounds heard within a dictated word that contains the letter *x*, students must count two sounds when accounting for the sounds the letter *x* represents. As an example if you dictate the word *box* and then ask your students how many sounds are in the word *box*, the correct answer is the word *box* contains four sounds- /b/, /o/, /k/ and /s/.

Dictation Procedure for Words that Contain the Letter *x*

1. The teacher pronounces the word two times. **"The word is *box, box*."**
2. The teacher identifies the number of sounds contained in the word and makes those sounds. The teacher says, **"This word has three letters but contains four sounds (and pronounces them slowly and clearly) - /b/, /o/** (short o sound), **third and fourth sounds /ks/."**

16

3. Students write the letters in the word on dry-erase marker board or on practice paper as they hear each individual sound within the word pronounced by the teacher.
4. The teacher pronounces the word a final time. The teacher says, ***"box."***
5. Students hold up their marker boards for the teacher to see. If the teacher sees a student has misspelled the word, the teacher will say to the student, **"Think about it."** The teacher will not tell the student how to spell the word but will instead pronounce the word again and exaggerate whatever element in the word the student has misspelled. Even if the student continues to misspell the word, the teacher does not tell the student the correct spelling of the word at this point.
6. The teacher asks students to say the word. The teacher says, **"Say the word."**
7. Students say, ***"box."***
8. The teacher asks how many sounds are in the word. The teacher asks, **"How many sounds?"**
9. Students identify the number of sounds in the word. Students reply, **"four."**
10. The teacher asks for the first sound in the word *box*. The teacher asks, **"first sound?"** Students do not say the name of the letter *b* but instead make the sound, **"/b/."** The teacher writes the letter *b* on the board.
11. The teacher asks for second sound in the word *box*. "The teacher asks, **"second sound?"** Students do not call out the name of the letter *o* but instead make the sound, **"/o/ "** (short *o* sound). The teacher writes the letter *o* on the board.
12. The teacher asks for the final two sounds in the word *box*. The teacher asks, **"third and fourth sounds?"** Students do not call out the name of the letter *x* but instead make the sounds, **"/ks/."** The teacher writes the letter *x* on the board.
13. Students check to make sure they have spelled the word correctly and make any changes in their spelling of the word at this time. If a word contains the letter teams *qu* or *ck*, those letter teams are underlined at this point. (Beginning on page 74 additional consonant teams are introduced.) If a word contains the letter *s* where *s* represents its second sound, the letter *s* is double underlined at this time.

Dictating Nonsense Words that Contain the Letter *s* Representing Its Second Sound
When dictating a **nonsense word** where the letter *s* represents the sound /z/ as in *di<u>s</u>*, the teacher must inform students prior to the time the students spell the word that one of the letters in the word they are about to spell will represent its second sound. **(Do not tell students that one of the letters in a word will represent its second sound when dictating real words where the letter *s* represents its second sound.)** Students must double underline the letter *s* when the letter *s* represents the sound /z/. **Students may only use the letter s to represent the /z/ sound when spelling nonsense words if they are first told by the teacher that one of the letters in the word represents its second sound; otherwise, they must use the letter z.**

Dictation Procedure for Nonsense Words Where the Letter *s* Represents Its Second Sound
1. The teacher pronounces the word two times. **"The word is *di<u>s</u>, di<u>s</u>."**
2. The teacher tells the students that one of the letters in the word will represent its second sound and also identifies the number of sounds contained in the word and makes those sounds. The teacher says, **"One of the letters in this word represents its second sound; the word contains three sounds (and pronounces them slowly and clearly) – /d/, /i/** (short i sound), **/z/."**
3. Students write the letters in the word on dry-erase marker board or on practice paper as they hear each individual sound within the word pronounced by the teacher.

4. The teacher pronounces the word a final time. The teacher says, *"dis̲."*
5. Students hold up their marker boards for the teacher to see. If the teacher sees a student has misspelled the word, the teacher will say to the student, **"Think about it."** The teacher will not tell the student how to spell the word but will instead pronounce the word again and exaggerate whatever element in the word the student has misspelled. Even if the student continues to misspell the word, the teacher does not tell the student the correct spelling of the word at this point.
6. The teacher asks students to say the word. The teacher says, **"Say the word."**
7. Students say, *"dis̲."*
8. The teacher asks how many sounds are in the word. The teacher asks, **"How many sounds?"**
9. Students identify the number of sounds in the word. Students reply, **"three."**
10. The teacher asks for the first sound in the word *dis̲*. The teacher asks, **"first sound?"** Students do not say the name of the letter *d* but instead make the sound, **"/d/."** The teacher writes the letter *d* on the board.
11. The teacher asks for second sound in the word *dis̲*. "The teacher asks, **"second sound?"** Students do not call out the name of the letter *i* but instead make the sound, **"/i/"** (short *i* sound). The teacher writes the letter *i* on the board.
12. The teacher asks for the third sound in the word *dis̲*. "The teacher asks, **"third sound?"** Students do not call out the name of the letter *s* but instead make the sound, **"/z/."** The teacher writes the letter *s* on the board.
13. Students check to make sure they have spelled the word correctly and make any changes in their spelling of the word at this time. Because this word contains the letter *s* where *s* represents its second sound, the letter *s* is double underlined at this time. If a word contains the letter teams *qu* or *ck*, those letter teams are underlined at this point. (Beginning on page 74 additional consonant teams are introduced.)

Page 5
Supplemental Materials

Flash Cards – Introduce Card Set A # 25 / Card Set C # 20. Review all cards previously introduced.

Information Teacher Presents or Reviews on this Page

The short *e* sound is introduced. The key word for short *e* is the word *egg*. The short *e* sound is the first sound you must make to say the word *egg*. In Lessons 12 and 13 the short *e* is followed by a consonant. In Lessons 14 and 15 the short sounds of *a* and *e* are reviewed, and the short sounds of *a* and *e* are followed by a consonant. For Lessons 14 and 15 review with your students the short sounds of *a* and *e*. It is vital to be precise when teaching the sounds of all letters but of particular importance when teaching the short sounds for each of the five vowels. Take as long as is necessary in these initial exercises. These basic sounds are the building blocks for the pronunciation of the entire English language, and thus these pages constitute the heart of the phonics program for teaching reading.

Student Exercises
Lesson 12 / Lesson 14

Students read the letter combinations in these lessons. (See the discussion of *Guided Oral Reading Practice* on pages 8 - 10.)
Lesson 13 (Quiz 6) / Lesson 15 (Quiz 7)
The teacher dictates the sounds represented by the letter combinations from these lessons. (See information under *Spelling Dictation* on pages 11 - 18.)

Teacher's Guide

Page 6
Supplemental Materials
Flash Cards – Review all cards previously introduced.
The Reader – Read pages 3-4 (1ˢᵗ Ed.) or pages 5-8 (2ⁿᵈ. Ed.) on completing page 6.

Information Teacher Presents or Reviews on this Page
This page consists of three and four letter words which all contain the short *e* sound. Review the short *e* sound.

Student Exercises
Lesson 16 / Lesson 18
Students read the words in these lessons. (See the discussion of *Guided Oral Reading Practice* on pages 8 - 10.)
Lesson 17 (Quiz 8) / Lesson 19 (Quiz 9)
The teacher dictates the words in these lessons. (See information under *Spelling Dictation* on pages 11 - 18.)

Page 7
Supplemental Materials
Flash Cards – Review all cards previously introduced.

Information Teacher Presents or Reviews on this Page
This page is a review page with words containing short *a* and *e*. Review the sounds for short *a* and short *e*.

Student Exercises
Lesson 20 / Lesson 22
Students read the words in these lessons. (See the discussion of *Guided Oral Reading Practice* on pages 8 - 10.)
Lesson 21 (Quiz 10) / Lesson 23 (Quiz 11)
The teacher dictates the words in these lessons. (See information under *Spelling Dictation* on pages 11 - 18.)

Page 8
Supplemental Materials
Flash Cards – Review all cards previously introduced.

Information Teacher Presents or Reviews on this Page
This page consists entirely of sentences. In addition to the word lists that are found on most pages in this book, it is also helpful for students to have the opportunity to read sentences whose words contain those phonic elements recently presented.

Student Exercises
Lesson 24 / Lesson 26
Students read the sentences in these lessons. (See the information that immediately follows regarding the instructional procedure to use for this page.)
Lesson 25 / Lesson 27
The teacher dictates the sentences from these lessons. (See the information that immediately follows regarding the instructional procedure to use for this page.)

Teacher's Guide
Procedure to Follow on Pages Consisting of Sentences

Throughout the first three sections of the book are located pages consisting entirely (*Sections One* and *Two*) or partly (*Section Three*) of sentences. These pages are evenly divided between nonsense sentences and sentences containing real words in the first two sections of the book; no nonsense words are used in the third section of the book. As in other lessons the instructional procedure is the same. Students are asked to read the sentences and then to spell the sentences. The procedure is somewhat modified to accommodate the fact that sentences are being presented rather than individual words in isolation.

Oral Reading Procedure With Sentences

Students read these sentences in a two-step process. The first time students read a sentence, students read each word in the sentence deliberately to make sure that they are correctly pronouncing each word in the sentence. After the students have correctly identified all of the words in the sentence, they reread the sentence and this time **read the sentence with expression**. The nonsense sentences are just that: nonsensical. They are, however, written to read and sound like an ordinary sentence would in English. Therefore in subsequent readings of these sentences, **students should attempt to read them as if they are speaking the sentence to another person in ordinary conversation**. Students have a lot of fun with this activity. Research has shown that guided oral reading practice helps to develop reading accuracy and fluency, skills that ultimately result in improved comprehension. For that reason students reread the sentences as many times as is necessary until they are able to read the sentences not only accurately but fluently and with expression as well. See page 9 for a list of five guided and repeated oral reading practice activities to use with these sentences. **Use both nonsense and real sentences for oral reading practice for all students regardless of their age.**

Spelling Dictation Procedure With Sentences

When you are dictating these sentences to your students, the procedure is the opposite of the procedure for oral reading. When dictating sentences for spelling, the teacher reads each sentence at least three times. The first two times a teacher reads a sentence to the students, the teacher reads the sentence fluently and with expression. Read both the nonsense sentences and the real sentences with expression. After the teacher reads the sentence twice with expression, she must read the sentence a third time and pronounce each word that is in bold individually and with exaggeration. **To hear sentence dictation exercises modeled, go to** www.weallcanread.com **and select the page titled** *Online Instruction.* **Listen to the dictation procedure modeled in Lessons 25 and 27.**

Repeat any word in bold as many times as is necessary so that students hear each individual sound in the word accurately. Remember to scan the words in each sentence prior to dictation to determine if any of the words contain one of the four elements that require a special dictation procedure. See pages 11 - 18 for more information.

All of the sentences contain some sight words; in the nonsense sentences these sight words enable the sentences to sound natural. Sight words are very common words, and students are almost certain to know them already; students know the spelling of sight words from memory. **(In these sentences the sight words are not in bold.) During dictation the teacher does not exaggerate the sounds within the sight words (the words not in bold) nor ask students to identify the number of sounds within those sight words. Students do not make any marks to the sight words such as underlining letter teams.** Only the words in bold are analyzed during the spelling dictation procedure to determine the number of sounds contained in them, the letter teams those words might contain, and starting on page 62 in the core book, the syllable pattern numbers to associate with the vowels in words.

Use both nonsense and real sentences for spelling dictation for students through the fifth grade. Use only the nonsense sentences for spelling dictation for students in the sixth grade, middle school, high school, and beyond. The two exceptions to this recommendation for sixth grade students and beyond would be in the instance where students in these grades read and spell less than eighty percent of the real words from any given page correctly or in the instance where students are learning English as a second language.

Page 9
Supplemental Materials
Flash Cards – Review all cards previously introduced.
The Reader – Read pages 5-6 (1ˢᵗ Ed.) or pages 9-12 (2ⁿᵈ. Ed.) on completing page 9.
The We All Can Read Phonics Game – Students play *Card Game One* upon completing this page.

Information Teacher Presents or Reviews on this Page
This page consists of two stories containing words with short *a* and short *e*. One story uses nonsense words; the other does not. In addition to the word lists that are found on most pages in this book, and the page containing sentences that is presented on the page immediately preceding this page, it is also helpful for students to have the opportunity to read stories whose words contain those phonic elements recently presented.

Student Exercises
Lesson 28 / Lesson 29
Students read the stories in these lessons. (See the information that immediately follows regarding the instructional procedure to use for this page.)

Procedure to Follow on Pages Consisting of Stories
Throughout the book are located pages consisting of stories. These pages are evenly divided between a nonsense word story and a real word story in the first two sections of the book; no nonsense words are used after the end of *Section Two*.

Oral Reading Procedure With Stories
Students read these stories but do not spell the words in them. The students' goal in reading these stories is for them to be able to read the stories with accuracy, fluency, and expression. Practice is the key to accomplish this task. The first time students read these stories they strive for accuracy; once accuracy is achieved, students reread these stories as many times as is necessary until they are able to read them not only with accuracy but with fluency and expression as well. The online audio files that accompany these stories are especially helpful for students to use to accomplish this goal. (Online subscription required.) Students read silently as they hear the stories read aloud on the online audio files. Students replay the online audio files as often as is necessary until they are able to read the stories with the same degree of skill as demonstrated on the online audio files. See page 9 for a list of five guided and repeated oral reading practice activities to use with these stories. **Use both nonsense and real stories for oral reading practice for all students regardless of their age.** (No nonsense words are used in the book after the end of *Section Two*.)

Teacher's Guide
Page 10
Supplemental Materials

Flash Cards – Introduce Card Set A # 26 / Card Set C # 21. Review all cards previously introduced.

Information Teacher Presents or Reviews on this Page

The short *o* sound is introduced. The key word for short *o* is the word *ostrich*. The short *o* sound is the first sound you must make to say the word *ostrich*. In Lessons 30 and 31 the short *o* is followed by a consonant. In Lessons 32 and 33 the short sounds of *a*, *e*, and *o* are followed by a consonant. Review with students the short sounds of *a*, *e*, and *o*. **Distinguishing between the short sounds of *e* and *i* can be particularly difficult. For this reason the sequence presented in introducing the vowels in this program is *a*, *e*, *o*, *u*, and only then *i*. The reason for introducing the *i* sound last is to enable the student to have as much time as is possible to learn thoroughly the short *e* sound first before being asked to articulate the closely-related short *i* sound.**

Student Exercises
Lesson 30 / Lesson 32

Students read the letter combinations in these lessons. (See the discussion of *Guided Oral Reading Practice* on pages 8 - 10.)

Lesson 31 (Quiz 12) / Lesson 33 (Quiz 13)

The teacher dictates the sounds represented by the letter combinations from these lessons. (See information under *Spelling Dictation* on pages 11 - 18.)

Page 11
Supplemental Materials

Flash Cards – Review all cards previously introduced.
The Reader – Read pages 7-8 (1st Ed.) or pages 13-16 (2nd. Ed.) on completing page 11.

Information Teacher Presents or Reviews on this Page

This page consists of three and four letter words which all contain the short *o* sound. Review the sound of short *o*.

Student Exercises
Lesson 34 / Lesson 36

Students read the words in these lessons. (See the discussion of *Guided Oral Reading Practice* on pages 8 - 10.)

Lesson 35 (Quiz 14) / Lesson 37 (Quiz 15)

The teacher dictates the words in these lessons. (See information under *Spelling Dictation* on pages 11 - 18.)

Page 12
Supplemental Materials

Flash Cards – Review all cards previously introduced.

Information Teacher Presents or Reviews on this Page

This page is a review page with words containing short *a*, *e*, and *o*. Review the sounds that short *a*, *e*, and *o* represent.

Teacher's Guide
Student Exercises
Lesson 38 / Lesson 40
Students read the words in these lessons. (See the discussion of *Guided Oral Reading Practice* on pages 8 - 10.)
Lesson 39 (Quiz 16) / Lesson 41 (Quiz 17)
The teacher dictates the words in these lessons. (See information under *Spelling Dictation* on pages 11 - 18.)

Page 13
Supplemental Materials
Flash Cards – Review all cards previously introduced.

Information Teacher Presents or Reviews on this Page
This page consists entirely of sentences. In addition to the word lists that are found on most pages in this book, it is also helpful for students to have the opportunity to read sentences whose words contain those phonic elements recently presented.

Student Exercises
Lesson 42 / Lesson 44
Students read the sentences in these lessons. (See the information provided under *Procedure to Follow on Pages Consisting of Sentences* located on pages 20 - 21.)
Lesson 43 / Lesson 45
The teacher dictates the sentences from these lessons. (See the information provided under *Procedure to Follow on Pages Consisting of Sentences* located on pages 20 - 21.)

Page 14
Supplemental Materials
Flash Cards – Review all cards previously introduced.
The Reader – Read pages 9-10 (1st Ed.) or pages 17-20 (2nd. Ed.) on completing page 14.
The We All Can Read Phonics Game – Students play *Card Game Two* upon completing this page.

Information Teacher Presents or Reviews on this Page
This page consists of two stories containing the elements identified at the top of the page in the title. One story uses nonsense words; the other does not. In addition to the word lists that are found on most pages in this book, and the page containing sentences that is presented on the page immediately preceding this page, it is also helpful for students to have the opportunity to read stories whose words contain those phonic elements recently presented.

Lesson 46 / Lesson 47
Students read the stories in these lessons. (See the information provided under *Oral Reading Procedure With Stories* located on page 21.)

Page 15
Supplemental Materials
Flash Cards – Introduce Card Set A # 27 / Card Set C # 22. Review all cards previously introduced.

Teacher's Guide
Information Teacher Presents or Reviews on this Page

The short *u* sound is introduced. The key word for short *u* is the word *umbrella*. The short *u* sound is the first sound you must make to say the word *umbrella*. In Lessons 48 and 49 the short *u* is followed by a consonant. In Lessons 50 and 51 the short sounds of *a, e, o,* and *u* are followed by a consonant. Review the short sounds of *a, e, o,* and *u*.

Student Exercises
Lesson 48 / Lesson 50

Students read the letter combinations in these lessons. (See the discussion of *Guided Oral Reading Practice* on pages 8 - 10.)
Lesson 49 (Quiz 18) / Lesson 51 (Quiz 19)

The teacher dictates the sounds represented by the letter combinations from these lessons. (See information under *Spelling Dictation* on pages 11 - 18.)

Page 16
Supplemental Materials

Flash Cards – Review all cards previously introduced.
The Reader – Read pages 11-12 (1st Ed.) or pages 21-24 (2nd. Ed.) on completing page 16.

Information Teacher Presents or Reviews on this Page

This page consists of three and four letter words that all contain the short *u* sound. Review the short *u* sound.

Student Exercises
Lesson 52 / Lesson 54

Students read the words in these lessons. (See the discussion of *Guided Oral Reading Practice* on pages 8 - 10.)
Lesson 53 (Quiz 20) / Lesson 55 (Quiz 21)

The teacher dictates the words in these lessons. (See information under *Spelling Dictation* on pages 11 - 18.)

Page 17
Supplemental Materials

Flash Cards – Review all cards previously introduced.

Information Teacher Presents or Reviews on this Page

This page is a review page with words containing short *a, e, o,* and *u*. Review the short sounds of *a, e, o,* and *u*.

Student Exercises
Lesson 56 / Lesson 58

Students read the words in these lessons. (See the discussion of *Guided Oral Reading Practice* on pages 8 - 10.)
Lesson 57 (Quiz 22) / Lesson 59 (Quiz 23)

The teacher dictates the words in these lessons. (See information under *Spelling Dictation* on pages 11 - 18.)

Page 18
Supplemental Materials

Flash Cards – Review all cards previously introduced.

Teacher's Guide
Information Teacher Presents or Reviews on this Page
This page consists entirely of sentences. In addition to the word lists that are found on most pages in this book, it is also helpful for students to have the opportunity to read sentences whose words contain those phonic elements recently presented.

Student Exercises
Lesson 60 / Lesson 62
Students read the sentences in these lessons. (See the information provided under *Procedure to Follow on Pages Consisting of Sentences* located on pages 20 - 21.)
Lesson 61 / Lesson 63
The teacher dictates the sentences from these lessons. (See the information provided under *Procedure to Follow on Pages Consisting of Sentences* located on pages 20 - 21.)

Page 19
Supplemental Materials
Flash Cards – Review all cards previously introduced.
The Reader – Read pages 13-14 (1ˢᵗ Ed.) or pages 25-28 (2ⁿᵈ. Ed.) on completing page 19.
The We All Can Read Phonics Game – Students play *Card Game Three* upon completing this page.

Information Teacher Presents or Reviews on this Page
This page consists of two stories containing the elements identified at the top of the page in the title. One story uses nonsense words; the other does not. In addition to the word lists that are found on most pages in this book, and the page containing sentences that is presented on the page immediately preceding this page, it is also helpful for students to have the opportunity to read stories whose words contain those phonic elements recently presented.

Lesson 64 / Lesson 65
Students read the stories in these lessons. (See the information provided under *Oral Reading Procedure With Stories* located on page 21.)

Page 20
Supplemental Materials
Flash Cards – Introduce Card Set A # 28 / Card Set C # 23. Review all cards previously introduced.

Information Teacher Presents or Reviews on this Page
The short *i* sound is introduced. The key word for short *i* is the word *igloo*. The short *i* sound is the first sound you must make to say the word *igloo*. In Lessons 66 and 67 the short *i* is followed by a consonant. In Lessons 68 and 69 the short sounds of *a, e, i, o,* and *u* are followed by a consonant. Review the short sounds of *a, e, i, o,* and *u*.

Student Exercises
Lesson 66 / Lesson 68
Students read the letter combinations in these lessons. (See the discussion of *Guided Oral Reading Practice* on pages 8 - 10.)
Lesson 67 (Quiz 24) / Lesson 69 (Quiz 25)
The teacher dictates the sounds represented by the letter combinations from these lessons. (See information under *Spelling Dictation* on pages 11 - 18.)

Teacher's Guide
Page 21
Supplemental Materials
Flash Cards – Review all cards previously introduced.
The Reader – Read pages 15-16 (1st Ed.) or pages 29-32 (2nd. Ed.) on completing page 21.

Information Teacher Presents or Reviews on this Page
This page consists of three and four letter words that all contain the short *i* sound. Review the short *i* sound.

Student Exercises
Lesson 70 / Lesson 72
Students read the words in these lessons. (See the discussion of *Guided Oral Reading Practice* on pages 8 - 10.)
Lesson 71 (Quiz 26) / Lesson 73 (Quiz 27)
The teacher dictates the words in these lessons. (See information under *Spelling Dictation* on pages 11 - 18.)

Pages 22 - 23
Supplemental Materials
Flash Cards – Review all cards previously introduced.

Information Teacher Presents or Reviews on these Pages
These are review pages with words containing short *a, e, i, o,* and *u*. Review the short sounds of *a, e, i, o,* and *u*. Write the five vowels on the board; ask individual students to make the sounds the letters represent as you point to those letters. Point to the letters in arbitrary order. Reverse the process. Make the sound of one of the five short vowels; ask students to write the letter that represents the sound you are making.

Student Exercises
Lesson 74 / Lesson 76 / Lesson 78 / Lesson 80
Students read the words in these lessons. (See the discussion of *Guided Oral Reading Practice* on pages 8 - 10.)
Lesson 75 (Quiz 28) / Lesson 77 (Quiz 29) / Lesson 79 (Quiz 30) / Lesson 81 (Quiz 31)
The teacher dictates the words in these lessons. (See information under *Spelling Dictation* on pages 11 - 18.)

Page 24
Supplemental Materials
Flash Cards – Review all cards previously introduced.

Information Teacher Presents or Reviews on this Page
This page consists entirely of sentences. In addition to the word lists that are found on most pages in this book, it is also helpful for students to have the opportunity to read sentences whose words contain those phonic elements recently presented.

Student Exercises
Lesson 82 / Lesson 84
Students read the sentences in these lessons. (See the information provided under *Procedure to Follow on Pages Consisting of Sentences* located on pages 20 - 21.)

Teacher's Guide
Lesson 83 / Lesson 85
The teacher dictates the sentences from these lessons.   (See the information provided under *Procedure to Follow on Pages Consisting of Sentences* located on pages 20 - 21.)

Page 25
Supplemental Materials
Flash Cards – Review all cards previously introduced.
The Reader – Read pages 17-18 (1ˢᵗ Ed.) or pages 33-36 (2ⁿᵈ. Ed.) on completing page 25.
The We All Can Read Phonics Game – Students play *Card Game Four* upon completing this page.

Information Teacher Presents or Reviews on this Page
This page consists of two stories containing the elements identified at the top of the page in the title. One story uses nonsense words; the other does not. In addition to the word lists that are found on most pages in this book, and the page containing sentences that is presented on the page immediately preceding this page, it is also helpful for students to have the opportunity to read stories whose words contain those phonic elements recently presented.

Lesson 86 / Lesson 87
Students read the stories in these lessons. (See the information provided under *Oral Reading Procedure With Stories* located on page 21.)

Page 26
Supplemental Materials
Flash Cards – Review all cards previously introduced.

Information Teacher Presents or Reviews on this Page
This page introduces the FLOSS Spelling Rule regarding one-syllable words that end in the letters *f, l, or s*.   Explain the rule found at the top of this page. Choose real words from page 26 or other words that illustrate this spelling rule, and write those words on the board. Chose at least one word that ends in *ff*, one that ends in *ll*, and one that ends in *ss*. Apply the rule at the top of page 26 to each of these words. See if students can think of any words on their own where this spelling rule applies.

Student Exercises
Lesson 88 / Lesson 90
Students read the words in these lessons. (See the discussion of *Guided Oral Reading Practice* on pages 8 - 10.)
Lesson 89 (Quiz 32) / Lesson 91 (Quiz 33)
The teacher dictates the words in these lessons. (See information under *Spelling Dictation* on pages 11 - 18.)

Page 27
Supplemental Materials
Flash Cards – Review all cards previously introduced.

Information Teacher Presents or Reviews on this Page
This page introduces the spelling rule regarding when to use the letter *c* or *k* when spelling a word containing the /k/ sound as the first sound in the word. Explain the rule found at the top of page 27. Choose real words from page 27 or think of other one-

syllable words that illustrate this spelling rule, and write those words on the board. Choose at least one word that begins with the letter *c* and at least one word that begins with the letter *k*. See if students can think of additional words on their own which begin with the letters *c* or *k*.

Student Exercises
Lesson 92 / Lesson 94

Students read the words in these lessons. (See the discussion of *Guided Oral Reading Practice* on pages 8 - 10.)

Lesson 93 (Quiz 34) / Lesson 95 (Quiz 35)

The teacher dictates the words in these lessons. (See information under *Spelling Dictation* on pages 11 - 18.)

Pages 28 – 29
Supplemental Materials

Blackline Masters – Duplicate pages one through four for students to take home.

Information Teacher Presents or Reviews on these Pages

Mastery Check and Review Number One – Read information found on page 28 in the core book.

Student Exercises
Lesson 96 through Lesson 100

See the box *Administering the Mastery Checks* immediately below.

Administering the Mastery Checks: Mastery Checks One through Eight

Students should be able to read and spell the words in the beginning mastery checks with a high degree of accuracy and fluency. It is not necessary to ask a student to read and spell every word from each lesson in these mastery checks. Choose a representative number of words under each lesson (at least ten words), and ask students to read and spell them. But if students struggle either reading or spelling the representative words chosen, the teacher should then have the students read and spell all of the words in that particular lesson. Failure to be able to read and spell these words with an eighty percent or higher degree of accuracy strongly suggests that a student is not sufficiently prepared to move into the next unit and that instead further review is required in previous lessons.

These mastery tests are primarily suitable for young students up to the fifth grade. Most students beyond fifth grade will be able to read and spell these words from memorization, regardless of how well they understand the phonics information that has been presented thus far in the program. Therefore this mastery check is of little diagnostic value for most students beyond the fifth grade; it is suggested that this test not be administered to students beyond the fifth grade unless the student is reading several grade levels below his age.

Do not administer these tests to sixth grade, middle school, or high school students unless students are reading at such a low level that they would be challenged by taking this test. Only a very small number of sixth grade, middle school, or high school students would fall into this category. If it becomes obvious while administering this test that the student knows the identity and the spelling of the words in these lists with a high degree of accuracy, discontinue the tests. There are a total of twenty-one mastery checks in the book. These mastery checks become progressively more challenging. Later in the program the mastery tests will provide a much more reliable indicator of the degree of progress students beyond the fifth grade are making.

Teacher's Guide
Page 30
Supplemental Materials

Posters – Display Poster titled *Beginning Consonant Blends*.
Flash Cards – Introduce Card Set A #'s 29-54. Review all cards previously introduced.

Information Teacher Presents or Reviews on this Page

Beginning consonant blends are introduced. A beginning consonant blend occurs before the vowel and consists of two or three consonant letters that are next to each other and do not form a consonant letter team. Instead each consonant letter retains its own sound and blends its sound together with the other consonant letters. **Consonant blends are not underlined.** Review with your students the sounds represented by each of the consonant blends in the individual boxes on this page. **When counting the number of sounds within a word that contains a consonant blend, each consonant blend consists of two or three individual sounds; count each of those sounds as an individual sound when adding up the total number of sounds within the word. As an example the word *sled* contains four individual sounds: /s/, /l/, /e/, /d/.**

Student Exercises
Lesson 101

Ask your students to make the sounds represented by the beginning blends listed in the individual boxes on this page. Ask students to think of words that begin with each of the blends listed on this page. Make a game out of this process, and call out numbers from 1 to 26 in an arbitrary order. When a student is assigned one of those numbers, he must make the sound of the beginning consonant blend in the box with that number and think of a word which contains that consonant blend. Reverse the process, and make the sounds represented by the consonant blends on this page. Then ask your students to spell those sounds.

Pages 31 – 32
Supplemental Materials

Flash Cards – Review all cards previously introduced.

Information Teacher Presents or Reviews on these Pages

Please note that in the *We All Can Read* program when you ask students to count the number of sounds heard within words that contain consonant blends, consonant blends are not counted as one single sound. As an example the consonant blend *bl* contains two sounds: /b/ and /l/; the word *bless* contains four individual sounds: /b/, /l/, /eh/ (short *e* sound), /s/. The consonant blend *str* contains three sounds: /s/, /t/, and /r/; the word *stress* contains five individual sounds: /s/, /t/, /r/, /eh/ (short *e* sound), /s/.

Student Exercises
Lesson 102 / Lesson 104 / Lesson 106 / Lesson 108

Students read the words in these lessons. (See the discussion of *Guided Oral Reading Practice* on pages 8 - 10.)

   Lesson 103 (Quiz 36) / Lesson 105 (Quiz 37) / Lesson 107 (Quiz 38) / Lesson 109 (Quiz 39)
The teacher dictates the words in these lessons. (See information under *Spelling Dictation* on pages 11 - 18.)

Teacher's Guide
Page 33
Supplemental Materials
Flash Cards – Review all cards previously introduced.

Information Teacher Presents or Reviews on this Page
This page consists entirely of sentences. In addition to the word lists that are found on most pages in this book, it is also helpful for students to have the opportunity to read sentences whose words contain those phonic elements recently presented.

Student Exercises
Lesson 110 / Lesson 112
Students read the sentences in these lessons. (See the information provided under *Procedure to Follow on Pages Consisting of Sentences* located on pages 20 - 21.)
Lesson 111 / Lesson 113
The teacher dictates the sentences from these lessons. (See the information provided under *Procedure to Follow on Pages Consisting of Sentences* located on pages 20 - 21.)

Page 34
Supplemental Materials
Flash Cards – Review all cards previously introduced.
The Reader – Read pages 19-20 (1st Ed.) or pages 37-40 (2nd. Ed.) on completing page 34.
The We All Can Read Phonics Game – Students play *Card Game Five* upon completing this page.

Information Teacher Presents or Reviews on this Page
This page consists of two stories containing the elements identified at the top of the page in the title. One story uses nonsense words; the other does not. In addition to the word lists that are found on most pages in this book, and the page containing sentences that is presented on the page immediately preceding this page, it is also helpful for students to have the opportunity to read stories whose words contain those phonic elements recently presented.

Lesson 114 / Lesson 115
Students read the stories in these lessons. (See the information provided under *Oral Reading Procedure With Stories* located on page 21.)

Page 35
Supplemental Materials
Blackline Masters – Duplicate pages five through seven for students to take home.

Information Teacher Presents or Reviews on this Page
Mastery Check and Review Number Two – Review the information found on page 28 in the core book.

Student Exercises
Lesson 116 through Lesson 120
See the box titled *Administering the Mastery Checks: Mastery Checks One through Eight* on page 28.

Teacher's Guide
Page 36
Supplemental Materials
Posters – Display Poster titled *Ending Consonant Blends*
Flash Cards – Introduce Card Set A #'s 55-71. Review all cards previously introduced.

Information Teacher Presents or Reviews on this Page
Ending consonant blends are introduced. An ending consonant blend occurs after the vowel and consists of two or three consonant letters that are next to each other in the same syllable and do not form a consonant letter team. Instead each consonant letter retains its own sound and blends its sound together with the other consonant letters. **Consonant blends are not underlined.** Review with your students the sounds represented by each of the ending consonant blends in the individual boxes on this page. When counting the number of sounds within a word that contains a consonant blend, each consonant blend consists of two or three individual sounds; count each of those sounds as an individual sound when adding up the total number of sounds within the word. As an example the word *bulb* contains four individual sounds: /b/, /u/, /l/, /b/.

Student Exercises
Lesson 121
Ask your students to make the sounds represented by the ending consonant blends listed in the individual boxes on this page. Ask students to think of words that end with each of the blends listed on this page. Make a game out of this process, and call out numbers from 1 to 17 in an arbitrary order. When a student is assigned one of those numbers, he must make the sound of the consonant blend in the box with that number and think of a word that contains that consonant blend. Reverse the process, and make the sounds represented by the consonant blends on this page. Then ask your students to spell those sounds.

Page 37
Supplemental Materials
Flash Cards – Review all cards previously introduced.

Information Teacher Presents or Reviews on this Page
This page presents letter combinations containing a short vowel followed by an ending consonant blend.

Student Exercises
Lesson 122 / Lesson 124
Students read the letter combinations in these lessons. (See the discussion of *Guided Oral Reading Practice* on pages 8 - 10.)
Lesson 123 (Quiz 40) / Lesson 125 (Quiz 41)
The teacher dictates the sounds represented by the letter combinations from these lessons. (See information under *Spelling Dictation* on pages 11 - 18.)

Page 38
Supplemental Materials
Flash Cards – Review all cards previously introduced.

Teacher's Guide
Information Teacher Presents or Reviews on this Page
Please note that in the *We All Can Read Program* when you ask students to count the number of sounds heard within words that contain consonant blends, consonant blends are not counted as one single sound. As an example the ending consonant blend *ft* contains two sounds: $/f/$ and $/t/$; the word *left* contains four sounds: $/l/$, $/e/$(short *e* sound), $/f/$, and $/t/$.

Student Exercises
Lesson 126 / Lesson 128
Students read the words in these lessons. (See the discussion of *Guided Oral Reading Practice* on pages 8 - 10.)
Lesson 127 (Quiz 42) / Lesson 129 (Quiz 43)
The teacher dictates the words in these lessons. (See information under *Spelling Dictation* on pages 11 - 18.)

Page 39
Supplemental Materials
Flash Cards – Review all cards previously introduced.

Information Teacher Presents or Reviews on this Page
This page consists entirely of sentences. In addition to the word lists that are found on most pages in this book, it is also helpful for students to have the opportunity to read sentences whose words contain those phonic elements recently presented.

Student Exercises
Lesson 130 / Lesson 132
Students read the sentences in these lessons. (See the information provided under *Procedure to Follow on Pages Consisting of Sentences* located on pages 20 - 21.)
Lesson 131 / Lesson 133
The teacher dictates the sentences from these lessons. (See the information provided under *Procedure to Follow on Pages Consisting of Sentences* located on pages 20 - 21.)

Page 40
Supplemental Materials
Flash Cards – Review all cards previously introduced.
The Reader – Read pages 21-22 (1st Ed.) or pages 41-44 (2nd. Ed.) on completing page 40.
The We All Can Read Phonics Game – Students play *Card Game Six* upon completing this page.

Information Teacher Presents or Reviews on this Page
This page consists of two stories containing the elements identified at the top of the page in the title. One story uses nonsense words; the other does not. In addition to the word lists that are found on most pages in this book, and the page containing sentences that is presented on the page immediately preceding this page, it is also helpful for students to have the opportunity to read stories whose words contain those phonic elements recently presented.

Lesson 134 / Lesson 135
Students read the stories in these lessons. (See the information provided under *Oral Reading Procedure With Stories* located on page 21.)

Teacher's Guide
Page 41
Supplemental Materials
Blackline Masters – Duplicate pages seven through nine for students to take home.

Information Teacher Presents or Reviews on this Page
Mastery Check and Review Number Three – Review the information found on page 28 in the core book.

Student Exercises
Lesson 136 through Lesson 139
See the box titled *Administering the Mastery Checks*: *Mastery Checks One through Eight* on page 28.

Pages 42 – 43
Supplemental Materials
Flash Cards – Review all cards previously introduced.

Information Teacher Presents or Reviews on these Pages
Words containing both beginning and ending consonant blends are introduced. These are the most challenging words introduced thus far in the program. Students must incorporate the sound of every letter in each word when reading the word. Students must listen very carefully to hear every sound in the word in order to spell the word correctly.

Student Exercises
Lesson 140 / Lesson 142 / Lesson 144 / Lesson 146
Students read the words in these lessons. (See the discussion of *Guided Oral Reading Practice* on pages 8 - 10.)
  Lesson 141 (Quiz 44) / Lesson 143 (Quiz 45) / Lesson 145 (Quiz 46) / Lesson 147 (Quiz 47)
The teacher dictates the words in these lessons. (See information under *Spelling Dictation* on pages 11 - 18.)

Page 44
Supplemental Materials
Flash Cards – Review all cards previously introduced.

Information Teacher Presents or Reviews on this Page
This page consists entirely of sentences. In addition to the word lists that are found on most pages in this book, it is also helpful for students to have the opportunity to read sentences whose words contain those phonic elements recently presented.

Student Exercises
Lesson 148 / Lesson 150
Students read the sentences in these lessons. (See the information provided under *Procedure to Follow on Pages Consisting of Sentences* located on pages 20 - 21.)
Lesson 149 / Lesson 151
The teacher dictates the sentences from these lessons. (See the information provided under *Procedure to Follow on Pages Consisting of Sentences* located on pages 20 - 21.)

Teacher's Guide
Page 45
Supplemental Materials

Flash Cards – Review all cards previously introduced.
The Reader – Read pages 23-24 (1st Ed.) or pages 45-48 (2nd. Ed.) on completing page 45.
The We All Can Read Phonics Game – Students play *Card Game Seven* upon completing this page.

Information Teacher Presents or Reviews on this Page

This page consists of two stories containing the elements identified at the top of the page in the title. One story uses nonsense words; the other does not. In addition to the word lists that are found on most pages in this book, and the page containing sentences that is presented on the page immediately preceding this page, it is also helpful for students to have the opportunity to read stories whose words contain those phonic elements recently presented.

Lesson 152 / Lesson 153

Students read the stories in these lessons. (See the information provided under *Oral Reading Procedure With Stories* located on page 21.)

Page 46
Supplemental Materials

Blackline Masters – Duplicate pages ten through eleven for students to take home.

Information Teacher Presents or Reviews on this Page

Mastery Check and Review Number Four – Review the information found on page 28 in the core book.

Student Exercises
Lesson 154 through Lesson 157

See the box titled *Administering the Mastery Checks: Mastery Checks One through Eight* on page 28.

Page 47
Supplemental Materials

Posters – Display Poster titled *Major Consonant Teams*
Flash Cards – Introduce Card Set A #'s 72-79 / Card Set B # 2 / Card Set C #'s 24-30. Retire Card Set C #'s 3, 16. Review all cards introduced that have not been retired.

Information Teacher Presents or Reviews on this Page

The following information is presented to students on this page:
1. **New consonant teams are introduced.** Explain to your students the difference between a consonant team and a consonant blend. **Consonant letter blends are composed of individual consonant letters clustered together that all retain their own individual sounds. Unlike the individual letters in consonant blends, the letters in consonant teams do not represent their own sounds and instead combine as a unit to represent a different sound.**
2. *ch* represents the first and last sound heard in the word <u>church</u>.
3. *tch* represents the last sound heard in the word *ma<u>tch</u>* (the same sound that ch represents). The team *tch* always follows a short vowel sound. Normally when a word ends in a short vowel sound followed immediately by the sound /ch/, we use the letter team <u>tch</u> to spell that sound: ca<u>tch</u>, hi<u>tch</u>, clu<u>tch</u>. (There are a few very common words

that are exceptions to this rule: such, much.) **Tell students to use the team *tch* when spelling nonsense words that end in a short vowel followed by the sound /ch/.**

4. *ck* represents the last sound in the word ro*ck*. **When a word ends in a short vowel followed by the sound /k/, use *ck* to spell that sound.**

5. *ng* represents the last sound in the word wi*ng*. **When a word ends in a short vowel followed by the sound /ng/, use *ng* to spell that sound.**

6. **The consonant teams *tch*, *ck*, and *ng* must come directly after a short vowel, never before the vowel.**

7. *ph* represents the first sound in the word *ph*one. **The team *ph* represents the same sound as does the letter *f*.**

8. *sh* represents the first sound in the word *sh*ell.

9. The consonant letter team *th* represents two different sounds. The first sound the team *th* represents is the first sound heard in the word *th*umb. This sound is the voiceless *th* sound. (See page 92 for more information.) When the team *th* represents its first sound, underline the *th* team one time. The second sound the team *th* represents is the first sound heard in the word *th*is. This sound is the voiced *th* sound. (See page 92 for more information.) The less frequently occurring second sound of *th* is marked by underlining the letter team twice.

10. The consonant team *wh* can be pronounced in one of two ways: w*h* = /w/ or /hw/. While each of these sounds is equally acceptable, the /w/ sound is the more common sound used by most people today.

Students should memorize these ten consonant teams. Notice that seven out of the ten consonant teams contain the letter *h*. **When students are spelling words that contain consonant teams, they are to underline those consonant teams. Consonant blends are never underlined. Also remember that when dictating nonsense words that contain the consonant letter teams *ph* and *wh*, the teacher must indicate to students that the word about to be dictated contains a consonant letter team.** Otherwise students might not know to use a consonant team and may instead use the letter *f* or the letter *w* instead of the consonant teams *ph* or *wh* to spell the nonsense word.

Consonant teams have been underlined in every word in the book up to this page. Beginning on this page consonant teams are not underlined in the main portion of the book, but the teams will be identified in the *Answer Key Section* that begins on page 263.

Student Exercises
Lesson 158

1. Ask your students to make the sounds represented by the consonant teams listed in the individual boxes on this page. Ask students to think of one-syllable words that contain these letter teams.

2. Reverse the process, and make the sounds represented by the consonant teams on this page. Then ask your students to write the consonant teams that represent those sounds. Divide the instructional period equally between these two activities.

3. After these new teams have been introduced to your students, periodically ask them to list as many of these teams as they can from memory. Continue to ask them on subsequent days to list these teams from memory until students are able to do so automatically.

Pages 48 – 49
Supplemental Materials

Flash Cards – Review all cards previously introduced that have not been retired.

Teacher's Guide
Information Teacher Presents or Reviews on these Pages
On these two pages the words all contain at least one of the consonant teams introduced on page 47.

Student Exercises
Lesson 159 / Lesson 161 / Lesson 163 / Lesson 165
Students read the words in these lessons. (See the discussion of *Guided Oral Reading Practice* on pages 8 - 10.)

Lesson 160 (Quiz 48) / Lesson 162 (Quiz 49) / Lesson 164 (Quiz 50) / Lesson 166 (Quiz 51)
The teacher dictates the words in these lessons. (See information under *Spelling Dictation* on pages 11 - 18.)

Page 50
Supplemental Materials
Flash Cards – Review all cards previously introduced that have not been retired.

Information Teacher Presents or Reviews on this Page
This page consists entirely of sentences. In addition to the word lists that are found on most pages in this book, it is also helpful for students to have the opportunity to read sentences whose words contain those phonic elements recently presented.

Student Exercises
Lesson 167 / Lesson 169
Students read the sentences in these lessons. (See the information provided under *Procedure to Follow on Pages Consisting of Sentences* located on pages 20 - 21.)

Lesson 168 / Lesson 170
The teacher dictates the sentences from these lessons. (See the information provided under *Procedure to Follow on Pages Consisting of Sentences* located on pages 20 - 21.)

Page 51
Supplemental Materials
Flash Cards – Review all cards previously introduced.
The We All Can Read Phonics Game – Students play *Card Game Eight* upon completing this page.

Information Teacher Presents or Reviews on this Page
This page consists of two stories containing the elements identified at the top of the page in the title. One story uses nonsense words; the other does not. In addition to the word lists that are found on most pages in this book, and the page containing sentences that is presented on the page immediately preceding this page, it is also helpful for students to have the opportunity to read stories whose words contain those phonic elements recently presented.

Lesson 171 / Lesson 172
Students read the stories in these lessons. (See the information provided under *Oral Reading Procedure With Stories* located on page 21.)

Page 52
Supplemental Materials
Flash Cards – Introduce Card Set A # 80 / Card Set B # 3 / Card Set C # 31. Retire Card Set C # 25. Review all cards previously introduced that have not been retired.
The Reader – Read pages 25-26 (1st Ed.) or pages 49-52 (2nd. Ed.) on completing page 52.

Teacher's Guide
Information Teacher Presents or Reviews on this Page
This page introduces the second sound for the letter *n*. Explain the rule found at the top of this page regarding when the letter *n* represents its second sound. Write words on the board that illustrate this rule. Ask students if they can think of any words where the letter *n* represents its second sound. See pages 60 - 61 in the core book for a list of words that contain the second sound for the letter *n*.

Lesson 173 / Lesson 175
Students read the words in these lessons. (See the discussion of *Guided Oral Reading Practice* on pages 8 - 10.)

Lesson 174 (Quiz 52) / Lesson 176 (Quiz 53)
The teacher dictates the words from these lessons. (See information under *Spelling Dictation* on pages 11 - 18.)

Student Exercises
Page 53
Blackline Masters – Duplicate pages eleven through thirteen for students to take home.

Information Teacher Presents or Reviews on this Page
Mastery Check and Review Number Five – Review the information found on page 28 in the core book.

Student Exercises
Lesson 177 through Lesson 181
See the box titled *Administering the Mastery Checks*: *Mastery Checks One through Eight* on page 28.

Page 54
Supplemental Materials
Flash Cards – Review all cards previously introduced that have not been retired.

Information Teacher Presents or Reviews on this Page
The chart on this page contains all of the blends and consonant teams presented thus far in the program. This chart is an excellent tool to use for reviewing these letter blends and letter teams.

Student Exercises
Lesson 182 / Lesson 183 / Lesson 184
Ask your students to make the sounds represented by the consonant blends and consonant teams listed in the individual boxes on this page. Ask students to think of words that contain a particular consonant blend or consonant team. Make a game out of this process and call out numbers from the boxes in each lesson in an arbitrary order. When a student is assigned one of those numbers, he must make the sound of the consonant blend or consonant team in the box with that number and think of a word that contains that consonant blend or consonant team. Reverse the process, and make the sounds represented by the consonant blends or consonant teams on this page. Then

ask your students to spell those sounds. **After you have reviewed each of these three individual lessons, review the entire page as a whole.** Call any number from 1 to 48; ask students to identify the sound represented by the blend or consonant team in the box they are assigned, and ask them to think of a word that uses that blend or consonant team. Reverse the process. Make the sounds represented by the consonant blends or consonant teams on this page. Then ask your students to spell those sounds.

Pages 55 – 56
Supplemental Materials
Flash Cards – Review all cards previously introduced that have not been retired.

Information Teacher Presents or Reviews on these Pages
Words with blends and consonant teams are introduced. These words are the most phonetically complex words presented thus far in the program. **Consonant blends are never underlined; consonant teams are always underlined.** Remember that when dictating nonsense words that contain the consonant letter teams *ph* or *wh*, you must indicate to your students that the word you are about to dictate contains a consonant letter team. Otherwise students might not know to use a consonant team and may instead use the letter *f* or the letter *w* instead of the consonant teams *ph* or *wh*.

Student Exercises
Lesson 185 / Lesson 187 / Lesson 189 / Lesson 191
Students read the words in these lessons. (See the discussion of *Guided Oral Reading Practice* on pages 8 - 10.)
  Lesson 186 (Quiz 54) / Lesson 188 (Quiz 55) / Lesson 190 (Quiz 56) / Lesson 192 (Quiz 57)
The teacher dictates the words in these lessons. (See information under *Spelling Dictation* on pages 11 - 18.)

Page 57
Supplemental Materials
Flash Cards – Review all cards previously introduced that have not been retired.

Information Teacher Presents or Reviews on this Page
This page consists entirely of sentences. In addition to the word lists that are found on most pages in this book, it is also helpful for students to have the opportunity to read sentences whose words contain those phonic elements recently presented.

Student Exercises
Lesson 193 / Lesson 195
Students read the sentences in these lessons. (See the information provided under *Procedure to Follow on Pages Consisting of Sentences* located on pages 20 - 21.)
Lesson 194 / Lesson 196
The teacher dictates the sentences from these lessons. (See the information provided under *Procedure to Follow on Pages Consisting of Sentences* located on pages 20 - 21.)

Page 58
Supplemental Materials
Flash Cards – Review all cards previously introduced.
The Reader – Read pages 27-28 (1st Ed.) or pages 53-56 (2nd. Ed.) on completing page 58.
The We All Can Read Phonics Game – Students play *Card Game Nine* upon completing this page.

Teacher's Guide
Information Teacher Presents or Reviews on this Page
This page consists of two stories containing the elements identified at the top of the page in the title. One story uses nonsense words; the other does not. In addition to the word lists that are found on most pages in this book, and the page containing sentences that is presented on the page immediately preceding this page, it is also helpful for students to have the opportunity to read stories whose words contain those phonic elements recently presented.

Lesson 197 / Lesson 198
Students read the stories in these lessons. (See the information provided under *Oral Reading Procedure With Stories* located on page 21.)

Page 59
Supplemental Materials
Blackline Masters – Duplicate pages thirteen through fifteen for students to take home.

Information Teacher Presents or Reviews on this Page
Mastery Check and Review Number Six – Review the information found on page 28 in the core book.

Student Exercises
Lesson 199 through Lesson 203
See the box titled *Administering the Mastery Checks: Mastery Checks One through Eight* on page 28.

Pages 60 - 61
Supplemental Materials
The Reader – Read pages 29-35 (1st Ed.) or pages 57-63 (2nd. Ed.) on completing page 61. **Blackline Masters** – Duplicate pages fifteen through nineteen for students to take home.

Information Teacher Presents or Reviews on these Pages
Mastery Check and Review Number Seven – Review the information found on page 28 in the core book.

Student Exercises
Lesson 204 through Lesson 211
See the box titled *Administering the Mastery Checks: Mastery Checks One through Eight* on page 28.

Section Two
The Six Major Syllable Patterns
At this point students should be reasonably competent at sounding out one-syllable words where the vowels all represent their short sounds; however, all vowels represent more than one sound. The long sound of a vowel is one where the vowel represents the sound of its own name as the letter *e* does in the word *be*. Once a student learns the long sound for each vowel, the next step for him is to learn in what situations the vowel will represent its short sound and in what situations the vowel will represent its long sound. There are six major syllable patterns. Once a student learns to recognize these six basic syllable patterns, identifying what sound the vowel will represent in a word becomes relatively easy. In *Section Two* each of the six major syllable patterns is explained.

Teacher's Guide

If you are using the video edition or the online edition of *We All Can Read* in conjunction with the core book, please note the term *syllable pattern* is not used in either the video or online editions. In the video edition the term *vowel rules* is used and in the audio files within the online edition the term *vowel groups* is used instead of the term *syllable patterns*. These phrases are interchangeable and all refer to the same concept.

Beginning in *Section Two* a system is introduced for marking the vowels to indicate the sounds they will represent. This system of marking vowels coupled with the already-introduced technique of underlining consonant teams and double underlining letters representing their second sounds, provides a comprehensive and sequential marking procedure for students to use to enable them to decode virtually any word in the language. This marking system is a most effective tool to use to insure that a student has thoroughly mastered the various component steps involved in decoding. Through the repetitive process of analyzing and marking each of thousands of words, a student is provided with an adequate supply of material to internalize the principles being taught.

Procedure for Marking Words in *Section Two*

1. Underline all vowel and consonant teams. If a word ends with a silent letter *e*, underline the letter *e* once to indicate it is silent; double underline any letter or letter team that represents its second sound.
2. Determine the syllable pattern number for the vowel or vowel team in the word, and write that number directly under the vowel or vowel team. Numbers written under vowels always indicate syllable patterns governing the sound the vowel will represent. No syllable pattern number is ever written under a silent *e*.

Page-by-Page Instructions for Section Two
Pages 62 - 63
Supplemental Materials

Flash Cards – Introduce Card Set A #'s 81-85 / Card Set B #'s 4-8 / Card Set C #'s 32-36. Review all cards previously introduced that have not been retired.
The We All Can Read Phonics Game – Students play *Card Game Ten* upon completing these pages.

Information Teacher Presents or Reviews on these Pages

These pages introduce syllable patterns one and two. Present the information found at the top of page 62 in core book. Choose several pairs of words listed under the heading *Real Words* from these pages, and write those words on the board. Identify which syllable pattern to assign to the vowel in each word of the word pairs. See if students can think of any word pairs on their own where these two syllable patterns would apply.

Student Exercises
Lesson 212 / Lesson 214 / Lesson 216 / Lesson 218

Students read the words in these lessons. (See the discussion of *Guided Oral Reading Practice* on pages 8 - 10.)
   Lesson 213 (Quiz 58) / Lesson 215 (Quiz 59) / Lesson 217 (Quiz 60) / Lesson 219 (Quiz 61)
The teacher dictates the word pairs from these lessons. (See the information in the box that immediately follows this paragraph titled *Dictation Procedure for Section Two*.) Dictate in word pairs just as the words are listed on this page. As an example do not dictate the word *sha* by itself; instead dictate the words *sha - shack*. **Students both spell and mark these words.**

Dictation Procedure for *Section Two*
Note the additional steps that begin with *Step 14*

1. The teacher pronounces the word two times. **"The word is** *shell, shell.***"**
2. The teacher identifies the number of sounds contained in the word and makes those sounds. The teacher says, **"three sounds** (and pronounces them slowly and clearly) - **/sh/, /e/** (short e sound), **/l/.**"
3. Students write the letters in the word on dry-erase marker board or on practice paper as they hear each individual sound within the word pronounced by the teacher.
4. The teacher pronounces the word a final time. The teacher says, *"shell."*
5. Students hold up their marker boards for the teacher to see. If the teacher sees a student has misspelled the word, the teacher will say to the student, **"Think about it."** The teacher will not tell the student how to spell the word but will instead pronounce the word again and exaggerate whatever element in the word the student has misspelled. Even if the student continues to misspell the word, the teacher does not tell the student the correct spelling of the word at this point.
6. The teacher asks students to say the word. The teacher says, **"Say the word."**
7. Students say, *"shell."*
8. The teacher asks how many sounds are in the word. The teacher asks, **"How many sounds?"**
9. Students identify the number of sounds in the word. Students reply, **"three."**
10. The teacher asks for the first sound in the word *shell*. The teacher asks, **"first sound?"** Students do not say the name of the letter team *sh* but instead make the sound, **"/sh/."** The teacher writes the letter team *sh* on the board.
11. The teacher asks for second sound in the word *shell*. "The teacher asks, **"second sound?"** Students do not call out the name of the letter *e* but instead make the sound, **"/e/"** (short e sound). The teacher writes the letter *e* on the board.
12. The teacher asks for the third sound in the word *shell*. "The teacher asks, **"third sound?"** Students do not call out the name of the letter *l* but instead make the sound, **"/l/."** The teacher writes the letters *ll* on the board. The teacher asks the students to recite the *FLOSS* spelling rule regarding words that end in the letters f, l, or s.
13. Students check to make sure they have spelled the word correctly and make any changes in their spelling of the word at this time.
14. The teacher tells the students to mark the word. **"Mark the word** *shell.***"** Students mark the word they have just spelled.
15. Students hold up their marker boards for the teacher to see. If the teacher sees a student has not marked the word correctly, the teacher will say to the student, **"Think about it."** Even if the student continues to not mark the word correctly, the teacher does not tell the student the correct marking of the word at this point.
16. The teacher marks the word on the board following the order of steps presented in *Procedure for Marking Words in Section Two* found on page 40. The teacher says, **"Let's mark the word. Step One?"**
17. If a word contains a letter team, students respond, **" Underline ___."** (They identify all letter teams for the teacher to underline.) If a letter or letter team represents its second sound, students will respond, **"Double underline ___."** (They identify the letters or letter teams to be double underlined.) If the word contains a silent e, students reply **"Underline the silent e."** If the word contains none of these elements, students reply, **"There is nothing to mark."** In the word *shell* students respond, **"Underline sh."**
18. The teacher asks, **"Step Two?"**

19. Students identify the correct syllable pattern to write under the vowel. Students respond, "**syllable pattern ___under ___.**" In the word *shell* students respond, "**syllable pattern one under e.**" The marking of the word is complete and students check to be sure they have marked the word correctly.

Pages 64 – 65
Supplemental Materials
Posters – Display Poster titled *Three Major Syllable Patterns*.
Flash Cards – Review all cards previously introduced that have not been retired.
The We All Can Read Phonics Game – Students play *Card Game Eleven* upon completing these pages.

Information Teacher Presents or Reviews on these Pages
These pages introduce syllable pattern three. Present the information found at the top of page 64 in the core book. Choose several pairs of words listed under the heading *Real Words* from these pages, and write those words on the board. Apply the rule for syllable pattern three listed at the top of page 64 along with the previously learned rule for syllable pattern one introduced on page 62 to the words in each of these word pairs. See if students can think of any word pairs on their own where these two syllable patterns would apply.

Student Exercises
Lesson 220 / Lesson 222 / Lesson 224 / Lesson 226
Students read the words in these lessons. (See the discussion of *Guided Oral Reading Practice* on pages 8 - 10.)
   Lesson 221 (Quiz 62) / Lesson 223 (Quiz 63) / Lesson 225 (Quiz 64) / Lesson 227 (Quiz 65)
The teacher dictates the word pairs from these lessons. (See information under *Dictation Procedure for Section Two* on pages 41 - 42.) Dictate in word pairs just as the words are listed on this page. As an example do not dictate the word *slim* by itself; instead dictate the words *slim - slime*. **Students both spell and mark these words.**

Page 66
Supplemental Materials
Flash Cards – Introduce Card Set A # 86 / Card Set B # 9 / Card Set C # 37. Retire Card Set B # 8. Review all cards previously introduced that have not been retired.

Information Teacher Presents or Reviews on this Page
Present the information found at the top of this page. Write words on the board that contain both the first and second long sounds of the letter *u*. The fact that the letter *u* represents two long sounds is a concept that can initially be difficult for some to grasp. The best way to teach this concept is often to contrast the first long sound of *u* in one word such as *cube* with the second long sound that *u* represents in another word such as *Luke*. According to the dictionary, the long *u* sound in some of these words such as *tune* may be pronounced as either /tyoon/ or /toon/. Before students see the words on this page, call out the words from this page, and ask students to put one finger up if the long *u* sound in the word represents its first long sound and two fingers up if the long *u* sound in the word represents its second long sound. In dictation tell students to count two sounds when accounting for the first long sound *u* represents, /y/ and /oo/.

Teacher's Guide
Student Exercises
Lesson 228

Students read the words in this lesson. (See the discussion of *Guided Oral Reading Practice* on pages 8 - 10.)

Lesson 229 (Quiz 66)

The teacher dictates the words from this lesson. (See information under *Dictation Procedure for Section Two* on pages 41 - 42.) **Students mark these words to indicate whether the letter *u* is making its first or second long sound.**

Page 67
Supplemental Materials

Flash Cards – Review all cards previously introduced that have not been retired.

Information Teacher Presents or Reviews on this Page

This page consists entirely of sentences. In addition to the word lists that are found on most pages in this book, it is also helpful for students to have the opportunity to read sentences whose words contain those phonic elements recently presented.

Student Exercises
Lesson 230 / Lesson 232

Students read the sentences in these lessons. (See the information provided under *Procedure to Follow on Pages Consisting of Sentences* located on pages 20 - 21.)

Lesson 231 / Lesson 233

The teacher dictates the sentences from these lessons. (See the information provided under *Procedure to Follow on Pages Consisting of Sentences* located on pages 20 - 21.)

Page 68
Supplemental Materials

Flash Cards – Review all cards previously introduced.
The Reader – Read pages 36-37 (1st Ed.) or pages 64-65 (2nd. Ed.) on completing page 68.

Information Teacher Presents or Reviews on this Page

This page consists of two stories containing the elements identified at the top of the page in the title. One story uses nonsense words; the other does not. In addition to the word lists that are found on most pages in this book, and the page containing sentences that is presented on the page immediately preceding this page, it is also helpful for students to have the opportunity to read stories whose words contain those phonic elements recently presented.

Lesson 234 / Lesson 235

Students read the stories in these lessons. (See the information provided under *Oral Reading Procedure With Stories* located on page 21.)

Page 69
Supplemental Materials

Blackline Masters – Duplicate pages twenty through twenty-two for students to take home.

Information Teacher Presents or Reviews on this Page

Mastery Check and Review Number Eight – Review the information found on page 28 in the core book.

Teacher's Guide
Student Exercises
Lesson 236 through Lesson 239
See the box titled *Administering the Mastery Checks*: *Mastery Checks One through Eight* on page 28.

Pages 70 – 71
Supplemental Materials
Flash Cards – Review all cards previously introduced that have not been retired.

Information Teacher Presents or Reviews on these Pages
Two pages review syllable patterns one, two, and three. Review each of the three syllable patterns. Write words on the board that illustrate each of these three syllable patterns. Ask students to think of one-syllable words that illustrate each of these three syllable patterns.

Student Exercises
Lesson 240 / Lesson 242 / Lesson 244 / Lesson 246
Students read the words in these lessons. (See the discussion of *Guided Oral Reading Practice* on pages 8 - 10.)
Lesson 241 (Quiz 67) / Lesson 243 (Quiz 68) / Lesson 245 (Quiz 69) / Lesson 247 (Quiz 70)
The teacher dictates words from these lessons. **Students both spell and mark these words.** (See information under *Dictation Procedure for Section Two* on pages 41 - 42.)

Page 72
Supplemental Materials
Flash Cards – Review all cards previously introduced that have not been retired.

Information Teacher Presents or Reviews on this Page
This page consists entirely of sentences. In addition to the word lists that are found on most pages in this book, it is also helpful for students to have the opportunity to read sentences whose words contain those phonic elements recently presented.

Student Exercises
Lesson 248 / Lesson 250
Students read the sentences in these lessons. (See the information provided under *Procedure to Follow on Pages Consisting of Sentences* located on pages 20 - 21.)
Lesson 249/ Lesson 251
The teacher dictates the sentences from these lessons. (See the information provided under *Procedure to Follow on Pages Consisting of Sentences* located on pages 20 - 21.)

Page 73
Supplemental Materials
Flash Cards – Review all cards previously introduced.
The Reader – Read pages 38-42 (1st Ed.) or pages 66-70 (2nd. Ed.) on completing page 73.
The We All Can Read Phonics Game – Students play *Card Game Twelve* upon completing this page.

Information Teacher Presents or Reviews on this Page
This page consists of two stories containing the elements identified at the top of the page in the title. One story uses nonsense words; the other does not. In addition to the word lists that are found on most pages in this book, and the page containing sentences

that is presented on the page immediately preceding this page, it is also helpful for students to have the opportunity to read stories whose words contain those phonic elements recently presented.

Lesson 252 / Lesson 253
Students read the stories in these lessons. (See the information provided under *Oral Reading Procedure With Stories* located on page 21.)

Page 74
Supplemental Materials
Posters – Display Poster titled *Syllable Pattern Four Teams.*
Flash Cards – Introduce Card Set A #'s 87-97 / Card Set B # 10 / Card Set C #'s 38-42. Retire Card Set C #'s 32, 33, 35, 36, 37. Review all cards previously introduced that have not been retired.

Information Teacher Presents or Reviews on this Page
Syllable pattern four teams are introduced. Explain Syllable Pattern Four, which is stated at the top of page 75. When certain vowels come together, they form teams where the first vowel represents its long sound, and the second vowel is silent. The vowel team *ue* represents two sounds. When *ue* has one line under it, *ue* represents the first long sound of *u*/yoo/ as in *cue*. When *ue* has two lines under it, *ue* represents the second long sound of *u* /oo/ as in *true*. The vowel team *ui* is always double underlined because it represents only the second long sound of the vowel *u* /oo/ as in *suit*. **Vowel teams are always underlined. Students should memorize these ten vowel teams.**

Student Exercises
Lesson 254
1. Ask students to make the sounds represented by the vowel teams listed in the individual boxes on this page. Ask students to think of one-syllable words that contain these syllable pattern four letter teams.
2. Reverse the process, and make the sounds represented by the vowel teams on this page. Next ask your students to write the vowel teams that represent those sounds. Divide the instructional period equally between these two activities.
3. After these new teams have been introduced to your students, periodically ask them to list as many of these teams as they can from memory. Continue to ask them on subsequent days to list the teams from memory until students are able to do so automatically.

A Word About Spelling
Starting from this page forward, do not use nonsense words for dictation any longer. Students are now introduced to two and sometimes three vowel teams that all represent the same identical sound. As an example the long *o* sound is represented by three teams: *oa, oe,* and *ow*. In addition the long o sound may also be found in words that end in a silent letter *e* such as in the word *hope*. Therefore nonsense words are no longer used for dictation in order to avoid confusion on the student's part.

Pages 75 - 76
Supplemental Materials
Flash Cards – Review all cards previously introduced that have not been retired.

Teacher's Guide
Information Teacher Presents or Reviews on these Pages
Students practice reading and spelling words that all contain syllable pattern four teams. Review syllable pattern four. Ask students to list as many of the syllable pattern four teams as they can from memory, and ask them to think of one-syllable words that contain each of those teams.

Student Exercises
Lesson 255 / Lesson 257 / Lesson 259 / Lesson 261
Students read the words in these lessons. (See the discussion of Guided Oral Reading Practice on pages 8 - 10.)

Lesson 256 / Lesson 260
The teacher does not dictate the nonsense words from these lessons. **Nonsense words are no longer used for dictation at this point in the program.** Instead students mark the words by underlining the letter teams found in these nonsense words and writing the correct syllable pattern number under the vowel in each word. (Syllable pattern numbers are written directly under the vowel; however, syllable pattern numbers are never written under the silent *e*.) As an alternative to marking words on dry-erase marker boards or practice paper, students may orally call out the letter teams found in each of these nonsense words and the syllable pattern number associated with the vowel in each word.

Lesson 258 (Quiz 71) / Lesson 262 (Quiz 72)
The teacher dictates the words from these lessons. **Students both spell and mark these words.** (See information under *Dictation Procedure for Section Two* on pages 41 - 42.)

Page 77
Supplemental Materials
Flash Cards – Review all cards previously introduced that have not been retired.

Information Teacher Presents or Reviews on this Page
This page consists entirely of sentences. In addition to the word lists that are found on most pages in this book, it is also helpful for students to have the opportunity to read sentences whose words contain those phonic elements recently presented.

Student Exercises
Lesson 263 / Lesson 265
Students read the sentences in these lessons. (See the information provided under *Procedure to Follow on Pages Consisting of Sentences* located on pages 20 - 21.)

Lesson 264
The teacher does not dictate the nonsense sentences from this lesson. **Nonsense words are no longer used for dictation at this point in the program.** Instead students mark the words in bold in these lessons by underlining the letter teams found in these nonsense words and writing the correct syllable pattern number under the vowel in each word. (Syllable pattern numbers are written directly under the vowel; however, syllable pattern numbers are never written under the silent *e*.) As an alternative to marking words on dry-erase marker boards or practice paper, students may orally call out the letter teams found in each of these nonsense words in the sentences and the syllable pattern number associated with the vowel in each word.

Lesson 266
The teacher dictates the sentences from this lesson. (See the information provided under *Procedure to Follow on Pages Consisting of Sentences* located on pages 20 - 21.)

Teacher's Guide
Page 78
Supplemental Materials

Flash Cards – Review all cards previously introduced.
The Reader – Read pages 43-44 upon completing page 78 in this book. 71-74
The We All Can Read Phonics Game – Students play *Card Game Thirteen* upon completing this page.

Information Teacher Presents or Reviews on this Page

This page consists of two stories containing the elements identified at the top of the page in the title. One story uses nonsense words; the other does not. In addition to the word lists that are found on most pages in this book, and the page containing sentences that is presented on the page immediately preceding this page, it is also helpful for students to have the opportunity to read stories whose words contain those phonic elements recently presented.

Lesson 267 / Lesson 268

Students read the stories in these lessons. (See the information provided under *Oral Reading Procedure With Stories* located on page 21.)

Pages 79 – 80
Supplemental Materials

Blackline Masters – Duplicate pages twenty-two through twenty-six for students to take home.

Information Teacher Presents or Reviews on these Pages

Mastery Check and Review Number Nine – Review the information found on page 28 in the core book.

Student Exercises
Lesson 269 through Lesson 275

See the box titled *Administering the Mastery Checks: Mastery Checks Nine through Thirteen* in the next paragraph. Dictate words as they are organized on these pages. As an example before dictating the words listed under the *ea* team found on page 79, you might say to your students, "The next group of words that I am about to dictate all contain the vowel team *ea*."

Administering the Mastery Checks: Mastery Checks Nine through Thirteen
Students should be able to read and spell the words in these mastery checks with a high degree of accuracy and fluency. It is not necessary to ask a student to read and spell every word from this list. Choose a representative number of words under each category in this list (at least ten words), and ask students to read and spell them. But if students struggle either reading or spelling the representative words chosen, the teacher should then have the students read and spell all of the words in that particular column. Failure to be able to read and spell these words with an eighty percent or higher degree of accuracy strongly suggests that a student is not sufficiently prepared to move into the next unit and instead requires additional review from previous lessons. **When a student is asked to spell any of these words, he should underline any consonant teams or vowel teams contained in the word he is spelling**; it is not necessary to write a syllable pattern number under the word. **Beginning with this mastery check, administer the remaining mastery tests to all students regardless of their age or grade level.**

Teacher's Guide
Pages 81 – 82
Supplemental Materials
Flash Cards – Review all cards previously introduced that have not been retired.

Information Teacher Presents or Reviews on these Pages
These two pages review syllable patterns one, two, three, and four. Review each of the four syllable patterns. Ask students to explain in their own words the four syllable patterns they have learned. Ask students to write one-syllable words that illustrate each of the four syllable patterns. Ask students to list all of the consonant teams they have learned and all syllable pattern four teams they have learned. Make this activity a competition by giving students a certain amount of time to list all of the teams they can remember; call *stop* after the time has elapsed, and see which student has listed the most number of consonant and vowel teams.

Student Exercises
Lesson 276 and Lesson 278 and Lesson 280 and Lesson 282
Students read the words in these lessons. (See the discussion of *Guided Oral Reading Practice* on pages 8 - 10.)

Lesson 277 / Lesson 281
The teacher does not dictate the nonsense words from these lessons. **Nonsense words are no longer used for dictation at this point in the program.** Instead students mark the words by underlining the letter teams found in these nonsense words and writing the correct syllable pattern number under the vowel in each word. (Syllable pattern numbers are written directly under the vowel; however, syllable pattern numbers are never written under the silent *e*.) As an alternative to marking words on dry-erase marker boards or practice paper, students may orally call out the letter teams found in each of these nonsense words and the syllable pattern number associated with the vowel in each word.

Lesson 279 (Quiz 73) / Lesson 283 (Quiz 74)
The teacher dictates words from these lessons. **Students both spell and mark these words.** (See information under *Dictation Procedure for Section Two* on pages 41 - 42.)

Page 83
Supplemental Materials
Flash Cards – Review all cards previously introduced that have not been retired.

Information Teacher Presents or Reviews on this Page
This page consists entirely of sentences. In addition to the word lists that are found on most pages in this book, it is also helpful for students to have the opportunity to read sentences whose words contain those phonic elements recently presented.

Student Exercises
Lesson 284 / Lesson 286
Students read the sentences in these lessons. (See the information provided under *Procedure to Follow on Pages Consisting of Sentences* located on pages 20 - 21.)

Lesson 285
The teacher does not dictate the nonsense sentences from this lesson. **Nonsense words are no longer used for dictation at this point in the program.** Instead students mark the words printed in bold by underlining the letter teams found in these nonsense words and writing the correct syllable pattern number under the vowel in each word. (Syllable pattern numbers are written directly under the vowel; however, syllable

pattern numbers are never written under the silent *e*.) As an alternative to marking the nonsense words from these sentences on dry-erase marker boards or practice paper, students may orally call out the letter teams found in each of the nonsense words in each sentence and the syllable pattern number associated with the vowel in each word.

Lesson 287

The teacher dictates the sentences from this lesson. (See the information provided under *Procedure to Follow on Pages Consisting of Sentences* located on pages 20 - 21.)

Page 84
Supplemental Materials

Flash Cards – Review all cards previously introduced.
The Reader – Read pages 45-51 (1ˢᵗ Ed.) or pages 75-81 (2ⁿᵈ. Ed.) on completing page 84.
The We All Can Read Phonics Game – Students play *Card Game Fourteen* upon completing this page.

Information Teacher Presents or Reviews on this Page

This page consists of two stories containing the elements identified at the top of the page in the title. One story uses nonsense words; the other does not. In addition to the word lists that are found on most pages in this book, and the page containing sentences that is presented on the page immediately preceding this page, it is also helpful for students to have the opportunity to read stories whose words contain those phonic elements recently presented.

Lesson 288 / Lesson 289

Students read the stories in these lessons. (See the information provided under *Oral Reading Procedure With Stories* located on page 21.)

Page 85
Supplemental Materials

Posters – Display Poster titled *Syllable Pattern Five Teams*.
Flash Cards – Introduce Card Set A #'s 98-103 / Card Set C #'s 43-45. Review all cards previously introduced that have not been retired.

Information Teacher Presents or Reviews on this Page

Syllable pattern five teams are introduced. Explain Syllable Pattern Five, which is stated at the top of page 86. A vowel when followed by the letter *r* will usually form a syllable pattern five team. The letters *ear* will normally form a syllable pattern five team when those letters are followed by a consonant sound. **Vowel teams are always underlined. Students should memorize these six vowel teams.**

Student Exercises
Lesson 290

1. Ask your students to make the sounds represented by the vowel teams listed in the individual boxes on this page. Ask students to think of one-syllable words that contain these letter teams.
2. Reverse the process, and make the sounds represented by the vowel teams on this page. Then ask students to write the vowel teams that represent those sounds. **Note that *er*, *ir*, *ur*, and *ear* all represent the same sound.**
3. After these new teams have been introduced to your students, periodically ask them to list as many of these teams as they can from memory. Continue to ask them on subsequent days to list the teams from memory until students are able to do so automatically.

Pages 86 - 87
Supplemental Materials
Flash Cards – Review all cards previously introduced that have not been retired.

Information Teacher Presents or Reviews on these Pages
Students practice reading and spelling words that all contain syllable pattern five teams. Review syllable pattern five. Ask students to list as many of the syllable pattern five teams as they can from memory, and ask them to think of one-syllable words that contain each of the syllable pattern five teams.

Student Exercises
Lesson 291 / Lesson 293 / Lesson 295 / Lesson 297
Students read the words in these lessons. (See the discussion of Guided Oral Reading Practice on pages 8 - 10.)
Lesson 292 / Lesson 296
The teacher does not dictate the nonsense words from these lessons. **Nonsense words are no longer used for dictation at this point in the program.** Instead students mark the words by underlining the letter teams found in these nonsense words and writing the correct syllable pattern number under the vowel in each word. (Syllable pattern numbers are written directly under the vowel; however, syllable pattern numbers are never written under the silent *e*.) As an alternative to marking words on dry-erase marker boards or practice paper, students may orally call out the letter teams found in each of these nonsense words and the syllable pattern number associated with the vowel in each word.
Lesson 294 (Quiz 75) / Lesson 298 (Quiz 76)
The teacher dictates the words from these lessons. **Students both spell and mark these words.** (See information under *Dictation Procedure for Section Two* on pages 41 - 42.)

Page 88
Supplemental Materials
Flash Cards – Review all cards previously introduced that have not been retired.

Information Teacher Presents or Reviews on this Page
This page consists entirely of sentences. In addition to the word lists that are found on most pages in this book, it is also helpful for students to have the opportunity to read sentences whose words contain those phonic elements recently presented.

Student Exercises
Lesson 299 / Lesson 301
Students read the sentences in these lessons. (See the information provided under *Procedure to Follow on Pages Consisting of Sentences* located on pages 20 - 21.)
Lesson 300
The teacher does not dictate the nonsense sentences from this lesson. **Nonsense words are no longer used for dictation at this point in the program.** Instead students mark the words in bold in these lessons by underlining the letter teams found in these nonsense words and writing the correct syllable pattern number under the vowel in each word. (Syllable pattern numbers are written directly under the vowel; however, syllable pattern numbers are never written under the silent *e*.) As an alternative to marking words on dry-erase marker boards or practice paper, students may orally call out the letter teams found in each of these nonsense words in the sentences and the syllable pattern number associated with the vowel in each word.

Teacher's Guide
Lesson 302

The teacher dictates the sentences from this lesson. (See the information provided under *Procedure to Follow on Pages Consisting of Sentences* located on pages 20 - 21.)

Page 89
Supplemental Materials

Flash Cards – Review all cards previously introduced.
The Reader – Read pages 52-53 (1ˢᵗ Ed.) or pages 82-85 (2ⁿᵈ. Ed.) on completing page 89.
The We All Can Read Phonics Game – Students play *Card Game Fifteen* upon completing this page.

Information Teacher Presents or Reviews on this Page

This page consists of two stories containing the elements identified at the top of the page in the title. One story uses nonsense words; the other does not. In addition to the word lists that are found on most pages in this book, and the page containing sentences that is presented on the page immediately preceding this page, it is also helpful for students to have the opportunity to read stories whose words contain those phonic elements recently presented.

Lesson 303 / Lesson 304

Students read the stories in these lessons. (See the information provided under *Oral Reading Procedure With Stories* located on page 21.)

Page 90
Supplemental Materials

Blackline Masters – Duplicate pages twenty-six through twenty-nine for students to take home.

Information Teacher Presents or Reviews on this Page

Mastery Check and Review Number Ten – Review the information found on page 28 in the core book.

Student Exercises
Lesson 305 through Lesson 309

See the box titled *Administering the Mastery Checks: Mastery Checks Nine through Thirteen* on page 47. Dictate words as they are grouped on this page. As an example before dictating the words listed under the *er* team found on page 90 in the core book, you might say to your students, "The next group of words which I am about to dictate all contain the vowel team *er*."

Pages 91 – 92
Supplemental Materials

Flash Cards – Review all cards previously introduced that have not been retired.

Information Teacher Presents or Reviews on these Pages

These two pages review syllable patterns one, two, three, four, and five. Review each of the five syllable patterns. Ask students to explain in their own words the five syllable patterns they have learned. Ask students to write one-syllable words that illustrate each of the five syllable patterns. Ask students to list all of the consonant teams they have learned, all syllable pattern four teams they have learned, and all syllable pattern five teams they have learned. Make this activity a competition by

Teacher's Guide

giving students a certain amount of time to list all of the teams they can remember; call *stop* after the time has elapsed, and see which student has listed the most number of consonant and vowel teams.

Student Exercises
Lesson 310 / Lesson 312 / Lesson 314 / Lesson 316

Students read the words in these lessons. (See the discussion of Guided Oral Reading Practice on pages 8 - 10.)

Lesson 311 / Lesson 315

The teacher does not dictate the nonsense words from these lessons. **Nonsense words are no longer used for dictation at this point in the program.** Instead students mark the words by underlining the letter teams found in these nonsense words and writing the correct syllable pattern number under the vowel in each word. (Syllable pattern numbers are written directly under the vowel; however, syllable pattern numbers are never written under the silent *e*.) As an alternative to marking words on dry-erase marker boards or practice paper, students may orally call out the letter teams found in each of these nonsense words and the syllable pattern number associated with the vowel in each word.

Lesson 313 (Quiz 77) / Lesson 317 (Quiz 78)

The teacher dictates the words from these lessons. **Students both spell and mark these words.** (See information under *Dictation Procedure for Section Two* on pages 41 - 42.)

Page 93
Supplemental Materials

Flash Cards – Review all cards previously introduced that have not been retired.

Information Teacher Presents or Reviews on this Page

This page consists entirely of sentences. In addition to the word lists that are found on most pages in this book, it is also helpful for students to have the opportunity to read sentences whose words contain those phonic elements recently presented.

Student Exercises
Lesson 318 and Lesson 320

Students read the sentences in these lessons. (See the information provided under *Procedure to Follow on Pages Consisting of Sentences* located on pages 20 - 21.)

Lesson 319

The teacher does not dictate the nonsense sentences from this lesson. **Nonsense words are no longer used for dictation at this point in the program.** Instead students mark the words printed in bold by underlining the letter teams found in these nonsense words and writing the correct syllable pattern number under the vowel in each word. (Syllable pattern numbers are written directly under the vowel; however, syllable pattern numbers are never written under the silent *e*.) As an alternative to marking the nonsense words from these sentences on dry-erase marker boards or practice paper, students may orally call out the letter teams found in each of the nonsense words in each sentence and the syllable pattern number associated with the vowel in each word.

Lesson 321

The teacher dictates the sentences from this lesson. (See the information provided under *Procedure to Follow on Pages Consisting of Sentences* located on pages 20 - 21.)

Teacher's Guide
Page 94
Supplemental Materials

Flash Cards – Review all cards previously introduced.
The Reader – Read pages 54-58 (1st Ed.) or pages 86-90 (2nd. Ed.) on completing page 94.
The We All Can Read Phonics Game – Students play *Card Game Sixteen* upon completing this page.

Information Teacher Presents or Reviews on this Page

This page consists of two stories containing the elements identified at the top of the page in the title. One story uses nonsense words; the other does not. In addition to the word lists that are found on most pages in this book, and the page containing sentences that is presented on the page immediately preceding this page, it is also helpful for students to have the opportunity to read stories whose words contain those phonic elements recently presented.

Lesson 322 / Lesson 323

Students read the stories in these lessons. (See the information provided under *Oral Reading Procedure With Stories* located on page 21.)

Page 95
Supplemental Materials

Posters – Display Poster titled *Syllable Pattern Six Teams*.
Flash Cards – Introduce Card Set A #'s 104-113 / Card Set B #'s 11-13 / Card Set C #'s 46-51. Retire Card Set C #'s 41, 42/ Review all cards previously introduced that have not been retired.

Information Teacher Presents or Reviews on this Page

Syllable pattern six teams are introduced. Explain the information that is presented at the top of page 96. Both syllable pattern four and syllable pattern six teams occur when two vowels come together and form a team. The difference between these two groups of vowel teams is that in syllable pattern four teams, the first vowel represents its name while with syllable pattern six teams, the first vowel does not represent its name. Due to regional pronunciation differences, some people will pronounce the *ew* team as making its first sound in some words while other individuals will pronounce the *ew* team in those same words as making its second sound. The word *stew* is an example of this. Some say /styoo/ while others will say /stoo/. In such instances either pronunciation is acceptable. Underline the *ew* team once when it represents the sound /yoo/ and twice when it represents the sound /oo/: f<u>ew</u>, thr<u>ew</u>. **Vowel teams are always underlined. Students should memorize these ten vowel teams.**

Student Exercises
Lesson 324

1. Ask your students to make the sounds represented by the vowel teams listed in the individual boxes on this page. Ask students to think of one-syllable words that contain these letter teams.
2. Reverse the process, and make the sounds represented by the vowel teams on this page. Next ask your students to write the vowel teams that represent those sounds. Note that many of these teams are pairs representing the same sound: <u>au</u>/<u>aw</u>, <u>oi</u>/<u>oy</u>, <u>ou</u>/<u>ow</u>.
3. After these new teams have been introduced to your students, periodically ask them to list as many of these teams as they can from memory. Continue to ask them on

Teacher's Guide

subsequent days to list the teams from memory until students are able to do so automatically.

Pages 96 - 98
Supplemental Materials
Flash Cards – Review all cards previously introduced that have not been retired.

Information Teacher Presents or Reviews on these Pages

Students practice reading and spelling words that all contain syllable pattern six teams. Review syllable pattern six. Ask students to list as many of the syllable pattern six teams as they can from memory, and ask them to think of one-syllable words that contain each of the syllable pattern six teams.

Student Exercises
Lesson 325 / Lesson 327 / Lesson 329 / Lesson 331 / Lesson 333 / Lesson 335

Students read the words in these lessons. (See the discussion of Guided Oral Reading Practice on pages 8 - 10.)

Lesson 326 / Lesson 330 / Lesson 334

The teacher does not dictate the nonsense words from these lessons. **Nonsense words are no longer used for dictation at this point in the program.** Instead students mark the words by underlining the letter teams found in these nonsense words and writing the correct syllable pattern number under the vowel in each word. (Syllable pattern numbers are written directly under the vowel; however, syllable pattern numbers are never written under the silent *e*.) As an alternative to marking words on dry-erase marker boards or practice paper, students may orally call out the letter teams found in each of these nonsense words and the syllable pattern number associated with the vowel in each word.

Lesson 328 (Quiz 79) / Lesson 332 (Quiz 80) / Lesson 336 (Quiz 81)

The teacher dictates the words from these lessons. **Students both spell and mark these words.** (See information under *Dictation Procedure for Section Two* on pages 41 - 42.)

Page 99
Supplemental Materials
Flash Cards – Review all cards previously introduced that have not been retired.

Information Teacher Presents or Reviews on this Page

This page consists entirely of sentences. In addition to the word lists that are found on most pages in this book, it is also helpful for students to have the opportunity to read sentences whose words contain those phonic elements recently presented.

Student Exercises
Lesson 337 / Lesson 339

Students read the sentences in these lessons. (See the information provided under *Procedure to Follow on Pages Consisting of Sentences* located on pages 20 - 21.)

Lesson 338

The teacher does not dictate the nonsense sentences from this lesson. **Nonsense words are no longer used for dictation at this point in the program.** Instead students mark the words in bold in these lessons by underlining the letter teams found in these nonsense words and writing the correct syllable pattern number under the vowel in each word. (Syllable pattern numbers are written directly under the vowel; however, syllable pattern numbers are never written under the silent *e*.) As an alternative to marking words on dry-erase marker boards or practice paper, students may orally call out the letter teams found in each of these nonsense words in the sentences and the syllable pattern number associated with the vowel in each word.

Lesson 340

The teacher dictates the sentences from this lesson. (See the information provided under *Procedure to Follow on Pages Consisting of Sentences* located on pages 20 - 21.)

Page 100
Supplemental Materials

Flash Cards – Review all cards previously introduced.
The Reader – Read pages 59-60 (1st Ed.) or pages 91-94 (2nd. Ed.) on completing page 100.
The We All Can Read Phonics Game – Students play *Card Game Seventeen* upon completing this page.

Information Teacher Presents or Reviews on this Page

This page consists of two stories containing the elements identified at the top of the page in the title. One story uses nonsense words; the other does not. In addition to the word lists that are found on most pages in this book, and the page containing sentences that is presented on the page immediately preceding this page, it is also helpful for students to have the opportunity to read stories whose words contain those phonic elements recently presented.

Lesson 341 / Lesson 342

Students read the stories in these lessons. (See the information provided under *Oral Reading Procedure With Stories* located on page 21.)

Page 101
Supplemental Materials

Blackline Masters – Duplicate pages twenty-nine through thirty-two for students to take home.

Information Teacher Presents or Reviews on this Page

Mastery Check and Review Number Eleven – Review the information found on page 28 in the core book.

Student Exercises
Lessons 343 through Lesson 350

See the box titled *Administering the Mastery Checks: Mastery Checks Nine through Thirteen* on page 47. Dictate words as they are grouped on these pages. As an example before dictating the words listed under the *au* team found on page 101 in the core book, you might say to your students, "The next group of words which I am about to dictate all contain the vowel team *au*."

Pages 102 – 103
Supplemental Materials

Posters – Display Poster titled *Six Major Syllable Patterns*.
Flash Cards – Review all cards previously introduced that have not been retired.

Information Teacher Presents or Reviews on these Pages

These two pages review syllable patterns one, two, three, four, five, and six. Review each of the six syllable patterns. Ask students to explain in their own words the six syllable patterns they have learned. Ask students to write one-syllable words that illustrate each of the six syllable patterns. Ask students to list all of the consonant teams they have learned, all syllable pattern four teams they have learned, all syllable pattern five teams they have learned, and all syllable pattern six teams they have learned. Make this activity a competition by giving students a certain amount of time to list all of the teams they can remember; call *stop* after the time has elapsed, and see which student has listed the most number of consonant and vowel teams.

Student Exercises
Lesson 351 / Lesson 353 / Lesson 355 / Lesson 357
Students read the words in these lessons. (See the discussion of *Guided Oral Reading Practice* on pages 8 - 10.)

Lesson 352 / Lesson 356
The teacher does not dictate the nonsense words from these lessons. **Nonsense words are no longer used for dictation at this point in the program.** Instead students mark the words by underlining the letter teams found in these nonsense words and writing the correct syllable pattern number under the vowel in each word. (Syllable pattern numbers are written directly under the vowel; however, syllable pattern numbers are never written under the silent *e*.) As an alternative to marking words on dry-erase marker boards or practice paper, students may orally call out the letter teams found in each of these nonsense words and the syllable pattern number associated with the vowel in each word.

Lesson 354 (Quiz 82) / Lesson 358 (Quiz 83)
The teacher dictates the words from these lessons. **Students both spell and mark these words.** (See information under *Dictation Procedure for Section Two* on pages 41 - 42.)

Page 104
Supplemental Materials
Flash Cards – Review all cards previously introduced that have not been retired.

Information Teacher Presents or Reviews on this Page
This page consists entirely of sentences. In addition to the word lists that are found on most pages in this book, it is also helpful for students to have the opportunity to read sentences whose words contain those phonic elements recently presented.

Student Exercises
Lesson 359 / Lesson 361
Students read the sentences in these lessons. (See the information provided under *Procedure to Follow on Pages Consisting of Sentences* located on pages 20 - 21.)

Lesson 360
The teacher does not dictate the nonsense sentences from this lesson. **Nonsense words are no longer used for dictation at this point in the program.** Instead students mark the words printed in bold by underlining the letter teams found in these nonsense words and writing the correct syllable pattern number under the vowel in each word. (Syllable pattern numbers are written directly under the vowel; however, syllable pattern numbers are never written under the silent *e*.) As an alternative to marking the nonsense words from these sentences on dry-erase marker boards or practice paper, students may orally call out the letter teams found in each of the nonsense words in each sentence and the syllable pattern number associated with the vowel in each word.

Teacher's Guide
Lesson 362
The teacher dictates the sentences from this lesson.   (See the information provided under *Procedure to Follow on Pages Consisting of Sentences* located on pages 20 - 21.)

Page 105
Supplemental Materials
Flash Cards – Review all cards previously introduced.
The Reader – Read pages 61-65 (1st Ed.) or pages 95-99 (2nd. Ed.) on completing page 105.
The We All Can Read Phonics Game – Students play *Card Game Eighteen* upon completing this page.

Information Teacher Presents or Reviews on this Page
This page consists of two stories containing the elements identified at the top of the page in the title. One story uses nonsense words; the other does not. In addition to the word lists that are found on most pages in this book, and the page containing sentences that is presented on the page immediately preceding this page, it is also helpful for students to have the opportunity to read stories whose words contain those phonic elements recently presented.

Lesson 363 / Lesson 364
Students read the stories in these lessons. (See the information provided under *Oral Reading Procedure With Stories* located on page 21.)

Page 106
Information Teacher Presents or Reviews on this Page
The chart on this page lists the six syllable patterns learned thus far in the program. This chart is an excellent tool to use for reviewing these six syllable patterns.

Student Exercises
Lesson 365
Students should be able to explain in their own words the six syllable patterns and to think of words that illustrate each of the six syllable patterns.

Page 107
Information Teacher Presents or Reviews on this Page
The chart on this page contains all of the consonant blends, consonant teams, and vowel teams presented thus far in the program. This chart is an excellent tool to use for reviewing these letter blends and letter teams.

Student Exercises
Lesson 366 through Lesson 369
Ask your students to make the sounds represented by the beginning consonant blends (Lesson 366), ending consonant blends (Lesson 367), consonant teams (Lesson 368), and vowel teams (Lesson 369) listed in the individual boxes on this page. Ask students to think of words that contain a particular beginning consonant blend (Lesson 366), ending consonant blend (Lesson 367), consonant team (Lesson 368), or vowel team (Lesson 369). Make a game out of this process, and call out numbers from the boxes in each particular lesson in an arbitrary order. When a student is assigned one of those numbers, he must make the sound of the consonant blend or consonant team or vowel team in the box with that number and think of a word that contains that consonant blend or consonant team or vowel team. Reverse the process, and make the sounds

represented by the consonant blends or consonant teams or vowel teams in each lesson. Then ask your students to write the letters or letter teams that represent those sounds. Students should be able to spell any of these consonant blends, consonant teams, or vowel teams when they hear these sounds dictated. When dictating vowel sounds for which more than one team represents that sound such as *ai/ay, ea/ee/ey, oa/oe/ow, er/ir/ur/ear, au/aw, oi/oy,* or *ou/ow,* students should be able to list all of the teams. **After reviewing the information in all four of these lessons, use the chart as a whole to review all of the elements listed.** Make a game out of this process, and call out numbers from any of the boxes from 1 to 72 in an arbitrary order. When a student is assigned one of those numbers, he must make the sound of the consonant blend or consonant team or vowel team in the box with that number and think of a word that contains that consonant blend or consonant team or vowel team. Reverse the process, and make the sounds represented by the consonant blends or letter teams in any of the 72 boxes. Ask students to write the letters or letter teams that represent those sounds.

Section Three
Multiple Syllable Words
Page 108
Supplemental Materials

Posters – Display Poster titled *Decoding Procedure Chart.*

Information Teacher Presents or Reviews on this Page

The emphasis in this program continues to focus upon teaching students to apply a systematic marking procedure for analyzing words phonetically. This marking system is a critical and unique aspect of the *We All Can Read* program. Through the application of the five steps listed in the box found on page 108 in the core book titled *Procedure for Marking and Decoding Word in Section Three,* students are given a specific set of steps to follow when analyzing and marking words. By repeating this analysis process with hundreds or perhaps even thousands of words, students will internalize this analysis process until it becomes automatic. In order to mark correctly the words that follow in *Section Three,* a student must have a very solid understanding of the phonetic foundation of English. It is through the careful marking of the words in this book that an understanding of this phonetic foundation of English is established on the student's part.

Review with your students the five individual steps contained in the box titled *Procedure for Marking and Decoding Words in Section Three* on page 108 in the core book. Tell students from this point forward to refer to this box when marking words from subsequent pages in *Section Three.* **No more nonsense words are used in the book.**

Page-by-Page Instructions for Section Three
Page 109
Supplemental Materials

Flash Cards – Review all cards previously introduced that have not been retired.

Information Teacher Presents or Reviews on this Page

The concept of two-syllable words is explained to students. Present the information found at the top of this page. Syllable rules indicate where words divide into syllables. **Each syllable can have one and only one vowel sound; each vowel sound in a word must have its own syllable.** If there is one vowel sound in a word, the word is a one-syllable word; if there are two vowel sounds in the word, the word is a two-syllable word. On this page we learn the first of two syllable rules that govern syllable division for most words.

Syllable Rule One is explained to students.
Syllable Rule One - When two vowels representing sounds are separated by one consonant, divide the word after the first vowel and before the consonant.

Draw a line between the letters where syllable division occurs. Start the line above the letters, and continue the line below the letters to avoid confusing the division line for another letter. Syllable rule numbers go above the letters, and syllable pattern numbers go below the letters. **Place the syllable rule number directly to the right side of the division line.**

	1			1				1	← Syllable Rule Numbers
si	lent		e	vict		pho	to		
•	•		•	•		•	•		
2	1		2	1		2	2		←Syllable Pattern Numbers

Student Exercises
Lesson 370
Students read the words in these lessons. (See the discussion of *Guided Oral Reading Practice* on pages 8 - 10.)
Lesson 371 (Quiz 84)
Dictate the words from this lesson for students to spell and to mark. Follow the procedure listed in the box titled *Dictation Procedure for Multiple Syllable Words* found immediately below this paragraph. Remind students to underline all vowel and consonant teams, to divide the word into syllables, to list the syllable rule number above the word, and to assign the appropriate syllable pattern number under each vowel in each syllable of the word.

The dictation procedure is modified in *Section Three*. There are many steps to follow when dictating multiple syllable words. While this procedure may at first glance seem daunting, after applying this procedure with a relatively small number of words, the procedure becomes an easily learned and automatic process for both the student and teacher to learn and apply.

Dictation Procedure for Multiple Syllable Words
1. *The teacher pronounces the word two times. **"The word is until, until."**
2. If the word contains more than one-syllable, the teacher identifies the number of syllables contained in the dictated word. If the word is a one-syllable word, the teacher does not identify the number of syllables in the word. In the word *until*, the teacher says, **"two syllables."**
3. The teacher pronounces the first syllable two times. **"The first syllable is un, un."**
4. The teacher identifies the number of sounds in the syllable and makes those sounds. **"two sounds** (and pronounces them slowly and clearly) - /u/ (short u sound), /n/."
5. Students write the letters in the syllable on dry-erase marker board or on practice paper as they hear each individual sound within the syllable pronounced by the teacher.
6. The teacher pronounces the first syllable a final time and says, **"un."**
7. The teacher pronounces the second syllable two times. **"The second syllable is til, til."**
8. The teacher identifies the number of sounds in the syllable and makes those

sounds. **"three sounds, /t/, /i/ (short i sound), /l/."**

9. Students write the letters in the syllable on dry-erase marker board or on practice paper as they hear each individual sound within the syllable pronounced by the teacher.

10. The teacher pronounces the second syllable a final time and says, **"til."**

11. The teacher pronounces the dictated word one final time and says **"until."**

12. Students hold up their marker boards for the teacher to see. If the teacher sees a student has misspelled the word, the teacher will say to the student, **"Think about it."** The teacher will not tell the student how to spell the word but will instead pronounce the word again and exaggerate whatever element in the word the student has misspelled. Even if the student continues to misspell the word, the teacher does not tell the student the correct spelling of the word at this point.

13. The teacher asks the students to say the word. The teacher says, **"Say the word."** Students reply, **"until."**

14. The teacher asks, **"how many syllables?"** (The teacher would not ask this question if the dictated word is a one-syllable word.)

15. The students reply, **"two."**

16. The teacher says, **"Say the first syllable. "**

17. Students respond, **"un."**

18. The teacher asks how many sounds are in the first syllable. **"How many sounds?"**

19. Students identify the number of sounds in the syllable. Students reply, **"two."**

20. The teacher asks for the first sound in the syllable *un*. **"first sound?"**

21. Students do not say the name of the letter *u* but instead make the short *u* sound. Students say, **"/u/"**. The teacher writes the letter *u* on the board.

22. The teacher asks for second sound in the syllable *un*. **"second sound?"**

23. Students do not call out the name of the letter *n* but instead make the *n* sound. Students say, **"/n/."** The teacher writes the letter *n* on the board.

24. The teacher asks students to say the second syllable. Students say, **"til."**

25. The teacher asks how many sounds are in second syllable. **"How many sounds?"**

26. Students identify the number of sounds in the syllable. Students reply, **"three."**

27. The teacher asks for first sound in the syllable *til*. **"first sound?"**

28. Students do not call out the name of the letter *t* but instead make the *t* sound. Students say, **"/t/."** The teacher writes the letter *t* on the board.

29. The teacher asks for second sound in the syllable *til*. **"second sound?"**

30. Students do not say the name of the letter *i* but instead make the short *i* sound. Students say, **"/i/."** The teacher writes the letter *i* on the board.

31. The teacher asks for the third sound in the syllable *til*. **"third sound?"**

32. Students do not call out the name of the letter *l* but instead make the *l* sound. Students say, **"/l/."** The teacher writes the letter *l* on the board.

33. Students check to make sure they have spelled the word correctly and make any changes in their spelling of the word at this time.

34. The teacher tells the students to mark the word. **"Mark the word *until*."** Students mark the word they have just spelled. (Follow the marking system listed in the box labeled *Procedure for Marking and Decoding Word in Section Three* on page 108 in the core book.)

35. Students hold up their marker boards for the teacher to see. If the teacher sees a student has not marked the word correctly, the teacher will say to the student, **"Think about it."** Even if the student continues to not mark the word correctly, the teacher does not tell the student the correct marking of the word at this point.

36. The teacher marks the word on the board. The teacher applies the marking system listed in the box labeled *Procedure for Marking and Decoding Word in Section Three* on page 108 in the core book. The teacher marks the word by following the specific

sequence of steps listed on page 108. The teacher says, "Let's mark the word. Step One?"

37. If a word contains a letter team, students respond, " Underline ___." (They identify those letter teams for the teacher to underline.) If a letter or letter team represents its second sound, students will respond, "Double underline ___" (They identify the letters or letter teams to be double underlined.) If the word contains a silent e, students reply "Underline the silent *e*." If the word contains none of these elements, students reply, "There is nothing to mark." In the word *until*, students say, "There is nothing to mark."

38. The teacher asks, "Step Two?"

39. Students respond, " Place dots under ___." (They identify the vowels or vowel teams in the word that represent a vowel sound.) In the word *until*, students say, "Place dots under *u* and *i*." The teacher places dots under the letters *u* and *i*.

40. The teacher asks, "Step Three?"

41. Students respond, "Divide the word between the letters ___ and ___ according to syllable rule ___". The teacher draws a division line between the appropriate letters and writes the syllable rule number that applies slightly to the right of the division line. In the word *until*, students say, "Divide the word between the letters *n* and *t* according to syllable rule two". (Syllable Rule Two is introduced in Lesson 37.) The teacher draws a division line between the letters *n* and *t* and writes the number two above the word and slightly to the right of the division line.

42. The teacher asks, "Step Four?"

43. Students identify the correct syllable pattern number to write under all the vowels that represent vowel sounds. Students respond, "syllable pattern ___ under ___ and syllable pattern ___ under ___." In the word *until*, students say, "syllable pattern one under *u* and syllable pattern one under *i*."

44. The marking of the word is complete and students check to be sure they have marked the word correctly. (Step Five from page 108 in the core book is omitted.)

*When dictating words for spelling, the teacher first pronounces the word without any special emphasis just as it would be spoken in normal conversation and makes sure that everyone understands the meaning of the word. **At this point if there is a discrepancy between the way a word is pronounced and the way a word is spelled, the teacher makes note of that fact to the students by saying, "spelling pronunciation" and then pronouncing the word as it is spelled. From that point forward in the dictation process the teacher pronounces the word as it is spelled, not as it is pronounced in normal conversation.** As an example the teacher would dictate the second syllable in the word *thousand* as /zand/ rather than pronouncing the second syllable as /zund/. **The teacher's pronunciation conforms to the spelling of the word as much as is possible.**

Page 110
Supplemental Materials
Posters – Display Poster titled *Dividing a Word Into Syllables*
Flash Cards – Review all cards previously introduced that have not been retired.

Information Teacher Presents or Reviews on this Page
The concept of two-syllable words is reviewed.
Syllable rules indicate where words divide into syllables. Each syllable can have one and only one vowel sound; each vowel sound in a word must have its own syllable. If there is one vowel sound in a word, the word is a one-syllable word; if there are two vowel sounds in the word, the word is a two-syllable word. Present the second of two syllable rules that govern syllable division for most words.

Teacher's Guide

Syllable Rule Two is explained to the students.

Syllable Rule Two - When two vowels representing sounds are separated by two or more consonants, divide the word between the first and second consonant letters.

Draw a line between the letters where syllable division occurs. Start the line above the letters, and continue the line below the letters so as to avoid confusing the division line for another letter. Syllable rule numbers go above the letters and syllable pattern numbers go under the vowels. **Place the syllable rule number directly to the right side of the division line.**

	2			2			2	←Syllable Rule Numbers
trol	ley		fil	ter		jel	lo	
•	•		•	•		•	•	
1	4		1	5		1	2	←Syllable Pattern Numbers

Student Exercises
Lesson 372 / Lesson 374

Students read the words in these lessons. (See the discussion of *Guided Oral Reading Practice* on pages 8 - 10.)

Lesson 373 (Quiz 85) / Lesson 375 (Quiz 86)

The teacher dictates the words from these lessons. **Students both spell and mark these words.** (See information under *Dictation Procedure for Multiple Syllable Words* on pages 59 - 61.)

Page 111
Supplemental Materials

Flash Cards – Review all cards previously introduced that have not been retired.

Information Teacher Presents or Reviews on this Page

This page reviews syllable rules one and two. Review the two syllable rules. Ask students to think of two-syllable words that illustrate these two rules. Review the specific steps involved in marking words listed in the box titled *Procedure for Marking and Decoding Word in Section Three* found on page 108 of the core book. Ask students to recite to you what those steps are. These steps need to be memorized by students; the process of marking words must become an automatic process on the students' part. Do not allow them to skip steps; insist they follow the steps in order.

Student Exercises
Lesson 376 / Lesson 378

Students read the words in these lessons. (See the discussion of Guided Oral Reading Practice on pages 8 - 10.)

Lesson 377 (Quiz 87) / Lesson 379 (Quiz 88)

The teacher dictates the words from these lessons. **Students both spell and mark these words.** (See information under *Dictation Procedure for Multiple Syllable Words* on pages 59 - 61.)

Page 112
Supplemental Materials

Flash Cards – Review all cards previously introduced that have not been retired.

Teacher's Guide
Information Teacher Presents or Reviews on this Page

This page introduces information regarding syllable division when a consonant team or consonant blend occurs between the vowels within a word. Explain the information presented at the top of this page.

Student Exercises
Lesson 380

Students read the words in these lessons. (See the discussion of Guided Oral Reading Practice on pages 8 - 10.)

Lesson 381 (Quiz 89)

The teacher dictates the words from these lessons. **Students both spell and mark these words.** (See information under *Dictation Procedure for Multiple Syllable Words* on pages 59 - 61.)

Page 113
Supplemental Materials

Flash Cards – Review all cards previously introduced that have not been retired.
The Reader – Read pgs. 66-73 (1st Ed.) or pgs. 100-109 (2nd. Ed.) on completing page 113.
The We All Can Read Phonics Game – Students play *Card Game Nineteen* upon completing this page.

Information Teacher Presents or Reviews on this Page

The first half of this page consists of sentences; the second half of this page consists of a story containing the elements identified at the top of the page in the title. In addition to the word lists that are found on most pages in this book, it is also helpful for students to have the opportunity to read sentences and stories whose words contain those phonic elements recently presented.

Student Exercises
Lesson 382

Students read the sentences in this lesson. (See the information provided under *Procedure to Follow on Pages Consisting of Sentences* located on pages 20 - 21.)

Lesson 383

The teacher dictates the sentences from this lesson. (See the information provided under *Procedure to Follow on Pages Consisting of Sentences* located on pages 20 - 21.)

Lesson 384

Students read this story. (See the information provided under *Oral Reading Procedure With Stories* located on page 21.)

Page 114
Supplemental Materials

Flash Cards – Introduce Card Set A # 114. Review all cards previously introduced that have not been retired.

Information Teacher Presents or Reviews on this Page

Syllable Pattern Seven is introduced. Explain the information presented at the top of page this page.

Teacher's Guide

Student Exercises
Lesson 385

Students read the words in this lesson. (See the discussion of Guided Oral Reading Practice on pages 8 - 10.)

Lesson 386 (Quiz 90)

The teacher dictates the words from this lesson. **Students both spell and mark these words.** (See information under *Dictation Procedure for Multiple Syllable Words* on pages 59 - 61.)

Page 115
Supplemental Materials

Flash Cards – Review all cards previously introduced that have not been retired.
The Reader – Read pgs. 74-75 (1ˢᵗ Ed.) or pgs. 110-113 (2ⁿᵈ. Ed.) on completing page 115.

Information Teacher Presents or Reviews on this Page

The first half of this page consists of sentences; the second half of this page consists of a story containing the elements identified at the top of the page in the title.   In addition to the word lists that are found on most pages in this book, it is also helpful for students to have the opportunity to read sentences and stories whose words contain those phonic elements recently presented.

Student Exercises
Lesson 387

Students read the sentences in this lesson. (See the information provided under *Procedure to Follow on Pages Consisting of Sentences* located on pages 20 - 21.)

Lesson 388

The teacher dictates the sentences from this lesson.   (See the information provided under *Procedure to Follow on Pages Consisting of Sentences* located on pages 20 - 21.)

Lesson 389

Students read this story. (See the information provided under *Oral Reading Procedure With Stories* located on page 21.)

Page 116
Supplemental Materials

Blackline Masters – Duplicate pages thirty-two through thirty-four for students to take home.

Information Teacher Presents or Reviews on this Page

Mastery Check and Review Number Twelve – Review the information found on page 28 in the core book.

Student Exercises
Lesson 390 / Lesson 391 / Lesson 392

See the box titled *Administering the Mastery Checks: Mastery Checks Nine through Thirteen* on page 47. Dictate words as they are grouped on these pages. As an example before dictating the words listed under the <u>le</u> team found on page 116 in the core book, you might say to your students, "The next group of words which I am about to dictate all contain the vowel team *le*."

Page 117
Supplemental Materials

Flash Cards – Review all cards previously introduced that have not been retired.

64

Teacher's Guide
Information Teacher Presents or Reviews on this Page
Review all seven syllable patterns and syllable rules one and two. Review the individual steps involved in marking words listed in the box titled *Procedure for Marking and Decoding Word in Section Three* found on page 108 of the book. Ask students to list all of the consonant and vowel teams learned thus far in the program. This review information can be presented as a game or contest. For instance the teacher might ask, "Who will be the first student to write on his paper all syllable pattern four teams we have learned?" Notice that at the top of this page are listed syllable pattern four teams. **The words on this page will all contain at least one syllable pattern four team.**

Lesson 393 / Lesson 395
Students read the words in these lessons. (See the discussion of Guided Oral Reading Practice on pages 8 - 10.)
Lesson 394 (Quiz 91) / Lesson 396 (Quiz 92)
The teacher dictates the words from these lessons. **Students both spell and mark these words.** (See information under *Dictation Procedure for Multiple Syllable Words* on pages 59 - 61.)

Page 118
Supplemental Materials
Flash Cards – Review all cards previously introduced that have not been retired.

Information Teacher Presents or Reviews on this Page
Review all seven syllable patterns and syllable rules one and two. Review the individual steps involved in marking words listed in the box titled *Procedure for Marking and Decoding Word in Section Three* found on page 108 in the core book. Ask students to list all of the consonant and vowel teams learned thus far in the program. This review information can be presented as a game or contest. For instance the teacher might ask, "Who will be the first student to write on his paper all syllable pattern five teams we have learned?" Notice that at the top of this page are listed syllable pattern five and syllable pattern six teams. **The words on this page will all contain either a syllable pattern five or syllable pattern six team.**

Student Exercises
Lesson 397 / Lesson 399
Students read the words in these lessons. (See the discussion of Guided Oral Reading Practice on pages 8 - 10.)
Lesson 398 (Quiz 93) / Lesson 400 (Quiz 94)
The teacher dictates the words from these lessons. **Students both spell and mark these words.** (See information under *Dictation Procedure for Multiple Syllable Words* on pages 59 - 61.)

Page 119
Supplemental Materials
Flash Cards – Review all cards previously introduced that have not been retired.

Information Teacher Presents or Reviews on this Page
The first half of this page consists of sentences; the second half of this page consists of a story containing the elements identified at the top of the page in the title. In addition to the word lists that are found on most pages in this book, it is also helpful for students to

have the opportunity to read sentences and stories whose words contain those phonic elements recently presented.

Student Exercises
Lesson 401
Students read the sentences in this lesson. (See the information provided under *Procedure to Follow on Pages Consisting of Sentences* located on pages 20 - 21.)
Lesson 402
The teacher dictates the sentences from this lesson. (See the information provided under *Procedure to Follow on Pages Consisting of Sentences* located on pages 20 - 21.)
Lesson 403
Students read this story. (See the information provided under *Oral Reading Procedure With Stories* located on page 21.)

Pages 120 - 121
Supplemental Materials
Flash Cards – Review all cards previously introduced that have not been retired.

Information Teacher Presents or Reviews on these Pages
Review all seven syllable patterns and syllable rules one and two. Review the individual steps involved in marking words listed in the box titled *Procedure for Marking and Decoding Word in Section Three* found on page 108 in the core book. Ask students to list all of the consonant and vowel teams learned thus far in the program. This review information can be presented as a game or contest. For instance the teacher might ask, "Who will be the first student to write on his paper all syllable pattern six teams we have learned?" Notice that at the top of these pages are listed syllable pattern four, syllable pattern five, and syllable pattern six teams. **The words on these pages contain either a syllable pattern four or syllable pattern five or syllable pattern six team.**

Student Exercises
Lesson 404 / Lesson 406 / Lesson 408 / Lesson 410
Students read the words in these lessons. (See the discussion of Guided Oral Reading Practice on pages 8 - 10.)
Lesson 405 (Quiz 95) / Lesson 407 (Quiz 96) / Lesson 409 (Quiz 97) / Lesson 411 (Quiz 98)
The teacher dictates the words from these lessons. **Students both spell and mark these words.** (See information under *Dictation Procedure for Multiple Syllable Words* on pages 59 - 61.)

Page 122
Supplemental Materials
Flash Cards – Review all cards previously introduced that have not been retired.
The We All Can Read Phonics Game – Students play *Card Game Twenty* upon completing this page.

Information Teacher Presents or Reviews on this Page
The first half of this page consists of sentences; the second half of this page consists of a story containing the elements identified at the top of the page in the title. In addition to the word lists that are found on most pages in this book, it is also helpful for students to have the opportunity to read sentences and stories whose words contain those phonic elements recently presented.

Student Exercises
Lesson 412
Students read the sentences in this lesson. (See the information provided under *Procedure to Follow on Pages Consisting of Sentences* located on pages 20 - 21.)

Lesson 413
The teacher dictates the sentences from this lesson. (See the information provided under *Procedure to Follow on Pages Consisting of Sentences* located on pages 20 - 21.)

Lesson 414
Students read this story. (See the information provided under *Oral Reading Procedure With Stories* located on page 21.)

Page 123
Supplemental Materials
Flash Cards – Introduce Card Set A #'s 115-117 / Card Set B #'s 14-16 / Card Set C #'s 52-54. Retire Card Set B #'s 4, 7,9. Retire Card Set C #'s 46, 48, 51. Review all cards previously introduced that have not been retired.

Information Teacher Presents or Reviews on this Page
This page introduces syllable pattern eight which is the final syllable pattern presented in this program. Explain syllable pattern eight which is listed at the top of page 123 in the core book. Syllable pattern eight describes the fact that three vowels, *a*, *o*, and *u* all represent an extra sound. Write several words on the board that illustrate the extra sound that each of these three vowels represents. See *Mastery Check and Review Chart Thirteen* on page 125 in the core book for words to select to illustrate syllable pattern eight.

Student Exercises
Lesson 415
Students read the words in this lesson. (See the discussion of Guided Oral Reading Practice on pages 8 - 10.)

Lesson 416 (Quiz 99)
The teacher dictates the words from this lesson. **Students both spell and mark these words.** (See information under *Dictation Procedure for Multiple Syllable Words* on pages 59 - 61.)

Page 124
Supplemental Materials
Flash Cards – Review all cards previously introduced that have not been retired.
The Reader – Read page 76 (1st Ed.) or pgs. 114-115 (2nd. Ed.) on completing page 124.

Information Teacher Presents or Reviews on this Page
The first half of this page consists of sentences; the second half of this page consists of a story containing the elements identified at the top of the page in the title. In addition to the word lists that are found on most pages in this book, it is also helpful for students to have the opportunity to read sentences and stories whose words contain those phonic elements recently presented.

Student Exercises
Lesson 417
Students read the sentences in this lesson. (See the information provided under *Procedure to Follow on Pages Consisting of Sentences* located on pages 20 - 21.)

Lesson 418

The teacher dictates the sentences from this lesson. (See the information provided under *Procedure to Follow on Pages Consisting of Sentences* located on pages 20 - 21.)

Lesson 419

Students read this story. (See the information provided under *Oral Reading Procedure With Stories* located on page 21.)

Page 125
Supplemental Materials

Blackline Masters – Duplicate pages thirty-five through thirty-six for students to take home.

Information Teacher Presents or Reviews on this Page

Mastery Check and Review Number Thirteen – Review the information found on page 28 in the core book.

Student Exercises
Lesson 420 / Lesson 421

See the box titled *Administering the Mastery Checks: Mastery Checks Nine through Thirteen* on page 47. Dictate words as they are grouped on these pages. As an example before dictating the words listed under the heading *a* on page 125 in the core book, you might say to your students, "The next group of words which I am about to dictate all contain the extra sound for the letter *a*."

Page 126
Information Teacher Presents or Reviews on this Page

The box on this page lists the eight syllable patterns learned in the program; it is an excellent tool to use for reviewing the eight syllable patterns.

Student Exercise
Lesson 422

The eight syllable patterns are listed on this page. Students should be able to explain in their own words all eight syllable patterns and to think of words that illustrate each of the eight syllable patterns.

Page 127
Supplemental Materials

Flash Cards – Review all cards previously introduced that have not been retired.

Information Teacher Presents or Reviews on this Page

This page introduces exceptions to syllable patterns one, two, and three. Review the information found at the top of this page. Write words on the board that illustrate the exceptions to these three groups.

Student Exercises
Lesson 423

Students read the words in this lesson. (See the discussion of Guided Oral Reading Practice on pages 8 - 10.)

Teacher's Guide
Lesson 424 (Quiz 100)
The teacher dictates the words from this lesson. **Students both spell and mark these words.** (See information under *Dictation Procedure for Multiple Syllable Words* on pages 59 - 61.)

Page 128
Supplemental Materials
Flash Cards – Review all cards previously introduced that have not been retired.
The Reader – Read page 77 (1st Ed.) or pages 116-117 (2nd. Ed.) on completing page 128.

Information Teacher Presents or Reviews on this Page
This page introduces situations where a vowel followed by the letter *r* will not form a vowel team. Present to your students the information found at the top of this page. Write words on the board that illustrate situations where the vowel plus the letter *r* do not combine to form a team.

Student Exercises
Lesson 425
Students read the words in this lesson. (See the discussion of Guided Oral Reading Practice on pages 8 - 10.)

Lesson 426 (Quiz 101)
The teacher dictates the words from these lessons. **Students both spell and mark these words.** (See information under *Dictation Procedure for Multiple Syllable Words* on pages 59 - 61.)

Pages 129 – 130
Supplemental Materials
Flash Cards – Review all cards previously introduced that have not been retired.

Information Teacher Presents or Reviews on these Pages
Review all eight syllable patterns and syllable rules one and two. Review the individual steps involved in marking words listed in the box titled *Procedure for Marking and Decoding Word in Section Three* found on page 108 in the core book. Notice that at the top of these pages are listed syllable pattern four, syllable pattern five, and syllable pattern six teams. Ask students to list all the consonant and vowel teams learned thus far in the program. This review information can be presented as a game or contest. For instance the teacher might ask, "Who will be the first student to write on his paper all syllable pattern six teams we have learned?"

Student Exercises
Lesson 427 / Lesson 429 / Lesson 431 / Lesson 433
Students read the words in these lessons. (See the discussion of Guided Oral Reading Practice on pages 8 - 10.)
Lesson 428 (Quiz 102) / Lesson 430 (Quiz 103) / Lesson 432 (Quiz 104) / Lesson 434 (Quiz 105)
The teacher dictates the words from these lessons. **Students both spell and mark these words.** (See information under *Dictation Procedure for Multiple Syllable Words* on pages 59 - 61.)

Page 131
Supplemental Materials
Flash Cards – Review all cards previously introduced that have not been retired.
The We All Can Read Phonics Game – Students play *Card Game Twenty-one* upon completing this page.

Teacher's Guide
Information Teacher Presents or Reviews on this Page

The first half of this page consists of sentences; the second half of this page consists of a story containing the elements identified at the top of the page in the title. In addition to the word lists that are found on most pages in this book, it is also helpful for students to have the opportunity to read sentences and stories whose words contain those phonic elements recently presented.

Student Exercises
Lesson 435

Students read the sentences in this lesson. (See the information provided under *Procedure to Follow on Pages Consisting of Sentences* located on pages 20 - 21.)

Lesson 436

The teacher dictates the sentences from this lesson. (See the information provided under *Procedure to Follow on Pages Consisting of Sentences* located on pages 20 - 21.)

Lesson 437

Students read this story. (See the information provided under *Oral Reading Procedure With Stories* located on page 21.)

Pages 132 - 133
Supplemental Materials

Flash Cards – Introduce Card Set A #'s 118-119 / Card Set B # 17 / Card Set C # 55. Retire Card Set C # 13. Review all cards previously introduced that have not been retired.

Information Teacher Presents or Reviews on this Page

In the chart on page 132 in the core book the second sounds for the letters *c* and *g* are introduced as are new consonant teams *ce*, *ge*, and *dge*. Tell your students that in the next few pages you will be introducing the rules which govern why the letters *c* and *g* sometimes represent their second sounds, and you will also introduce the rules which indicate why and when the letters *c* and *e* sometimes join together to form a team and why and when the letters *g* and *e* sometimes join together to form a team. Review the information at the top of page 133 in the core book with your students. Select words from page 135 in the core book to write on the board where the letter *c* represents its second sound and where the letters *c* and *e* combine to form a consonant team. **Please emphasize to students that *ce* is only a consonant team when the letter *e*'s sole purpose in following the letter *c* is to cause the letter *c* to represent its second sound as in the word *tran̲ce̲*.** The letters *c* and *e* do not form a consonant team in the word *trace* because the letter *e* in this word does more than cause the letter c to represent its second sound; the silent *e* also causes the letter *a* to represent its long sound.

Student Exercises
Lesson 438 / Lesson 440

Students read the words in these lessons. (See the discussion of Guided Oral Reading Practice on pages 8 - 10.)

Lesson 439 (Quiz 106) / Lesson 441 (Quiz 107)

The teacher dictates the words from these lessons. **Students both spell and mark these words.** (See information under *Dictation Procedure for Multiple Syllable Words* on pages 59 - 61.)

Teacher's Guide
Page 134
Supplemental Materials
Flash Cards – Review all cards previously introduced that have not been retired.
The Reader – Read page 78 (1st Ed.) or pages 118-119 (2nd. Ed.) on completing page 134.
The We All Can Read Phonics Game – Students play *Card Game 22* upon completing this page.

Information Teacher Presents or Reviews on this Page
The first half of this page consists of sentences; the second half of this page consists of a story containing the elements identified at the top of the page in the title. In addition to the word lists that are found on most pages in this book, it is also helpful for students to have the opportunity to read sentences and stories whose words contain those phonic elements recently presented.

Student Exercises
Lesson 442
Students read the sentences in this lesson. (See the information provided under *Procedure to Follow on Pages Consisting of Sentences* located on pages 20 - 21.)
Lesson 443
The teacher dictates the sentences from this lesson. (See the information provided under *Procedure to Follow on Pages Consisting of Sentences* located on pages 20 - 21.)
Lesson 444
Students read this story. (See the information provided under *Oral Reading Procedure With Stories* located on page 21.)

Page 135
Supplemental Materials
Blackline Masters – Duplicate pages thirty-six through thirty-nine for students to take home.
Information Teacher Presents or Reviews on this Page
Mastery Check and Review Number Fourteen – Review the information found on page 28 in the core book.
Student Exercises
Lesson 445 / Lesson 446
See the box titled *Administering the Mastery Checks: Mastery Checks Fourteen through Twenty-one* that immediately follows this paragraph. Dictate words as they are grouped on the mastery check. As an example before dictating the words listed under the heading <u>ce</u> on page 135 in the core book, you might say to your students, "The next group of words which I am about to dictate all contain the consonant letter team *ce*."

Administering the Mastery Checks:
Mastery Checks Fourteen through Twenty-one
Many of the words in these word lists are more challenging than words in previous *Mastery Check and Review Lists*. A student should be able to read the words in these word lists accurately; however, spelling many of these words will prove more challenging. Because of the complexity of some of the words in these lists, a student's inability to spell these words at an eighty percent or higher degree of accuracy does not necessarily indicate that a student has not learned the information presented in these units. **The ability to read these words accurately thus becomes the determining factor regarding whether or not a student is sufficiently prepared to continue on to the next set of lessons. A student's ability to spell these words accurately is no longer used as**

---

the determining factor to evaluate whether or not a student has learned the information sufficiently well to be able to continue on to the next set of lessons.

It is not necessary to ask a student to read every word from these lists. Choose a representative number of words under each category in this list (at least ten words), and ask students to read them. But if students struggle reading the representative words chosen, the teacher should then have the students read all of the words in that particular column. Spelling these words is more problematic. Because many of these words are more challenging, it is not to be expected that students will always be able to spell these words with an eighty percent degree of accuracy, nor is it necessary that they be able to do so. Obviously many words in these lists would prove extremely difficult for students in the early grades. Older students in middle school and high school and adults should be held to a higher standard; however, some students in the upper grades as well as some adults may find some of these words to be too complex for their current level of spelling acquisition ability. Judgment on the teacher's part is required to determine which words are appropriate to dictate to students depending on the students' age and developmental level. The teacher should feel free to not dictate any words from these lists that he or she feels may be too difficult for students. **When a student is asked to spell any of these words, he should underline any consonant teams or vowel teams contained in the word he is spelling; however it is not necessary to assign syllable pattern numbers to the vowels or syllable rule numbers to the syllables.**

Page 136
Supplemental Materials
Flash Cards – Introduce Card Set A's # 120-122/ Card Set B # 18/ Card Set C # 56. Retire Card Set C # 6. Review all cards previously introduced that have not been retired.

Information Teacher Presents or Reviews on this Page
Review the information at the top of this page with your students. Write words on the board from page 138 in the core book which illustrate when the letter *g* represents its second sound and when the letters *g* and *e* combine to form a consonant team. **Please emphasize to students that *ge* is only a consonant team when the letter *e*'s sole purpose in following the letter *g* is to cause the letter *g* to represent its second sound as in the word *charge*.** The letters *g* and *e* do not form a consonant team in the word *change* because the letter *e* in this word does more than cause the letter *g* to represent its second sound; the silent *e* also causes the letter *a* to represent its long sound. English words don't end in the letter *j*; the consonant team *dge* is used at the end of a word to represent the sound /j/ when it follows directly after a short vowel sound as in the words *fudge* and *wedge*. Use the letters *g* and *e* to represent the sound /j/ at the end of a word when the /j/ sound is preceded by any vowel sound other than a short vowel sound as in the words *page* and *barge*.

Student Exercises
Lesson 447 / Lesson 449
Students read the words in these lessons. (See the discussion of Guided Oral Reading Practice on pages 8 - 10.)

Teacher's Guide

Lesson 448 (Quiz 108) / Lesson 450 (Quiz 109)

The teacher dictates the words from these lessons. **Students both spell and mark these words.** (See information under *Dictation Procedure for Multiple Syllable Words* on pages 59 - 61.)

Page 137
Supplemental Materials

Flash Cards – Review all cards previously introduced that have not been retired.
The Reader – Read page 79 (1st Ed.) or pages 120-121 (2nd. Ed.) on completing page 137.
The We All Can Read Phonics Game – Students play *Card Game Twenty-three* upon completing this page.

Information Teacher Presents or Reviews on this Page

The first half of this page consists of sentences; the second half of this page consists of a story containing the elements identified at the top of the page in the title. In addition to the word lists that are found on most pages in this book, it is also helpful for students to have the opportunity to read sentences and stories whose words contain those phonic elements recently presented.

Student Exercises
Lesson 451

Students read the sentences in this lesson. (See the information provided under *Procedure to Follow on Pages Consisting of Sentences* located on pages 20 - 21.)

Lesson 452

The teacher dictates the sentences from this lesson. (See the information provided under *Procedure to Follow on Pages Consisting of Sentences* located on pages 20 - 21.)

Lesson 453

Students read this story. (See the information provided under *Oral Reading Procedure With Stories* located on page 21.)

Page 138
Supplemental Materials

Blackline Masters – Duplicate pages thirty-nine through forty-one for students to take home.

Information Teacher Presents or Reviews on this Page

Mastery Check and Review Number Fifteen – Review the information found on page 28 in the core book.

Student Exercises
Lesson 454 / Lesson 455 / Lesson 456

See the box titled *Administering the Mastery Checks: Mastery Checks Fourteen through Twenty-one* on pages 71 - 72. Dictate words as they are grouped on these pages. As an example before dictating the words listed under the heading *ge* on page 138 in the core book, you might say to your students, "The next group of words which I am about to dictate all contain the consonant letter team *ge*."

Pages 139 - 140
Supplemental Materials

Flash Cards – Introduce Card Set A #'s 123-126 / Card Set B # 19 / Card Set C #'s 57-59. Retire Card Set C #'s 23, 34, 39. Review all cards previously introduced that have not been retired.

Teacher's Guide
Information Teacher Presents or Reviews on this Page

The six jobs for the letter *y* are introduced on these two pages along with the rules which govern in what situations the letter *y* will represent its various sounds. Students have already learned that the letter *y* is part of the vowel teams *ay*, *ey*, and *oy* (listed as the fifth job of *y* on page 139 in the core book, and they have also learned that the letter *y* functions as a consonant at the beginning of any syllable (listed as the sixth job of *y* on page 139). Review those functions of *y*, which students have already learned in the program. After reviewing that information, introduce to them the other four jobs of *y*, which are listed on page 139 under the heading *The Six Jobs of y - Job One*, *Job Two*, *Job Three*, and *Job Four*. Begin with *Job One*.

1. Select from *Mastery Check Sixteen* on page 144 in the core book several words under the column labeled *y as short i sound*. Put these words on the board, and use them to illustrate the fact that *y* represents the short *i* sound when it is the only vowel in a syllable and is followed by a consonant as in the words *gym* and *cymbal*.

2. Select from *Mastery Check Sixteen* on page 144 in the core book several words under the column labeled *y-as-long-i sound*. Put these words on the board, and use them to illustrate the fact that *y* represents the long *i* sound when it is the only vowel in a syllable and is the last letter in the syllable as in the words *dry* and *shy*.

3. Select from *Mastery Check Sixteen* on page 144 in the core book several words under the column labeled *y-as-long-e-sound*. Put these words on the board, and use them to illustrate the fact that *y* represents the long *e* sound when it occurs by itself at the end of any syllable after the first syllable in a word as in the words *gently* and *navy*.

4. Put the words *style* and *type* on the board, and use them to illustrate the fact that *y* represents the long *i* sound when two vowels in one syllable are separated by one or more consonants, and the first vowel is the letter *y*, and the second vowel is a silent letter *e*.

Student Exercise
Lesson 457

On page 140 students make the sounds represented by the letters and letter teams in the eight boxes on this page. Students should be able to explain in their own words the six jobs of the letter *y* as listed on pages 139-140 and to think of words which illustrate each of the six jobs of the letter *y*.

Page 141
Supplemental Materials

Flash Cards – Review Card Set A #'s 123-126 / Card Set B # 19/ Card Set C #'s 57-59. Retire Card Set C #'s 23, 34, 39. Review all other cards previously introduced that have not been retired.

Information Teacher Presents or Reviews on this Page

Review the information from pages 139 and 140 with your students. Words on this page will contain the letter *y* representing the short and long sound of *i* and the long *e* sound. Write words on the board that illustrate when the letter *y* represents those three sounds. Select at least two words that illustrate *y* representing each of those three sounds and discuss the rules that govern why the letter *y* is representing those three sounds in the words you have chosen. (A list of words containing *y* representing those three sounds is found on page 144 in the core book.)

Teacher's Guide

Student Exercises
Lesson 458 / Lesson 460
Students read the words in these lessons. (See the discussion of Guided Oral Reading Practice on pages 8 - 10.)

Lesson 459 (Quiz 110) / Lesson 461 (Quiz 111)
The teacher dictates the words from these lessons. **Students both spell and mark these words.** (See information under *Dictation Procedure for Multiple Syllable Words* on pages 59 - 61.)

Page 142
Supplemental Materials
Flash Cards – Review all cards previously introduced that have not been retired.

Information Teacher Presents or Reviews on this Page
Refer to the *Information Teacher Presents or Reviews on this Page* section for pages 139 – 140 found on page 74. Review again the information listed in that passage with your students. Write sample words on the board that illustrate each of the six jobs of *y*, and discuss why the letter *y* represents the sound it does in each of the words you choose to write on the board. (Select words from page 144 in the core book.)

Student Exercises
Lesson 462 / Lesson 464
Students read the words in these lessons. (See the discussion of Guided Oral Reading Practice on pages 8 - 10.)

Lesson 463 (Quiz 112) / Lesson 465 (Quiz 113)
The teacher dictates the words from these lessons. **Students both spell and mark these words.** (See information under *Dictation Procedure for Multiple Syllable Words* on pages 59 - 61.)

Page 143
Supplemental Materials
Flash Cards – Review all cards previously introduced that have not been retired.
The Reader – Read page 80 (1st Ed.) or pages 122-123 (2nd. Ed.) on completing page 143.
The We All Can Read Phonics Game – Students play *Card Game Twenty-four* upon completing this page.

Information Teacher Presents or Reviews on this Page
The first half of this page consists of sentences; the second half of this page consists of a story containing the elements identified at the top of the page in the title. In addition to the word lists that are found on most pages in this book, it is also helpful for students to have the opportunity to read sentences and stories whose words contain those phonic elements recently presented.

Student Exercises
Lesson 466
Students read the sentences in this lesson. (See the information provided under *Procedure to Follow on Pages Consisting of Sentences* located on pages 20 - 21.)
Lesson 467
The teacher dictates the sentences from this lesson. (See the information provided under *Procedure to Follow on Pages Consisting of Sentences* located on pages 20 - 21.)

Teacher's Guide
Lesson 468

Students read this story. (See the information provided under *Oral Reading Procedure With Stories* located on page 21.)

Page 144
Supplemental Materials

Blackline Masters – Duplicate pages forty-one through forty-two for students to take home.

Information Teacher Presents or Reviews on this Page

Mastery Check and Review Number Sixteen – Review the information found on page 28 in the core book.

Student Exercises
Lesson 469 / Lesson 470 / Lesson 471

See the box titled *Administering the Mastery Checks: Mastery Checks Fourteen through Twenty-one* on pages 71 - 72. Dictate words as they are grouped on these pages. As an example before dictating the words listed under the heading *y-as-long-e-sound* on page 144 in the core book, you might say to your students, "The next group of words which I am about to dictate all contain the letter *y* at the end of each word which will represent the long *e* sound."

Pages 145 – 146
Supplemental Materials

Flash Cards – Review all cards previously introduced that have not been retired.

Information Teacher Presents or Reviews on these Pages

Review all eight syllable patterns and syllable rules one and two. Notice that at the top of these pages are listed syllable pattern four, syllable pattern five, and syllable pattern six teams. Review the individual specific steps involved in marking words listed in the box titled *Procedure for Marking and Decoding Word in Section Three* found on page 108 in the core book. Ask students to list all the consonant and vowel teams learned thus far in the program. This review information can be presented as a game or contest. For instance the teacher might ask, "Who will be the first student to write on his marker board or practice paper one word which illustrates each of the eight syllable patterns we have learned?"

Student Exercises
Lesson 472 / Lesson 474 / Lesson 476 / Lesson 478

Students read the words in these lessons. (See the discussion of Guided Oral Reading Practice on pages 8 - 10.)

Lesson 473 (Quiz 114) / Lesson 475 (Quiz 115) / Lesson 477 (Quiz 116) / Lesson 479 (Quiz 117)
The teacher dictates the words from these lessons. **Students both spell and mark these words.** (See information under *Dictation Procedure for Multiple Syllable Words* on pages 59 - 61.)

Pages 147– 148
Supplemental Materials

Flash Cards – Review all cards previously introduced that have not been retired.

Information Teacher Presents or Reviews on these Pages

These two pages introduce three syllable words. No new or special steps are added when decoding or spelling three syllable words; the same procedures are used as used to decode and spell two syllable words. Notice that at the top of these pages are listed syllable pattern four, syllable pattern five, and syllable pattern six teams. Review all eight syllable patterns and syllable rules one and two. Review the individual specific steps involved in marking words listed in the box titled *Procedure for Marking and Decoding Word in Section Three* found on page 108 in the core book. Ask students to list all the consonant and vowel teams learned thus far in the program. This review information can be presented as a game or contest. For instance the teacher might ask, "Who will be the first student to write on his marker board or practice paper one word which illustrates each of the two-syllable rules we have learned?"

Student Exercises
Lesson 480 / Lesson 482 / Lesson 484 / Lesson 486
Students read the words in these lessons. (See the discussion of Guided Oral Reading Practice on pages 8 - 10.)
Lesson 481 (Quiz 118) / Lesson 483 (Quiz 119) / Lesson 485 (Quiz 120) / Lesson 487 (Quiz 121)
The teacher dictates the words from these lessons. **Students both spell and mark these words.** (See information under *Dictation Procedure for Multiple Syllable Words* on pages 59 - 61.)

Page 149
Supplemental Materials
Flash Cards – Review all cards previously introduced that have not been retired.

Information Teacher Presents or Reviews on this Page
Syllable Rule Three is introduced; this is the final syllable rule taught in this program. Present the information listed at the top of this page. Choose words from this page that illustrate syllable rule three and write them on the board. Ask students to think of other words that contain syllables where two vowels are next to one another in a word, and yet those vowels do not join together to form a team.

Student Exercises
Lesson 488 / Lesson 490
Students read the words in these lessons. (See the discussion of Guided Oral Reading Practice on pages 8 - 10.)
Lesson 489 (Quiz 122) / Lesson 491 (Quiz 123)
The teacher dictates the words from these lessons. **Students both spell and mark these words.** (See information under *Dictation Procedure for Multiple Syllable Words* on pages 59 - 61.)

Page 150
Supplemental Materials
Flash Cards – Review all cards previously introduced that have not been retired.
The Reader – Read page 81 (1st Ed.) or pages 124-125 (2nd. Ed.) on completing page 150.
The We All Can Read Phonics Game – Students play *Card Game Twenty-five* upon completing this page.

Information Teacher Presents or Reviews on this Page
The first half of this page consists of sentences; the second half of this page consists of a story containing the elements identified at the top of the page in the title. In addition to the word lists that are found on most pages in this book, it is also helpful for students to

have the opportunity to read sentences and stories whose words contain those phonic elements recently presented.

Student Exercises
Lesson 492

Students read the sentences in this lesson. (See the information provided under *Procedure to Follow on Pages Consisting of Sentences* located on pages 20 - 21.)

Lesson 493

The teacher dictates the sentences from this lesson. (See the information provided under *Procedure to Follow on Pages Consisting of Sentences* located on pages 20 - 21.)

Lesson 494

Students read this story. (See the information provided under *Oral Reading Procedure With Stories* located on page 21.)

Page 151
Supplemental Materials

Flash Cards – Introduce Card Set A #'s 127-134 / Card Set B #'s 20-22 / Card Set C #'s 60-65. Retire Card Set C #'s 5, 7, 12, 26. Review all cards previously introduced that have not been retired.

Information Teacher Presents or Reviews on this Page

In the chart on this page eight new consonant teams are introduced. Present to your students the information found at the top of page 152 in the core book. Select from *Mastery Check Seventeen* on pages 155-156 in the core book several words listed under the heading for each of the new teams presented in the chart on this page. Put these words on the board, and use them to illustrate the sounds represented by these eight new consonant teams.

Student Exercises
Lesson 495

1. Ask your students to make the sounds represented by the consonant teams listed in the individual boxes on this page. Ask students to think of words that contain these consonant letter teams.
2. Reverse the process, and make the sounds represented by the consonant teams on this page. Next ask your students to spell those sounds. Note that the teams *ci*, *si*, and *ti* all represent the same sound.

Pages 152 – 153
Supplemental Materials

Flash Cards – Review all cards previously introduced that have not been retired.

Information Teacher Presents or Reviews on these Pages

Students practice reading and spelling words which all contain one of the eight new consonant teams introduced on the last page. Review the eight new consonant teams. Ask students to list as many of these new consonant teams as they can from memory, and ask them to think of words that contain each of those teams. Notice at the top of each of these pages is found a list of the eight consonant teams just introduced. Students may find it helpful to refer to this list when marking words.

Student Exercises
Lesson 496 / Lesson 498 / Lesson 500 / Lesson 502

Students read the words in these lessons. (See the discussion of Guided Oral Reading Practice on pages 8 - 10.)

Teacher's Guide

Lesson 497 (Quiz 124) / Lesson 499 (Quiz 125) / Lesson 501 (Quiz 126) / Lesson 503 (Quiz 127)
The teacher dictates the words from these lessons. **Students both spell and mark these words.** (See information under *Dictation Procedure for Multiple Syllable Words* on pages 59 - 61.)

Page 154
Supplemental Materials
Flash Cards – Review all cards previously introduced that have not been retired.
The Reader – Read page 82 (1st Ed.) or pages 126-127 (2nd. Ed.) on completing page 154.
The We All Can Read Phonics Game – Students play *Card Game Twenty-six* upon completing this page.

Information Teacher Presents or Reviews on this Page
The first half of this page consists of sentences; the second half of this page consists of a story containing the elements identified at the top of the page in the title. In addition to the word lists that are found on most pages in this book, it is also helpful for students to have the opportunity to read sentences and stories whose words contain those phonic elements recently presented.

Student Exercises
Lesson 504
Students read the sentences in this lesson. (See the information provided under *Procedure to Follow on Pages Consisting of Sentences* located on pages 20 - 21.)
Lesson 505
The teacher dictates the sentences from this lesson. (See the information provided under *Procedure to Follow on Pages Consisting of Sentences* located on pages 20 - 21.)
Lesson 506
Students read this story. (See the information provided under *Oral Reading Procedure With Stories* located on page 21.)

Pages 155 - 156
Supplemental Materials
Blackline Masters – Duplicate pages forty-two through forty-eight for students to take home.

Information Teacher Presents or Reviews on this Page
Mastery Check and Review Number Seventeen – Review the information found on page 28 in the core book.

Student Exercises
Lesson 507 through Lesson 513
See the box titled *Administering the Mastery Checks: Mastery Checks Fourteen through Twenty-one* on pages 71 - 72. Dictate words as they are grouped on these pages. As an example before dictating the words listed under the heading *si* on page 155 in the core book, you might say to your students, "The next group of words which I am about to dictate all contain the consonant letter team *si*."

Teacher's Guide
Page 157
Supplemental Materials

Flash Cards – Introduce Card Set A #'s 135-139 / Card Set B #'s 23-25 / Card Set C #'s 66-68. Retire Card Set C #'s 38, 58, 59. Review all cards previously introduced that have not been retired.

Information Teacher Presents or Reviews on this Page

In the chart on this page eight vowel teams are listed; some of these teams were presented earlier in the program; some are presented for the first time on this page. These teams are grouped together in pairs; each team is listed twice on this page. For instance the vowel team *ey* is listed in one box as a syllable-pattern-four-team representing the long *e* sound, and in another box the vowel team *ey* is listed as a syllable-pattern-six-team representing the long *a* sound. Remind students that according to the marking system in this book, when a vowel team represents the long sound of the first vowel in the vowel team, the vowel team is classified as a syllable pattern *four* team. When a vowel team does not represent the long sound of the first vowel in the vowel team, then the vowel team is classified as a syllable pattern *six* team except when the letter *r* is part of the vowel team. Review this information that is found at the top of page 158 in the core book. Select from *Mastery Check Eighteen* on page 161 in the core book several words listed under the heading for each of the new teams presented in the chart on this page. Put these words on the board, and use them to illustrate the sounds represented by these eight vowel teams.

Student Exercises
Lesson 514

1. Ask your students to make the sounds represented by the vowel teams listed in the individual boxes on this page. Ask students to think of words that contain these vowel teams.
2. Reverse the process, and make the sounds represented by the vowel teams on this page. Then ask your students to spell those sounds.

Pages 158 – 159
Supplemental Materials

Flash Cards – Review all cards previously introduced that have not been retired.

Information Teacher Presents or Reviews on these Pages

Students practice reading and spelling words which all contain one of the eight vowel teams introduced on the last page. Review the eight vowel teams. Ask students to list as many of these new vowel teams as they can from memory, and ask them to think of words that contain each of those teams. Notice at the top of pages 158 - 159 a list is found with the eight vowel teams introduced. Students may find it helpful to refer to this list when marking words.

Student Exercises
Lesson 515 / Lesson 517 / Lesson 519 / Lesson 521

Students read the words in these lessons. (See the discussion of Guided Oral Reading Practice on pages 8 - 10.)

Lesson 516 (Quiz 128) / **Lesson 518 (Quiz 129)** / **Lesson 520 (Quiz 130)** / **Lesson 522 (Quiz 131)**
The teacher dictates the words from these lessons. **Students both spell and mark these words.** (See information under *Dictation Procedure for Multiple Syllable Words* on pages 59 - 61.)

Teacher's Guide
Page 160
Supplemental Materials

Flash Cards – Review all cards previously introduced that have not been retired.
The Reader – Read page 83 (1st Ed.) or pages 128-129 (2nd. Ed.) on completing page 160.
The We All Can Read Phonics Game – Students play *Card Game Twenty-seven* upon completing this page.

Information Teacher Presents or Reviews on this Page

The first half of this page consists of sentences; the second half of this page consists of a story containing the elements identified at the top of the page in the title. In addition to the word lists that are found on most pages in this book, it is also helpful for students to have the opportunity to read sentences and stories whose words contain those phonic elements recently presented.

Student Exercises
Lesson 523

Students read the sentences in this lesson. (See the information provided under *Procedure to Follow on Pages Consisting of Sentences* located on pages 20 - 21.)

Lesson 524

The teacher dictates the sentences from this lesson. (See the information provided under *Procedure to Follow on Pages Consisting of Sentences* located on pages 20 - 21.)

Lesson 525

Students read this story. (See the information provided under *Oral Reading Procedure With Stories* located on page 21.)

Page 161
Supplemental Materials

Blackline Masters – Duplicate pages forty-nine through fifty-two for students to take home.

Information Teacher Presents or Reviews on this Page

Mastery Check and Review Number Eighteen – Review the information found on page 28 in the core book.

Student Exercises
Lesson 526 through Lesson 529

See the box titled *Administering the Mastery Checks: Mastery Checks: Fourteen through Twenty-one* on pages 71 - 72. Dictate words as they are grouped on these pages. As an example before dictating the words listed under the syllable pattern six team *ei* found on page 161, you might say to your students, "The next group of words which I am about to dictate all contain the syllable pattern six team *ei*."

Pages 162 – 163
Supplemental Materials

Flash Cards – Review all cards previously introduced that have not been retired.

Information Teacher Presents or Reviews on this Page

The three major spelling rules for adding suffixes are presented on page 162; the lessons applying those rules are on page 163. Present each spelling rule one at a time and have students work in the corresponding lessons for that spelling rule. As an example, present spelling rule one on page 162 and then assign students Lesson 530 and then

Teacher's Guide

Lesson 531 on page 163. Next present spelling rule two on page 162 and then assign students Lesson 532 and then Lesson 533 on page 163. Finally present spelling rule three on page 162 and then assign students Lesson 534 and then Lesson 535 on page 163.

Student Exercises
Lesson 530 / Lesson 532 / Lesson 534

Students read the word pairs in these lessons. (See the discussion of Guided Oral Reading Practice on pages 8 - 10.)

Lesson 531 (Quiz 132) / Lesson 533 (Quiz 133) / Lesson 535 (Quiz 134)

The teacher dictates the word pairs from these lessons. Dictate in word pairs just as the words are listed on this page. As an example do not dictate the word *cry* by itself; instead dictate the words *cry - crying*. **Students both spell and mark these word pairs.** (See information under *Dictation Procedure for Multiple Syllable Words* on pages 59 - 61.)

Page 164
Supplemental Materials

Flash Cards – Review all cards previously introduced that have not been retired.

Information Teacher Presents or Reviews on this Page

The five major spelling rules for forming the plurals of words are presented on page 164; the lessons applying those rules are located directly under the rules. Present spelling rules one and two and then assign students Lesson 536 and Lesson 537 on this page. Next present spelling rules three, four, and five and then assign students Lesson 538 and Lesson 539 from this page.

Student Exercises
Lesson 536 / Lesson 538

Students read the word pairs in these lessons. (See the discussion of Guided Oral Reading Practice on pages 8 - 10.)

Lesson 537 (Quiz 135) / Lesson 539 (Quiz 136)

The teacher dictates the word pairs from these lessons. Dictate in word pairs just as the words are listed on this page. As an example do not dictate the word *elf* by itself; instead dictate the words *elf - elves*. **Students both spell and mark these word pairs.** (See information under *Dictation Procedure for Multiple Syllable Words* on pages 59 - 61.)

Page 165
Supplemental Materials

Flash Cards – Introduce Card Set A #'s 140-141 / Card Set B # 26 / Card Set C #'s 69-70. Retire Card Set C #'s 2, 14. Review all cards previously introduced that have not been retired.

Information Teacher Presents or Reviews on this Page

The letter team *ed* is introduced. Present the information listed at the top of this page. Write words on the board that end in the letter *d* followed by the letter team *ed* and words that end in the letter *t* followed by the letter team *ed*. Choose words from this page or other words you can think of that end in a consonant other than *d* or *t* followed by the consonant letter team *ed*. Present the first and second sounds that the consonant team *ed* represents when the *ed* team is not preceded by the letters *d* or *t*, and write them on the board. Ask students to think of other words that end in *ed* where *ed* represents past tense. Ask them what sound the *ed* team represents in those words.

Teacher's Guide
Student Exercises
Lesson 540
Students read the words in this lesson. (See the discussion of Guided Oral Reading Practice on pages 8 - 10.)

Lesson 541 (Quiz 137)
The teacher dictates the words from this lesson. **Students both spell and mark these words.** (See information under *Dictation Procedure for Multiple Syllable Words* on pages 59 - 61.)

Page 166
Supplemental Materials
Flash Cards – Review all cards previously introduced that have not been retired.
The Reader – No pages (1ˢᵗ Ed.). Read pages 130-131 (2ⁿᵈ. Ed.) on completing page 166.

Information Teacher Presents or Reviews on this Page
The first half of this page consists of sentences; the second half of this page consists of a story containing the elements identified at the top of the page in the title. In addition to the word lists that are found on most pages in this book, it is also helpful for students to have the opportunity to read sentences and stories whose words contain those phonic elements recently presented.

Student Exercises
Lesson 542
Students read the sentences in this lesson. (See the information provided under *Procedure to Follow on Pages Consisting of Sentences* located on pages 20 - 21.)

Lesson 543
The teacher dictates the sentences from this lesson. (See the information provided under *Procedure to Follow on Pages Consisting of Sentences* located on pages 20 - 21.)

Lesson 544
Students read this story. (See the information provided under *Oral Reading Procedure With Stories* located on page 21.)

Page 167
Supplemental Materials
Flash Cards – Introduce Card Set A #'s 142-148 / Card Set B #'s 27-30 / Card Set C #'s 71-77. Retire Card Set C #'s 20, 22, 44, 45, 52, 66, 68. Review all cards previously introduced that have not been retired.

Information Teacher Presents or Reviews on this Page
In the chart on this page seven vowel teams are listed. Review the information found at the top of page 168 in the core book with students. Vowel teams augh and eigh are four-letter vowel teams where the vowel teams do not represent the long sound of the first vowel in each of the two vowel teams; thus both teams are classified as syllable pattern six teams. The letters *gh* at the end of both of these teams form part of the four letter vowel teams. Vowel team *igh* is a three-letter vowel team, where the vowel team represents the long sound of the first vowel in the vowel team; thus this team is classified as a syllable pattern four team. Previously we learned that *ea* is a vowel team that represents the long *e* sound as in the word *eat*; *ea* in this instance is classified as a syllable pattern four team. The vowel team *ea* also represents another sound, the short *e* sound, as in the word *bread*. The vowel team *ea* in the instance where it represents the short *e* sound is classified as a syllable pattern six team because the first vowel, *e*, does not represent the

long *e* sound. Earlier in the program the vowel team *ou* was introduced as representing the sound /ou/ as in *out*; when *ou* is double-underlined, it represents the short *u* sound as in the word *double*. In both of these instances the vowel team *ou* is classified as a syllable pattern six team because in neither instance does the letter *o* represent the long *o* sound. The *ou* team is double underlined when it represents the short *u* sound. Finally on this page both the vowel team *ar* and the vowel team *or* represent their second sounds and thus are double underlined. Both of these teams represent a second sound when they are preceded by the sound /w/. The second sound for the team *ar* is /or/ as in *warm*, and the second sound for the team *or* is /er/ as in *work*. Select from *Mastery Check Nineteen* on page 171 in the core book several words listed under the heading for each of the new teams presented in the chart on this page. Put these words on the board, and use them to illustrate the sounds represented by these seven vowel teams.

Student Exercises
Lesson 545

1. Ask your students to make the sounds represented by the vowel teams listed in the individual boxes on this page. Ask students to think of words that contain these vowel teams.
2. Reverse the process, and make the sounds represented by the vowel teams on this page. Then ask your students to spell those sounds.

Pages 168 – 169
Supplemental Materials

Flash Cards – Review all cards previously introduced that have not been retired.

Information Teacher Presents or Reviews on these Pages

Students practice reading and spelling words that all contain one of the seven vowel teams introduced on the last page. Review the seven vowel teams. Ask students to list as many of these new vowel teams as they can from memory, and ask them to think of words that contain each of those teams. Notice at the top of each of these pages is found a list of the seven vowel teams introduced. Students may find it helpful to refer to this list when marking words.

Student Exercises
Lesson 546 / Lesson 548 / Lesson 550 / Lesson 552

Students read the words in these lessons. (See the discussion of Guided Oral Reading Practice on pages 8 - 10.)

Lesson 547 (Quiz 138) / Lesson 549 (Quiz 139) / Lesson 551 (Quiz 140) / Lesson 553 (Quiz 141)
The teacher dictates the words from these lessons. **Students both spell and mark these words.** (See information under *Dictation Procedure for Multiple Syllable Words* on pages 59 - 61.)

Page 170
Supplemental Materials

Flash Cards – Review all cards previously introduced that have not been retired.
The Reader – Read page 84 (1st Ed.) or pages 132-133 (2nd. Ed.) on completing page 170.
The We All Can Read Phonics Game – Students play *Card Game Twenty-eight* upon completing this page.

Teacher's Guide
Information Teacher Presents or Reviews on this Page

The first half of this page consists of sentences; the second half of this page consists of a story containing the elements identified at the top of the page in the title. In addition to the word lists that are found on most pages in this book, it is also helpful for students to have the opportunity to read sentences and stories whose words contain those phonic elements recently presented.

Student Exercises
Lesson 554

Students read the sentences in this lesson. (See the information provided under *Procedure to Follow on Pages Consisting of Sentences* located on pages 20 - 21.)

Lesson 555

The teacher dictates the sentences from this lesson. (See the information provided under *Procedure to Follow on Pages Consisting of Sentences* located on pages 20 - 21.)

Lesson 556

Students read this story. (See the information provided under *Oral Reading Procedure With Stories* located on page 21.)

Page 171
Supplemental Materials

Blackline Masters – Duplicate pages fifty-two through fifty-five for students to take home.

Information Teacher Presents or Reviews on this Page

Mastery Check and Review Number Nineteen – Review the information found on page 28 in the core book.

Student Exercises
Lesson 557 through Lesson 561

See the box titled *Administering the Mastery Checks: Mastery Checks Fourteen through Twenty-one* on pages 71 - 72. Dictate words as they are grouped on these pages. As an example, before dictating the words listed under the vowel team *augh* found on page 171 in the core book, you might say to your students, "The next group of words that I am about to dictate all contain the vowel team *augh*."

Page 172
Supplemental Materials

Flash Cards – Introduce Card Set A #'s 149-156 / Card Set B # 31 / Card Set C #'s 78-83. Retire Card Set C #'s 4, 10, 55, 62, 63, 65. Review all cards previously introduced that have not been retired.

Information Teacher Presents or Reviews on this Page

In the chart eight new consonant teams are introduced. Select from *Mastery Check Twenty* on page 176 in the core book several words listed under the heading for each of the new teams presented in the chart on this page. Put these words on the board, and use them to illustrate the sounds represented by these eight new consonant teams. The letter team *ch* represents three sounds. **When a letter team represents its third sound, students draw a dotted underline under the team to indicate that the team is representing its third sound.** Note additional information listed at the top of page 173.

Teacher's Guide
Student Exercises
Lesson 562

1. Ask your students to make the sounds represented by the consonant teams listed in the individual boxes on this page. Ask students to think of words that contain these consonant letter teams.

2. Reverse the process, and make the sounds represented by the consonant teams on this page. Next ask your students to spell those sounds.

Pages 173 – 174
Supplemental Materials

Flash Cards – Review all cards previously introduced that have not been retired.

Information Teacher Presents or Reviews on these Pages

Students practice reading and spelling words that all contain one of the eight new consonant teams introduced on page 172 in the core book. Review the eight new consonant teams. Ask students to list as many of these new consonant teams as they can from memory, and ask them to think of words that contain each of those teams. Notice at the top of each of these pages is found a list of the eight consonant teams just introduced. Students may find it helpful to refer to this list when marking words.

Student Exercises
Lesson 563 / Lesson 565 / Lesson 567 / Lesson 569

Students read the words in these lessons. (See the discussion of Guided Oral Reading Practice on pages 8 - 10.)

Lesson 564 (Quiz 142) / Lesson 566 (Quiz 143) / Lesson 568 (Quiz 144) / Lesson 570 (Quiz 145)

The teacher dictates the words from these lessons. **Students both spell and mark these words.** (See information under *Dictation Procedure for Multiple Syllable Words* on pages 59 - 61.)

Page 175
Supplemental Materials

Flash Cards – Review all cards previously introduced that have not been retired.
The Reader – Read page 85 (1ˢᵗ Ed.) or pages 134-135 (2ⁿᵈ. Ed.) on completing page 175.
The We All Can Read Phonics Game – Students play *Card Game Twenty-nine* upon completing this page.

Information Teacher Presents or Reviews on this Page

The first half of this page consists of sentences; the second half of this page consists of a story containing the elements identified at the top of the page in the title. In addition to the word lists that are found on most pages in this book, it is also helpful for students to have the opportunity to read sentences and stories whose words contain those phonic elements recently presented.

Student Exercises
Lesson 571

Students read the sentences in this lesson. (See the information provided under *Procedure to Follow on Pages Consisting of Sentences* located on pages 20 - 21.)
Lesson 572

The teacher dictates the sentences from this lesson. (See the information provided under *Procedure to Follow on Pages Consisting of Sentences* located on pages 20 - 21.)

Teacher's Guide
Lesson 573

Students read this story. (See the information provided under *Oral Reading Procedure With Stories* located on page 21.)

Page 176
Supplemental Materials

Blackline Masters – Duplicate pages fifty-six through fifty-nine for students to take home.

Information Teacher Presents or Reviews on this Page

Mastery Check and Review Number Twenty – Review the information found on page 28 in the core book.

Student Exercises
Lesson 574 through Lesson 579

See the box titled *Administering the Mastery Checks: Mastery Checks: Fourteen through Twenty-one* on pages 71 - 72. Dictate words as they are grouped on these pages. As an example before dictating the words listed under the consonant team <u>gn</u> found on page 176 in the core book, you might say to your students, "The next group of words that I am about to dictate all contain the consonant team <u>gn</u>."

Pages 177 – 178
Supplemental Materials

Flash Cards – Review all cards previously introduced that have not been retired.

Information Teacher Presents or Reviews on these Pages

These two pages introduce four syllable words. No new or special steps are added when decoding or spelling four syllable words; the same procedures are used as used to decode and spell two and three syllable words. Review all eight syllable patterns and syllable rules one, two, and three. Review the specific steps involved in marking words listed in the box titled *Procedure for Marking and Decoding Word in Section Three* found on page 108 in the core book. Ask students to list all the consonant and vowel teams learned thus far in the program. This review information can be presented as a game or contest. For instance the teacher might say, "I am going to give you two minutes to write down as many consonant teams as you can; the student who can write down the most teams wins the game."

Student Exercises
Lesson 580 / Lesson 582 / Lesson 584 / Lesson 586

Students read the words in these lessons. (See the discussion of Guided Oral Reading Practice on pages 8 - 10.)

Lesson 581 (Quiz 146) / Lesson 583 (Quiz 147) / Lesson 585 (Quiz 148) / Lesson 587 (Quiz 149)
The teacher dictates the words from these lessons. **Students both spell and mark these words.** (See information under *Dictation Procedure for Multiple Syllable Words* on pages 59 - 61.)

Page 179
Supplemental Materials

Flash Cards – Review all cards previously introduced that have not been retired.
The Reader – No pages (1st Ed.). Read pages 136-137 (2nd. Ed.) on completing page 179.

Teacher's Guide

The We All Can Read Phonics Game – Students play *Card Game Thirty* upon completing this page.

Information Teacher Presents or Reviews on this Page

The first half of this page consists of sentences; the second half of this page consists of a story containing the elements identified at the top of the page in the title. In addition to the word lists that are found on most pages in this book, it is also helpful for students to have the opportunity to read sentences and stories whose words contain those phonic elements recently presented.

Student Exercises
Lesson 588

Students read the sentences in this lesson. (See the information provided under *Procedure to Follow on Pages Consisting of Sentences* located on pages 20 - 21.)

Lesson 589

The teacher dictates the sentences from this lesson. (See the information provided under *Procedure to Follow on Pages Consisting of Sentences* located on pages 20 - 21.)

Lesson 590

Students read this story. (See the information provided under *Oral Reading Procedure With Stories* located on page 21.)

Page 180
Supplemental Materials

Flash Cards – Introduce Card Set A #'s 157-161 / Card Set B #'s 32-33 / Card Set C #'s 84-86. Retire Card Set B # 28 and Card Set C #'s 40, 53, 75. Review all cards previously introduced that have not been retired.

Information Teacher Presents or Reviews on this Page

Five vowel teams are listed on the chart on this page. Review with students the information found at the top of page 181 in the core book. The vowel team ou represents a total of four different sounds. Thus far we have learned that ou represents the sound /ou/ as in *out* and /uh/ (short *u* sound) as in *double*. On this page the final two sounds that the vowel team ou represents are listed. In the word *soul*, ou represents the long *o* sound; in this word underline the ou team, and write the number *four* under it. In the word *soup* the vowel team ou represents the sound /oo/; in this word draw a dotted underline under the ou team, and write the number *six* under it. A dotted underline in the word *soup* indicates that the team ou is making its third sound as a syllable-pattern-six-team. The letters *o*, *u*, and *r* will normally join together and form a syllable-pattern-five-team when they are followed by a consonant letter such as in the word *journey*; notice that in the word *journey*, the three letters our form a team even when the consonant which follows the our vowel team is in the next syllable. Vowel team ough is a four-letter vowel team that represents many sounds. By far the most common sound the team ough represents is the long *o* sound as in the word *dough*. When the vowel team ough represents the long *o* sound, underline the team, and write the number *four* under the team. In all other instances where the team ough represents any other sound, underline the ough team, and write the number *six* under it. Select from *Mastery Check Twenty-one* on page 183 in the core book several words listed under the heading for each of the new teams presented in the chart on this page. Put these words on the board, and use them to illustrate the sounds represented by these five vowel teams.

Teacher's Guide
Student Exercises
Lesson 591

1. Ask your students to make the sounds represented by the vowel teams listed in the individual boxes on this page. Ask students to think of words that contain these vowel teams.

2. Reverse the process. and make the sounds represented by the vowel teams on this page. Then ask your students to spell those sounds.

Page 181
Supplemental Materials

Flash Cards – Review all cards previously introduced that have not been retired.

Information Teacher Presents or Reviews on this Page

Students practice reading and spelling words that all contain one of the five vowel teams introduced on the last page. Review the five vowel teams. Ask students to list as many of these new vowel teams as they can from memory, and ask them to think of words that contain each of those teams. Notice at the top of this page is found a list of the five vowel teams introduced. Students may find it helpful to refer to this list when marking words.

Student Exercises
Lesson 592 / Lesson 594

Students read the words in these lessons. (See the discussion of Guided Oral Reading Practice on pages 8 - 10.)

Lesson 593 (Quiz 150) / Lesson 595 (Quiz 151)

The teacher dictates the words from these lessons. **Students both spell and mark these words.** (See information under *Dictation Procedure for Multiple Syllable Words* on pages 59 - 61.)

Page 182
Supplemental Materials

Flash Cards – Review all cards previously introduced that have not been retired.
The Reader – Read page 86 (1st Ed.) or pages 138-139 (2nd. Ed.) on completing page 182.
The We All Can Read Phonics Game – Students play *Card Game Thirty-one* upon completing this page.

Information Teacher Presents or Reviews on this Page

The first half of this page consists of sentences; the second half of this page consists of a story containing the elements identified at the top of the page in the title. In addition to the word lists that are found on most pages in this book, it is also helpful for students to have the opportunity to read sentences and stories whose words contain those phonic elements recently presented.

Student Exercises
Lesson 596

Students read the sentences in this lesson. (See the information provided under *Procedure to Follow on Pages Consisting of Sentences* located on pages 20 - 21.)

Lesson 597

The teacher dictates the sentences from this lesson. (See the information provided under *Procedure to Follow on Pages Consisting of Sentences* located on pages 20 - 21.)

Teacher's Guide
Lesson 598

Students read this story. (See the information provided under *Oral Reading Procedure With Stories* located on page 21.)

Page 183
Supplemental Materials

Blackline Masters – Duplicate pages fifty-nine through sixty-one for students to take home.

Information Teacher Presents or Reviews on this Page

Mastery Check and Review Number Twenty-one – Review the information found on page 28 in the core book.

Student Exercises
Lesson 599 through Lesson 602

See the box titled *Administering the Mastery Checks: Mastery Checks Fourteen through Twenty-one* on pages 71 - 72. Dictate words as they are grouped on these pages. As an example before dictating the words listed under the vowel team *our* found on page 183 in the core book, you might say to your students, "The next group of words that I am about to dictate all contain the vowel team *our*."

Pages 184 - 185
Supplemental Materials

Flash Cards – Review all cards previously introduced that have not been retired.

Information Teacher Presents or Reviews on these Pages

These two pages introduce four, five, and six-syllable words. No new or special steps are added when decoding or spelling four, five, and six syllable words; the same procedures are used as used to decode and spell two and three syllable words. Review all eight syllable patterns and syllable rules one, two, and three. Review the individual specific steps involved in marking words listed in the box titled *Procedure for Marking and Decoding Word in Section Three* found on page 108 in the core book. Ask students to list all the consonant and vowel teams learned thus far in the program. This review information can be presented as a game or contest. For instance the teacher might say, "I am going to give you two minutes to write down as many syllable pattern four teams as you can; the student who can write down the most teams wins the game."

Student Exercises
Lesson 603 / Lesson 605 / Lesson 607 / Lesson 609

Students read the words in these lessons. (See the discussion of Guided Oral Reading Practice on pages 8 - 10.)

Lesson 604 (Quiz 152) / Lesson 606 (Quiz 153) / Lesson 608 (Quiz 154) / Lesson 610 (Quiz 155)

The teacher dictates the words from these lessons. **Students both spell and mark these words.** (See information under *Dictation Procedure for Multiple Syllable Words* on pages 59 - 61.)

Page 186
Supplemental Materials

Flash Cards – Review all cards previously introduced that have not been retired.
The Reader – Read pgs. 87-88 (1st Ed.) or pgs. 140-141 (2nd. Ed.) on completing page 186.
The We All Can Read Phonics Game – Students play Card Game Thirty-two upon completing this page.

Information Teacher Presents or Reviews on these Pages

The first half of this page consists of sentences; the second half of this page consists of a story containing the elements identified at the top of the page in the title. In addition to the word lists that are found on most pages in this book, it is also helpful for students to have the opportunity to read sentences and stories whose words contain those phonic elements recently presented.

Student Exercises
Lesson 611

Students read the sentences in this lesson. (See the information provided under *Procedure to Follow on Pages Consisting of Sentences* located on pages 20 - 21.)

Lesson 612

The teacher dictates the sentences from this lesson. (See the information provided under *Procedure to Follow on Pages Consisting of Sentences* located on pages 20 - 21.)

Lesson 613

Students read this story. (See the information provided under *Oral Reading Procedure With Stories* located on page 21.)

Additional Information Regarding Consonant Sounds
Classifying Consonant Sounds

Consonants can be subdivided in several different ways. One way to think about consonant sounds is by determining whether or not a sound is made with a sudden burst of air which once released causes the sound to stop or if instead the sound can be made to go on as long as we have air left to utter the sound. (All vowel sounds can be produced as long as breath is available.) We call these two basic groups of consonant sounds *stop consonants* and *go consonants*. Stop consonant sounds are made with a sudden release of air while go consonant sounds are made by gradually releasing air.

Stop and Go consonants

Stop Consonants	b	d	g	j	k	p	t	w	y
Go Consonants	f	h	l	m	n	r	s	v	z

Another category for consonants is one in which sounds are divided according to whether or not they are voiced. A voiced sound is one in which the vocal cords are made to vibrate when producing that sound; a voiceless sound is one in which the vocal cords do not vibrate during the production of a particular sound. Many consonant sounds can be paired together so that the consonant sounds are produced in an almost identical manner except that one sound is voiced (vocal cords vibrate), and the other sound is voiceless (vocal chords do not vibrate). Students can monitor whether or not their vocal cords are vibrating during the production of a particular sound by placing their hands on the larynx (Adam's apple).

Consonant Pairs

Voiceless Consonant Sounds	p	t	k	ch	f	s	sh	th-thin
Voiced Consonant Sounds	b	d	g	j	v	z	zh	th-this

Nasal Consonants

Finally the consonants *m* and *n* are called nasal consonants because the sounds for those letters must come through the nose. As an experiment begin to make the /m/ or /n/ sound as in the word *map* or *nut*, and pinch the tip of your nose while still making the /m/ or /n/ sound. By pinching the nose, you immediately stop the /m/ or /n/ sound from being made, thus demonstrating how air is directed out through the nose when making these two nasal sounds. (There are a total of three nasal sounds in English; the third nasal sound is the sound made by the consonant team *ng* as in the word *sing*.)

The Mechanics of Speech Production

All sounds begin with air being exhaled. We have different parts in our mouth and throat that enable us to influence the air stream as it rushes out of our mouth to produce different sounds for speech. The major speech parts are the tongue, lips, teeth, upper mouth, jaw, and vocal chords.

Teacher's Guide

What follows is a brief description of how we form various consonant sounds. A description of the mechanics of how we produce sounds can never be precise because a specific sound can be correctly made by a variety of different mouth positions. The following descriptions are general guidelines for the production of consonant sounds.

Most students already know how to articulate correctly the consonant sounds. The purpose in providing the information in this section is to create an opportunity for students to discover for themselves that speech is composed of discrete sounds and to enable students to have a way to think about what they are doing in order to create a specific sound. It is unnecessary for the student, the teacher, or the tutor to memorize this information. Discussing the mechanics of speech production causes students, often for the first time, to think about the individual sounds that makeup the English language. Again it is important to stress that students should not be asked to memorize this information, nor should they be tested on this information. The following section on speech production is also intended for teachers as a reference guide in the event they are confronted with a student who has difficulty making a particular sound or series of sounds. *(It is helpful though not necessary for each student to use a small pocket mirror when exploring the various mouth positions we use to produce different sounds.)*

Sounds Created With Both Lips

b Vocal cords vibrate. The letter *b* is a stop consonant. Lips come together to hold the air. Lips open to release the air. The sound explodes across the lips.

p Vocal cords do not vibrate. The letter *p* is a stop consonant. Lips come together to hold the air. Lips open to release the air. The sound explodes across the lips. (The only difference between the sounds of *b* and *p* is one of voicing.)

m Vocal cords vibrate. The letter *m* is a go consonant. Lips are closed, and air and sound are directed out through the nose. The tongue is usually flat, and teeth open a small amount.

w Vocal cords vibrate. The letter *w* is a stop consonant. Lips are rounded and pushed out.

Sounds Created With Upper Teeth and Lower Lips

f Vocal cords do not vibrate. The letter *f* is a go consonant. The lower lip is raised to touch upper front teeth while air is directed around teeth, causing a resulting sound like air leaking from a tire.

v Vocal cords vibrate. The letter *v* is a go consonant. The lower lip is raised to touch the upper front teeth while air is directed around the teeth. (The only difference between the sounds of *v* and *f* is one of voicing.)

Sounds Created by Placing Tip of Tongue On or Near
the Ridge of Gum Directly Behind Upper Teeth

t Vocal cords do not vibrate. The letter *t* is a stop consonant. The tongue creates an airtight seal against the ridge of the upper gum and teeth prior to release of air.

d Vocal cords vibrate. The letter *d* is a stop consonant. The tongue creates an airtight seal against the ridge of the upper gum and teeth prior to release of air. (The only difference between the sounds of *d* and *t* is one of voicing.)

n Vocal cords vibrate. The letter *n* is a go consonant. The tongue creates an airtight seal against the ridge of upper gum and teeth. Air and sound are directed out through the nose; lips and teeth are slightly open.

j Vocal cords vibrate. The letter *j* is a stop consonant. The tongue touches the ridge of the gum behind the upper teeth. The tongue creates an airtight seal against the ridge of the upper gum and teeth prior to release of air. Lips are pushed out and slightly rounded. As air is released, it is directed through the upper teeth to create a sound of friction.

l Vocal cords vibrate. The letter *l* is a go consonant. The tongue is rolled and touches either the point at which the upper gum line and the upper teeth meet or the point at the ridge of the gum behind the upper teeth. Teeth are open slightly. The sides of the tongue are open, permitting air to flow around the tongue and out of the mouth.

Sounds Created With Other Mouth Positions

s Vocal cords do not vibrate. The letter *s* is a go consonant. The tip of the tongue's position can vary. Lips are slightly open. Air is directed out over the front teeth, causing a noticeable sound of friction.

z Vocal cords vibrate. The letter *z* is a go consonant. The tip of the tongue's position can vary. Lips are slightly open. Air is directed out over the front teeth, causing a noticeable sound of friction. Less force is used in the production of this sound than in the production of the *s* sound.

r Vocal cords vibrate. The letter *r* is a go consonant. The main portion of the tongue points upwards. Teeth and lips are slightly open.

y Vocal cords vibrate. The letter *y* is a stop consonant. The tip of the tongue is placed behind the lower front teeth, and the lips are slightly opened.

k Vocal cords do not vibrate. The letter *k* is a stop consonant. The tip of the tongue usually is lowered. Air is held in the back of the mouth and then released in an explosive manner between the tongue and the roof of the mouth. Lips and teeth are slightly open.

g Vocal cords vibrate. The letter *g* is a stop consonant. The tip of the tongue usually is lowered. Air is in the back of the mouth and then released between the tongue and the roof of the mouth with less force than is done with the letter *k*. Lips and teeth are slightly open.

h Vocal cords do not vibrate. The letter *h* is a go consonant. The lips, teeth, and tongue are not involved in the production of this sound. Because the breath makes only a slight noise as it leaves the mouth, it must be exhaled through the mouth with greater force than most other sounds require in order for the sound to be heard.

How to Form Lower Case Letters

a   b   c   d

e   f   g   h   i

j   k   l   m   n

o   p   q   r

s   t   u   v

w   x   y   z

95

How to Form Upper Case Letters

A B C D

E F G H I

J K L M N

O P Q R

S T U V

W X Y Z

Student Assessment Procedure

Because this program is sequential, it is critical that students demonstrate mastery in each lesson in this program before being permitted to proceed to subsequent lessons. The teacher can determine whether or not a student has sufficiently mastered the information and skills contained in any lesson by evaluating a student's performance in the three following skill areas: **1) the ability of the student to read the words on the page accurately, 2) the ability of the student to read the words on the page fluently, and 3) the ability of the student to spell the words on the page correctly.**

Two assessment procedures follow. The *Informal Student Assessment Procedure* (pages 103 - 116) provides a detailed evaluation procedure to document and track a student's progress as he or she proceeds through the entire program lesson-by-lesson. Five separate competencies are tracked and evaluated throughout the entire program. Those five competencies measured are as follows:

1. The ability of a student to **read words** contained in a lesson **accurately**.
2. The ability of the student to **read words** contained in a lesson **fluently**.
3. The ability of the student to **spell words** contained in a lesson **correctly**.
4. The ability of the student to **mark words** contained in a lesson **correctly**.
5. The ability of the student to **score eighty percent or higher** on **spelling quizzes correlated to specific lessons**.

Some of the above categories are easier to measure in a classroom setting than are others. The ability of students to spell and mark words can be determined by administering a group spelling and marking quiz where students are asked both to spell and mark dictated words. Students turn in their papers, and the teacher can then grade those papers. Measuring a student's ability to read accurately and fluently, on the other hand, requires that a teacher spend individual one-on-one time with each student as often as is practicable in order to hear how accurately and fluently the student is able to read. Determining whether a student is reading accurately and fluently cannot be accomplished only by listening to a group of students read in unison. It is possible to receive some limited feedback of oral reading skills of individual students by listening to them read in a group setting; but some one-to-one time is also essential.

Ideally the teacher would evaluate each student's oral reading skills at the point in each lesson indicated on the *Informal Student Assessment Procedure and Chart* (pages 103 - 116). Evaluating a student's oral reading skills presents no problems in the context of one-to-one instruction or even in small group instruction. However, monitoring oral reading skills for individuals within the context of an entire classroom of students is more problematic.

Two evaluation strategies are suggested for evaluating a student's reading accuracy and fluency levels: an informal evaluation procedure and a more formal assessment procedure. If possible alternate between the informal and formal evaluation procedures. For the first evaluation cycle, use the informal procedure. After each student has been evaluated informally, administer the more formal procedure for the next evaluation cycle. Because evaluation is an ongoing activity, evaluate each student once each week if possible using either the informal or formal evaluation procedure. If it is not possible to evaluate each student once each week, then evaluate each student as often as is practicable alternating between the informal and formal procedures. A discussion of the two contrasting evaluation procedures now follows.

Informal Accuracy and Fluency Assessment Procedure - Evaluate each student once each week if at all possible. Find a quiet corner and select the most recent lesson that you have completed from the core book. (**Do not use the lessons from the Mastery Word Lists for this evaluation.**) Ask the student to read for you. You want to determine if the student is able to read the words on the page **1) accurately** and **2) fluently**. These competencies can be determined simply by listening to your student read. Give each student approximately one minute to read the words from the selected lesson. Is he able to read most of the words (approximately ninety-five percent of the words) accurately? Is he able to read the words fluently? (Is he able to read words at a pace where the words flow effortlessly or relatively effortlessly, or does he struggle and stumble?) Are the student's accuracy and fluency levels improving or remaining stagnant over a period of weeks and months? The *Informal Student Assessment Procedure and Chart* that begins on page 103 relies upon this informal assessment procedure for the teacher to determine if a student has sufficiently demonstrated competency in the columns labeled *A* for *Reads Accurately* and *F* for *Reads Fluently*.

The second oral reading evaluation, The *Formal Reading Accuracy and Fluency Assessment Procedure* (page 101), is more formal and precise and has two alternate formats.

Formal Reading Accuracy and Fluency Assessment Procedure - Find a quiet corner to administer the reading accuracy and fluency assessment procedure. Open the core book to the most recent lesson completed that contains either sentences or a story. As an example if you currently are working on page 22 in the core book, then go back to either page 18 (sentences) or page 19 (stories) to administer the oral reading assessment. Never use a lesson in the book ahead of the lesson you are currently presenting to students. Note that real word sentences and stories are easier to read than are nonsense word sentences and stories. Students will almost always read faster and with a higher rate of accuracy when reading from the real word sentences and stories. **Therefore, to obtain the most accurate measurement possible, it is recommended that real word sentences or stories be used exclusively for the oral reading assessment.**

The next step is to determine which lesson format is most appropriate to use with your student – a lesson that contains sentences or a lesson that contains a short story. Usually it is best to use a lesson consisting of sentences for very low-performing readers who read at speeds less than sixty words-per-minute. Sentences are far more psychologically manageable for these students; large blocks of text can intimidate and discourage them. On the other hand, if a student might possibly be able to read all of the words in the real sentences within a lesson in less than one minute, then for that student it is necessary to use lessons that contain stories for the oral reading assessment test.

If time permits prior to administering the oral reading assessment, allow the student the opportunity to warm up by reading the lesson in the book that occurs immediately before the lesson that is to be used for the assessment. Students may read lessons that contain either real words or nonsense words for the warm-up.

Give each student exactly one minute to read the words from the identified lesson. Do not provide any feedback to your student as to whether or not he is reading the words correctly. Keep a count of the total number of words a student does not read correctly; misread words, substituted words, and skipped words all constitute errors. If a student corrects himself without prompting, accept whatever answer he identifies as his final answer. If a student is unable to read a word after three-to-four seconds, say the word for him and have him continue on to the next word. When the minute is over, tell the student to stop.

Record **A) Number of Words Read Correctly** in the first space provided on the *Formal Student Accuracy and Fluency Assessment Procedure and Chart* (page 101), **B) Total Number of Words Read** in the second space provided. Write the student's **C) Reading Accuracy Score** in the third space provided. Determine a student's accuracy score by dividing the number of words read correctly by the number of total words read. Multiply that figure by 100%. As an example if a student reads 110 words correctly out of a total of 120 words, divide the number 110 by the number 120; the amount is .916. Multiply .916 by 100; the amount is 91.6. Therefore the accuracy rate is 91.6 %. Record **D) Words Read Correctly Per Minute Rate** in the fourth space provided on the chart. The number of words a student reads in one minute minus the number of words a student has misread equals the number of words read correctly per minute. If a student reads 120 words in one minute and has misread 10 words, then the number of words read correctly per minute for that student is 110 words per minute or 110 wpm.

To determine the number of words in the lessons with sentences, consult the numbers found at the end of each sentence. The first number indicates the number of words in that sentence; the second figure indicates the cumulative number of words contained in that lesson up to the end of the current sentence. The third figure (found only in the lessons with real sentences) refers to the cumulative number of words on that page up to the end of the current sentence including the number of words contained in the nonsense sentences. As an example, consult the nonsense sentences under Lessons 24 and 25 on page eight in the book. Sentence three contains six words and there are a total of twenty words contained in sentences one through three. Sentence nine contains eight words and there are a total of sixty-four words in the nine sentences under Lessons 24 and 25. Now consult the sentences contained under Lessons 26 and 27. Sentence three contains nine words and there are a total of twenty-three words in sentences one through three under Lessons 26 and 27. The third number refers to the total number of words contained in all of the sentences on this page starting from the top of the page. A total of eighty-seven words are contained in the sentences starting from sentence one under Lessons 24 and 25 to sentence number three under Lessons 26 and 27. Sentence nine under Lessons 26 and 27 contains nine words and there are a total of seventy-four words in Lessons 26 and 27 and a total of 138 words found in all of the sentences on this page.

To determine the number of words in the lessons with short stories, consult the numbers found at the end of each line in each paragraph. The number at the end of each line represents the cumulative number of words found in the passage up to the end of that line.

By administering either of these oral reading assessment procedures to five students each day, the teacher can evaluate an entire class of twenty-five students in a one-week cycle. Teachers will find that a minute and one-half to two minutes per student will provide enough time to evaluate and record the results for each student. Students will also come to understand their role in the assessment procedure, and their understanding and cooperation will further help to streamline the process. The teacher also might find it possible to evaluate one or two students before class actually begins.

Students should be able to read with 95 to 100 percent accuracy. Desirable word per minute rates increase with the age of the student. First grade students should read between 60 to 80 words per minute by the end of the year. Second grade students should read from 90 to 115 words per minute by the end of the academic year. Students by the second half of third grade should be able to read 120 words per minute and by fifth grade students should be able to read at a rate of 150 words per minute. Beyond the fifth grade students should be able to read grade level material at a minimum speed of 150 words per minute with good comprehension.

Fluency is not just measured in speed alone. Prosody or expression, the rhythm of spoken language, is also a crucial element to develop with students. Students should be able to read orally with the same intonation and phrasing as they would use to converse in normal spoken conversation. Emphasize and develop prosody while practicing fluency skills with your students.

Formal Student Accuracy and Fluency Assessment Procedure and Chart

Student's Name/Date	Lesson #				Lesson #				Lesson #				Lesson #			
	A	B	C	D	A	B	C	D	A	B	C	D	A	B	C	D
1.																
2.																
3.																
4.																
5.																
6.																
7.																
8.																
9.																
10.																
11.																
12.																
13.																
14.																
15.																
16.																
17.																
18.																
19.																
20.																
21.																
22.																
23.																
24.																
25.																
26.																

At the top of each lesson number column, write the lesson number you are using to test the student. Under each lesson number column, write **A) Number of Words Read Correctly** in one minute's time in the first space provided, **B) Total Number of Words Read** in the second space provided, and **C) Reading Accuracy Score** in the third space. Determine a student's accuracy score by dividing the number of words read correctly by the number of total words read and then multiply by 100%. (See page 99 for more information regarding determining a student's accuracy score.) In the fourth column enter the **D) Words Read Correctly Per Minute Rate** which is the number of words a student reads in one minute minus the number of words a student has misread which equals the number of words read correctly per minute.
Go to http://www.weallcanread.com/downloads.html to print additional copies of this chart.

Student reads words in lesson **Accurately (A)**, **Fluently (F)**, **Spells (S)** and **Marks (M)** each word correctly and scores 80% or higher on **Quiz (Q)**. Check each box when task completed. **Date (D)** each lesson completed.

VHS Video Guide	Video CD Guide	Book Page Guide	**Informal Student Assessment Procedure and Chart** Student's Name _____	A	F	S	M	Q	D
1	1	1	**Lesson 1** – Introduction of the consonant letters and sounds they represent	X	X	X	X	X	
1	1	2	**Lesson 2** – The consonant letters – Oral Reading			X	X	X	
1	1	2	**Lesson 3/Quiz 1** – The consonant letters – Dictation	X	X				
1	1	3	**Lesson 4** – Short *a* followed by a consonant – Oral Reading			X	X	X	
1	1	3	**Lesson 5/Quiz 2** – Short *a* followed by a consonant – Dictation	X	X				
1	1	3	**Lesson 6** – Short *a* followed by a consonant – Oral Reading			X	X	X	
1	1	3	**Lesson 7/Quiz 3** – Short *a* followed by a consonant – Dictation	X	X				
1	1	4	**Lesson 8** – Nonsense words with short *a* – Oral Reading			X	X	X	
1	1	4	**Lesson 9/Quiz 4** – Nonsense words with short *a* – Dictation	X	X				
1	1	4	**Lesson 10** – Real words with short *a* – Oral Reading			X	X	X	
1	1	4	**Lesson 11/Quiz 5** – Real words with short *a* – Dictation	X	X				
1	2	5	**Lesson 12** – Nonsense words with short *e* – Oral Reading			X	X	X	
1	2	5	**Lesson 13/Quiz 6** – Nonsense words with short *e* – Dictation	X	X				
1	2	5	**Lesson 14** – Nonsense words with short *a* and *e* – Oral Reading			X	X	X	
1	2	5	**Lesson 15/Quiz 7** – Nonsense words with short *a* and *e* – Dictation	X	X				
1	2	6	**Lesson 16** – Nonsense words with short *e* – Oral Reading			X	X	X	
1	2	6	**Lesson 17/Quiz 8** – Nonsense words with short *e* – Dictation	X	X				
1	2	6	**Lesson 18** – Real words with short *e* – Oral Reading			X	X	X	
1	2	6	**Lesson 19/Quiz 9** – Real words with short e – Dictation	X	X				
1	2	7	**Lesson 20** – Nonsense words with short *a* and *e* – Oral Reading			X	X	X	
1	2	7	**Lesson 21/Quiz 10** – Nonsense words with short *a* and *e* – Dictation	X	X				
2	3	7	**Lesson 22** – Real words with short *a* and *e* – Oral Reading			X	X	X	
2	3	7	**Lesson 23/Quiz 11** – Real words with short *a* and *e* – Dictation	X	X				
2	3	8	**Lesson 24** – Nonsense sentences with short *a* and *e* – Oral Reading			X	X	X	
2	3	8	**Lesson 25** – Nonsense sentences with short *a* and *e* –Dictation	X	X			X	
2	3	8	**Lesson 26** – Real sentences with short *a* and *e* – Oral Reading			X	X	X	
2	3	8	**Lesson 27** – Real sentences with short *a* and *e* – Dictation	X	X			X	
2	3	9	**Lesson 28** – Nonsense word story with short *a* and *e* – Oral Reading			X	X	X	
2	3	9	**Lesson 29** – Real word story with short *a* and *e* – Oral Reading			X	X	X	
2	4	10	**Lesson 30** – Nonsense words with short *o* – Oral Reading			X	X	X	
2	3	10	**Lesson 31/Quiz 12** – Nonsense words with short *o* – Dictation	X	X				
2	4	10	**Lesson 32** – Nonsense words with short *a, e,* and *o* – Oral Reading			X	X	X	
2	4	10	**Lesson 33/Quiz 13** – Nonsense words with short *a, e,* and *o* – Dictation	X	X				
2	4	11	**Lesson 34** – Nonsense words with short *o* – Oral Reading			X	X	X	
2	4	11	**Lesson 35/Quiz 14** – Nonsense words with short *o* – Dictation	X	X				
2	4	11	**Lesson 36** – Real words with short *o* – Oral Reading			X	X	X	
2	4	11	**Lesson 37/Quiz 15** – Real words with short *o* – Dictation	X	X				
2	4	12	**Lesson 38** – Nonsense words with short *a, e,* and *o* – Oral Reading			X	X	X	
2	4	12	**Lesson 39/Quiz 16** – Nonsense words with short *a, e,* and *o* – Dictation	X	X				
2	4	12	**Lesson 40** – Real words with short *a,* e, and *o* – Oral Reading			X	X	X	
2	4	12	**Lesson 41/Quiz 17** – Real words with short *a, e,* and *o* – Dictation	X	X				
2	4	13	**Lesson 42** – Nonsense sentences with short *a, e,* and *o* – Oral Reading			X	X	X	
2	4	13	**Lesson 43** – Nonsense sentences with short *a, e,* and *o* – Dictation	X	X			X	
2	4	13	**Lesson 44** – Real sentences with short *a, e,* and *o* – Oral Reading			X	X	X	
2	4	13	**Lesson 45** – Real sentences with short *a, e,* and *o* – Dictation	X	X			X	
2	4	14	**Lesson 46** – Nonsense word story with short *a, e,* and *o* – Oral Reading			X	X	X	
2	4	14	**Lesson 47** – Real word story with short *a, e,* and *o* – Oral Reading			X	X	X	
2	4	15	**Lesson 48** – Nonsense words with short u – Oral Reading			X	X	X	
2	4	15	**Lesson 49/Quiz 18** – Nonsense words with short u – Dictation	X	X				
3	5	15	**Lesson 50** – Nonsense words with short *a, e, o,* and *u* – Oral Reading			X	X	X	
3	5	15	**Lesson 51/Quiz 19** – Nonsense words with short *a, e, o,* and *u* – Dictation	X	X				
3	5	16	**Lesson 52** – Nonsense words with short *u* – Oral Reading			X	X	X	
3	5	16	**Lesson 53/Quiz 20** – Nonsense words with short *u* – Dictation	X	X				
3	5	16	**Lesson 54** – Real words with short *u* – Oral Reading			X	X	X	

Student reads words in lesson **Accurately (A)**, **Fluently (F)**, **Spells (S)** and **Marks (M)** each word correctly and scores 80% or higher on **Quiz (Q)**. Check each box when task completed. **Date (D)** each lesson completed.

VHS Video Guide	Video CD Guide	Book Page Guide	Informal Student Assessment Procedure and Chart — Student's Name _____	A	F	S	M	Q	D
3	5	16	**Lesson 55/Quiz 21** – Real words with short *u* – Dictation	X	X				
3	5	17	**Lesson 56** – Nonsense words with short *a, e, o,* and *u* – Oral Reading			X	X	X	
3	5	17	**Lesson 57/Quiz 22** – Nonsense words with short *a, e, o,* and *u* – Dictation	X	X				
3	5	17	**Lesson 58** – Real words with short *a, e, o,* and *u* – Oral Reading			X	X	X	
3	5	17	**Lesson 59/Quiz 23** – Real words with short *a, e, o,* and *u* – Dictation	X	X				
3	6	18	**Lesson 60** – Nonsense sentences with short *a, e, o,* and *u* – Oral Reading			X	X	X	
3	6	18	**Lesson 61** – Nonsense sentences with short *a, e, o,* and *u* – Dictation	X	X			X	
3	6	18	**Lesson 62** – Real sentences with short *a, e, o,* and *u* – Oral Reading			X	X	X	
3	6	18	**Lesson 63** – Real sentences with short *a, e, o,* and *u* – Dictation	X	X			X	
3	6	19	**Lesson 64** – Nonsense word story with short *a, e, o,* and *u* – Oral Reading			X	X	X	
3	6	19	**Lesson 65** – Real word story with short *a, e, o,* and *u* – Oral Reading			X	X	X	
3	6	20	**Lesson 66** – Nonsense words with short *i* – Oral Reading			X	X	X	
3	6	20	**Lesson 67/Quiz 24** – Nonsense words with short *i* – Dictation	X	X				
3	6	20	**Lesson 68** – Nonsense words with short *a, e, i, o,* and *u* – Oral Reading			X	X	X	
3	6	20	**Lesson 69/Quiz 25** – Nonsense words with short *a, e, i, o,* and *u* – Dictation	X	X				
3	6	21	**Lesson 70** – Nonsense words with short *i* – Oral Reading			X	X	X	
3	6	21	**Lesson 71/Quiz 26** – Nonsense words with short *i* – Dictation	X	X				
3	6	21	**Lesson 72** – Real words with short *i* – Oral Reading			X	X	X	
3	6	21	**Lesson 73/Quiz 27** – Real words with short *i* – Dictation	X	X				
3	6	22	**Lesson 74** – Nonsense words with short *a, e, i, o,* and *u* – Oral Reading			X	X	X	
3	6	22	**Lesson 75/Quiz 28** – Nonsense words with short *a, e, i, o,* and *u* – Dictation	X	X				
4	7	22	**Lesson 76** – Real words with short *a, e, i, o,* and *u* – Oral Reading			X	X	X	
4	7	22	**Lesson 77/Quiz 29** – Real words with short *a, e, i, o,* and *u* – Dictation	X	X				
4	7	23	**Lesson 78** – Nonsense words with short *a, e, i, o,* and *u* – Oral Reading			X	X	X	
4	7	23	**Lesson 79/Quiz 30** – Nonsense words with short *a, e, i, o,* and *u* – Dictation	X	X				
4	7	23	**Lesson 80** – Real words with short *a, e, i, o,* and *u* – Oral Reading			X	X	X	
4	7	23	**Lesson 81/Quiz 31** – Real words with short *a, e, i, o,* and *u* – Dictation	X	X				
4	7	24	**Lesson 82** – Nonsense sentences with short *a, e, i, o,* and *u* – Oral Reading			X	X	X	
4	7	24	**Lesson 83** – Nonsense sentences with short *a, e, i, o,* and *u* – Dictation	X	X			X	
4	7	24	**Lesson 84** – Real sentences with short *a, e, i, o,* and *u* – Oral Reading			X	X	X	
4	7	24	**Lesson 85** – Real sentences with short *a, e, i, o,* and *u* – Dictation	X	X			X	
4	7	25	**Lesson 86** – Nonsense word story with short *a, e, i, o,* and *u* – Oral Reading			X	X	X	
4	7	25	**Lesson 87** – Real word story with short *a, e, i, o,* and *u* – Oral Reading			X	X	X	
4	7	26	**Lesson 88** – Nonsense words ending in *ff, ll, ss* – Oral Reading			X	X	X	
4	7	26	**Lesson 89/Quiz 32** – Nonsense words ending in *ff, ll, ss* – Dictation	X	X				
4	7	26	**Lesson 90** – Real words ending in *ff, ll, ss* – Oral Reading			X	X	X	
4	7	26	**Lesson 91/Quiz 33** – Real words ending in *ff, ll, ss* – Dictation	X	X				
4	7	27	**Lesson 92** – Nonsense words beginning with *c* or *k* – Oral Reading			X	X	X	
4	7	27	**Lesson 93/Quiz 34** – Nonsense words beginning with *c* or *k* – Dictation	X	X				
4	8	27	**Lesson 94** – Real words beginning with *c* or *k* – Oral Reading			X	X	X	
4	8	27	**Lesson 95/Quiz 35** – Real words beginning with *c* or *k* – Dictation	X	X				
4	8	29	**Lesson 96** – Mastery Check 1 – short *a*				X	X	
4	8	29	**Lesson 97** – Mastery Check 1 – short *e*				X	X	
4	8	29	**Lesson 98** – Mastery Check 1 – short *i*				X	X	
4	8	29	**Lesson 99** – Mastery Check 1 – short *o*				X	X	
4	8	29	**Lesson 100** – Mastery Check 1 – short *u*				X	X	
4	8	30	**Lesson 101** – Introducing beginning consonant blends				X	X	
5	9	31	**Lesson 102** – Nonsense words/beginning blends – Oral Reading			X	X	X	
5	9	31	**Lesson 103/Quiz 36** – Nonsense words/beginning blends – Dictation	X	X				
5	9	31	**Lesson 104** – Real words/beginning blends – Oral Reading			X	X	X	
5	9	31	**Lesson 105/Quiz 37** – Real words/beginning blends – Dictation	X	X				
5	9	32	**Lesson 106** – Nonsense words/beginning blends – Oral Reading			X	X	X	
5	9	32	**Lesson 107/Quiz 38** – Nonsense words/beginning blends – Dictation	X	X				
5	9	32	**Lesson 108** – Real words/beginning blends – Oral Reading			X	X	X	

Student reads words in lesson **Accurately (A)**, **Fluently (F)**, **Spells (S)** and **Marks (M)** each word correctly and scores 80% or higher on **Quiz (Q)**. Check each box when task completed. **Date (D)** each lesson completed.

VHS Video Guide	Video CD Guide	Book Page Guide	Informal Student Assessment Procedure and Chart / Student's Name _____	A	F	S	M	Q	D
5	9	32	**Lesson 109/Quiz 39** – Real words/beginning blends – Dictation	X	X				
5	9	33	**Lesson 110** – Nonsense sentences /beginning consonant blends – Oral Reading			X	X	X	
5	9	33	**Lesson 111** – Nonsense sentences / beginning consonant blends – Dictation	X	X			X	
5	9	33	**Lesson 112** – Real sentences / beginning consonant blends – Oral Reading			X	X	X	
5	9	33	**Lesson 113** – Real sentences / beginning consonant blends – Dictation	X	X			X	
5	9	34	**Lesson 114** – Nonsense word story/beginning consonant blends–Oral Reading			X	X	X	
5	9	34	**Lesson 115** – Real word story / beginning consonant blends – Oral Reading			X	X	X	
5	9	35	**Lesson 116** – Mastery Check 2 – beginning consonant blends/short *a*				X	X	
5	9	35	**Lesson 117** – Mastery Check 2 – beginning consonant blends/short *e*				X	X	
5	9	35	**Lesson 118** – Mastery Check 2 – beginning consonant blends/short *i*				X	X	
5	9	35	**Lesson 119** – Mastery Check 2 – beginning consonant blends/short *o*				X	X	
5	9	35	**Lesson 120** – Mastery Check 2 – beginning consonant blends/short *u*				X	X	
5	9	36	**Lesson 121** – Introducing ending consonant blends				X	X	
5	9	37	**Lesson 122** – Nonsense words/ending blends – Oral Reading			X	X	X	
5	9	37	**Lesson 123/Quiz 40** – Nonsense words/ending blends – Dictation	X	X				
5	9	37	**Lesson 124** – Real words/ ending blends – Oral Reading			X	X	X	
5	9	37	**Lesson 125/Quiz 41** – Nonsense words/ending blends – Dictation	X	X				
5	9	38	**Lesson 126** – Nonsense words/ending blends – Oral Reading			X	X	X	
5	9	38	**Lesson 127/Quiz 42** – Nonsense words/ending blends – Dictation	X	X				
5	10	38	**Lesson 128** – Real words/ ending blends – Oral Reading			X	X	X	
5	10	38	**Lesson 129/Quiz 43** – Real words/ending blends – Dictation	X	X				
5	10	39	**Lesson 130** – Nonsense sentences / ending consonant blends – Oral Reading			X	X	X	
5	10	39	**Lesson 131** – Nonsense sentences / ending consonant blends – Dictation	X	X			X	
5	10	39	**Lesson 132** – Real sentences / ending consonant blends – Oral Reading			X	X	X	
5	10	39	**Lesson 133** – Real sentences / ending consonant blends – Dictation	X	X			X	
5	10	40	**Lesson 134** – Nonsense word story / ending consonant blends – Oral Reading			X	X	X	
5	10	40	**Lesson 135** – Real word story / ending consonant blends – Oral Reading			X	X	X	
5	10	41	**Lesson 136** – Mastery Check 3 – short vowels / ending blends – short *a*				X	X	
5	10	41	**Lesson 137** – Mastery Check 3 – short vowels / ending blends – short *e*				X	X	
5	10	41	**Lesson 138** – Mastery Check 3 – short vowels / ending blends – short *i*				X	X	
5	10	41	**Lesson 139** – Mastery Check 3 – short vowels / ending blends – short *o + u*				X	X	
5	10	42	**Lesson 140** – Nonsense words/beginning and ending blends – Oral Reading			X	X	X	
5	10	42	**Lesson 141/Quiz 44** – Nonsense words/beginning / ending blends – Dictation	X	X				
5	10	42	**Lesson 142** – Real words/beginning and ending blends – Oral Reading			X	X	X	
5	10	42	**Lesson 143/Quiz 45** – Real words/beginning and ending blends – Dictation	X	X				
5	10	43	**Lesson 144** – Nonsense words/beginning and ending blends – Oral Reading			X	X	X	
5	10	43	**Lesson 145/Quiz 46** – Nonsense words/beginning / ending blends – Dictation	X	X				
5	10	43	**Lesson 146** – Real words/beginning and ending blends – Oral Reading			X	X	X	
5	10	43	**Lesson 147/Quiz 47** – Real words/beginning and ending blends – Dictation	X	X				
5	10	44	**Lesson 148** – Nonsense sentences beginning/ending blends – Oral Reading			X	X	X	
5	10	44	**Lesson 149** – Nonsense sentences beginning/ending blends – Dictation	X	X			X	
5	10	44	**Lesson 150** – Real sentences beginning/ending blends – Oral Reading			X	X	X	
5	10	44	**Lesson 151** – Real sentences beginning/ending blends – Dictation	X	X			X	
5	10	45	**Lesson 152** – Nonsense word story beginning/ending blends – Oral Reading			X	X	X	
5	10	45	**Lesson 153** – Real word story beginning/ending blends – Oral Reading			X	X	X	
5	10	46	**Lesson 154** – Mastery Check 4 – vowels / beginning + ending blends – short *a*				X	X	
5	10	46	**Lesson 155** – Mastery Check 4 – vowels / beginning + ending blends – short *e*				X	X	
5	10	46	**Lesson 156** – Mastery Check 4 – vowels / beginning + ending blends – short *i*				X	X	
5	10	46	**Lesson 157** – Mastery Check 4 – vowels / beginning + ending blends – *o + u*				X	X	
5	10	47	**Lesson 158** – Introduction of consonant teams					X	
6	11	48	**Lesson 159** – Nonsense words/consonant teams – Oral Reading			X	X	X	
6	11	48	**Lesson 160/Quiz 48** – Nonsense words/consonant teams – Dictation	X	X				
6	11	48	**Lesson 161** – Real words/consonant teams – Oral Reading			X	X	X	
6	11	48	**Lesson 162/Quiz 49** – Real words/consonant teams – Dictation	X	X				

Student reads words in lesson **Accurately (A)**, **Fluently (F)**, **Spells (S)** and **Marks (M)** each word correctly and scores 80% or higher on **Quiz (Q)**. Check each box when task completed. **Date (D)** each lesson completed.

VHS Video Guide	Video CD Guide	Book Page Guide	**Informal Student Assessment Procedure and Chart** Student's Name _____	A	F	S	M	Q	D
6	11	49	**Lesson 163** – Nonsense words/consonant teams – Oral Reading			X	X	X	
6	11	49	**Lesson 164/Quiz 50** – Nonsense words/consonant teams – Dictation	X	X				
6	11	49	**Lesson 165** – Real words/consonant teams – Oral Reading			X	X	X	
6	11	49	**Lesson 166/Quiz 51** – Real words/consonant teams – Dictation	X	X				
6	11	50	**Lesson 167** – Nonsense sentences with consonant teams – Oral Reading			X	X	X	
6	11	50	**Lesson 168** – Nonsense sentences with consonant teams – Dictation	X	X			X	
6	11	50	**Lesson 169** – Real sentences with consonant teams – Oral Reading			X	X	X	
6	11	50	**Lesson 170** – Real sentences with consonant teams – Dictation	X	X			X	
6	11	51	**Lesson 171** – Nonsense word story with consonant teams – Oral Reading			X	X	X	
6	11	51	**Lesson 172** – Real word story with consonant teams – Oral Reading			X	X	X	
6	11	52	**Lesson 173** – Nonsense words/second sound of n and ng – Oral Reading			X	X	X	
6	11	52	**Lesson 174/Quiz 52** – Nonsense words/ second sound of n and ng – Dictation	X	X				
6	11	52	**Lesson 175** – Real words/ second sound of n and ng – Oral Reading			X	X	X	
6	11	52	**Lesson 176 /Quiz 53** – Real words/ second sound of n and ng – Dictation	X	X				
6	11	53	**Lesson 177** – Mastery Check 5 – short vowels / consonant teams – short *a*					X	
6	11	53	**Lesson 178** – Mastery Check 5 – short vowels / consonant teams – short *e*					X	
6	11	53	**Lesson 179** – Mastery Check 5 – short vowels / consonant teams – short *i*					X	
6	11	53	**Lesson 180** – Mastery Check 5 – short vowels / consonant teams – short *o*					X	
6	11	53	**Lesson 181** – Mastery Check 5 – short vowels / consonant teams – short *u*					X	
6	11	54	**Lesson 182** – Review of beginning consonant blends				X	X	
6	11	54	**Lesson 183** – Review of ending consonant blends				X	X	
6	11	54	**Lesson 184** – Review of major consonant teams					X	
6	12	55	**Lesson 185** – Nonsense words/blends and consonant teams – Oral Reading			X	X	X	
6	12	55	**Lesson 186/Quiz 54** – Nonsense words/blends + consonant teams – Dictation	X	X				
6	12	55	**Lesson 187** – Real words/blends and consonant teams – Oral Reading			X	X	X	
6	12	55	**Lesson 188/Quiz 55** – Real words/blends and consonant teams – Dictation	X	X				
6	12	56	**Lesson 189** – Nonsense words/blends and consonant teams – Oral Reading			X	X	X	
6	12	56	**Lesson 190/Quiz 56** – Nonsense words/blends + consonant teams – Dictation	X	X				
6	12	56	**Lesson 191** – Real words/blends and consonant teams – Oral Reading			X	X	X	
6	12	56	**Lesson 192/Quiz 57** – Real words/blends and consonant teams – Dictation	X	X				
6	12	57	**Lesson 193** – Nonsense sentences / blends + consonant teams – Oral Reading			X	X	X	
6	12	57	**Lesson 194** – Nonsense sentences / blends + consonant teams – Dictation	X	X			X	
6	12	57	**Lesson 195** – Real sentences / blends + consonant teams – Oral Reading			X	X	X	
6	12	57	**Lesson 196** – Real sentences / blends + consonant teams – Dictation	X	X			X	
6	12	58	**Lesson 197** – Nonsense word story / blends + consonant teams – Oral Reading			X	X	X	
6	12	58	**Lesson 198** – Real word story / blends + consonant teams – Oral Reading			X	X	X	
6	12	59	**Lesson 199** – Mastery Check 6–short vowels/blends/consonant teams– short *a*					X	
6	12	59	**Lesson 200** – Mastery Check 6–short vowels/blends/consonant teams – short *e*					X	
6	12	59	**Lesson 201** – Mastery Check 6– short vowels/blends/consonant teams– short *i*					X	
6	12	59	**Lesson 202** – Mastery Check 6–short vowel/blends/consonant teams – short *o*					X	
6	12	59	**Lesson 203** – Mastery Check 6–short vowels/blends/consonant teams– short *u*					X	
6	12	60	**Lesson 204** – Mastery Check 7 – short vowels / consonant team *ck*					X	
6	12	60	**Lesson 205** – Mastery Check 7 – short vowels / consonant team *ch*					X	
6	12	60	**Lesson 206** – Mastery Check 7 – short vowels / consonant team *tch*					X	
6	12	60–61	**Lesson 207** – Mastery Check 7 – short vowels / the second sound of n					X	
6	12	61	**Lesson 208** – Mastery Check 7 – short vowels / consonant team *ng*					X	
6	12	61	**Lesson 209** – Mastery Check 7 – short vowels / consonant team *sh*					X	
6	12	61	**Lesson 210** – Mastery Check 7 – short vowels / consonant team *th*					X	
6	12	61	**Lesson 211** – Mastery Check 7 – short vowels / 2nd sound of *th* and *wh*					X	
7	13	62	**Lesson 212** – Nonsense words/syllable patterns one and two – Oral Reading			X	X	X	
7	13	62	**Lesson 213/Quiz 58** – Nonsense words/syllable patterns 1 and 2 – Dictation	X	X				
7	13	62	**Lesson 214** – Real words/syllable patterns 1 and 2 – Oral Reading			X	X	X	
7	13	62	**Lesson 215/Quiz 59** – Real words/syllable patterns 1 and 2 – Dictation	X	X				
7	13	63	**Lesson 216** – Nonsense words/syllable patterns 1 and 2 – Oral Reading			X	X	X	

Student reads words in lesson **Accurately (A)**, **Fluently (F)**, **Spells (S)** and **Marks (M)** each word correctly and scores 80% or higher on **Quiz (Q)**. Check each box when task completed. **Date (D)** each lesson completed.

VHS Video Guide	Video CD Guide	Book Page Guide	Informal Student Assessment Procedure and Chart Student's Name _____	A	F	S	M	Q	D
7	13	63	**Lesson 217/Quiz 60** – Nonsense words/syllable patterns 1 and 2 – Dictation	X	X				
7	13	63	**Lesson 218** – Real words/syllable patterns 1 and 2 – Oral Reading			X	X	X	
7	13	63	**Lesson 219/Quiz 61** – Real words/syllable patterns 1 and 2 – Dictation	X	X				
7	14	64	**Lesson 220** – Nonsense words/syllable patterns 1 and 3 – Oral Reading			X	X	X	
7	14	64	**Lesson 221/Quiz 62** – Nonsense words/syllable patterns 1 + 3 – Dictation	X	X				
7	14	64	**Lesson 222** – Real words/syllable patterns 1 and 3 – Oral Reading			X	X	X	
7	14	64	**Lesson 223/Quiz 63** – Real words/syllable patterns 1 and 3 – Dictation	X	X				
7	14	65	**Lesson 224** – Nonsense words/syllable patterns 1 and 3 – Oral Reading			X	X	X	
7	14	65	**Lesson 225/Quiz 64** – Nonsense words/syllable patterns 1 + 3 – Dictation	X	X				
7	14	65	**Lesson 226** – Real words/syllable patterns 1 and 3 – Oral Reading			X	X	X	
7	14	65	**Lesson 227/Quiz 65** – Real words/syllable patterns 1 and 3 – Dictation	X	X				
8	15	66	**Lesson 228** – Real words/The two long vowel sounds of *u* – Oral Reading			X	X	X	
8	15	66	**Lesson 229/Quiz 66** – Real words/The two long vowel sounds of *u* – Dictation	X	X				
8	15	67	**Lesson 230** – Nonsense sentences / syllable pattern 3 words – Oral Reading			X	X	X	
8	15	67	**Lesson 231** – Nonsense sentences / syllable pattern 3 words – Dictation	X	X			X	
8	15	67	**Lesson 232** – Real sentences / syllable pattern 3 words – Oral Reading			X	X	X	
8	15	67	**Lesson 233** – Real sentences / syllable pattern 3 words – Dictation	X	X			X	
8	15	68	**Lesson 234** – Nonsense word story / syllable pattern 3 words – Oral Reading			X	X	X	
8	15	68	**Lesson 235** – Real word story / syllable pattern 3 words – Oral Reading			X	X	X	
8	15	69	**Lesson 236** – Mastery Check 8 – the vowels *a* + e / consonant letter / silent *e*					X	
8	15	69	**Lesson 237** – Mastery Check 8 – the vowel *i* / consonant letter / silent *e*					X	
8	15	69	**Lesson 238** – Mastery Check 8 – the vowel *o* / consonant letter / silent *e*					X	
8	15	69	**Lesson 239** – Mastery Check 8 – the vowel *u* / consonant letter / silent *e*					X	
8	15	70	**Lesson 240** – Nonsense words/syllable patterns 1, 2, + 3 – Oral Reading			X	X	X	
8	15	70	**Lesson 241/Quiz 67** – Nonsense words/ syllable patterns 1, 2, 3 – Dictation	X	X				
8	16	70	**Lesson 242** – Real words/ syllable patterns 1, 2, and 3 – Oral Reading			X	X	X	
8	16	70	**Lesson 243/Quiz 68** – Real words/ syllable patterns 1, 2, 3 – Dictation	X	X				
8	16	71	**Lesson 244** – Nonsense words/ syllable patterns 1, 2, 3 – Oral Reading			X	X	X	
8	16	71	**Lesson 245/Quiz 69** – Nonsense words/ syllable patterns 1, 2, 3 – Dictation	X	X				
8	16	71	**Lesson 246** – Real words/ syllable patterns 1, 2, and 3 – Oral Reading			X	X	X	
8	16	71	**Lesson 247/Quiz 70** – Real words/ syllable patterns 1, 2, 3 – Dictation	X	X				
8	16	72	**Lesson 248** – Nonsense sentences syllable patterns 1 to 3 – Oral Reading			X	X	X	
8	16	72	**Lesson 249** – Nonsense sentences syllable patterns 1 to 3 – Dictation	X	X			X	
8	16	72	**Lesson 250** – Real sentences syllable patterns 1 to 3 – Oral Reading			X	X	X	
8	16	72	**Lesson 251** – Real sentences syllable patterns 1 to 3 – Dictation			X	X	X	
8	16	73	**Lesson 252** – Nonsense word story syllable patterns 1 to 3 – Oral Reading			X	X	X	
8	16	73	**Lesson 253** – Real word story syllable patterns 1 to 3 – Oral Reading	X	X			X	
8	16	74	**Lesson 254** – Introduction of syllable pattern 4 teams					X	
8	16	75	**Lesson 255** – Nonsense words/syllable pattern 4 teams – Oral Reading			X	X	X	
8	16	75	**Lesson 256** – Nonsense words/ syllable pattern 4 teams – Identify Teams	X	X	X		X	
8	16	75	**Lesson 257** – Real words/ syllable pattern 4 teams – Oral Reading			X	X	X	
8	16	75	**Lesson 258/Quiz 71** – Real words/ syllable pattern 4 teams – Dictation	X	X				
8	16	76	**Lesson 259** – Nonsense words/ syllable pattern 4 teams – Oral Reading			X	X	X	
8	16	76	**Lesson 260** – Nonsense words/ syllable pattern 4 teams – Identify Teams	X	F	X		X	
8	16	76	**Lesson 261** – Real words/ syllable pattern 4 teams – Oral Reading			X	X	X	
8	16	76	**Lesson 262/Quiz 72** – Real words/ syllable pattern 4 teams – Dictation	X	X				
8	16	77	**Lesson 263** – Nonsense sentences with syllable pattern 4 words – Oral Reading			X	X	X	
8	16	77	**Lesson 264**–Identify teams in nonsense sentences with syllable pattern 4 words	X	X	X		X	
8	16	77	**Lesson 265** – Real sentences with syllable pattern 4 words – Oral Reading			X	X	X	
8	16	77	**Lesson 266** – Real sentences with syllable pattern 4 words – Dictation	X	X			X	
8	16	78	**Lesson 267**–Nonsense word story with syllable pattern 4 words–Oral Reading			X	X	X	
8	16	78	**Lesson 268** – Real word story with syllable pattern 4 words – Oral Reading			X	X	X	
8	16	79	**Lesson 269** – Mastery Check 9 – syllable pattern 4 teams – *ai*					X	
8	16	79	**Lesson 270** – Mastery Check 9 – syllable pattern 4 teams – *ay*					X	

Student reads words in lesson **Accurately** (A), **Fluently** (F), **Spells** (S) and **Marks** (M) each word correctly and scores 80% or higher on **Quiz** (Q). Check each box when task completed. **Date** (D) each lesson completed.

VHS Video Guide	Video CD Guide	Book Page Guide	Informal Student Assessment Procedure and Chart Student's Name _____	A	F	S	M	Q	D
8	16	79	**Lesson 271** – Mastery Check 9 – syllable pattern 4 teams – *ea*					X	
8	16	79–80	**Lesson 272** – Mastery Check 9 – syllable pattern 4 teams – *ee*					X	
8	16	80	**Lesson 273** – Mastery Check 9 – syllable pattern 4 teams – *oa*					X	
8	16	80	**Lesson 274** – Mastery Check 9 – syllable pattern 4 teams – *ow*					X	
8	16	80	**Lesson 275** – Mastery Check 9 – syllable pattern 4 teams – *ue*, 2nd sound *ue, ui*					X	
8	16	81	**Lesson 276** – Nonsense words/syllable patterns 1 through 4 – Oral Reading			X	X	X	
8	16	81	**Lesson 277** – Nonsense words/syllable patterns 1 through 4 – Identify groups	X	X	X		X	
8	16	81	**Lesson 278** – Real words/ syllable patterns one through four – Oral Reading			X	X	X	
8	16	81	**Lesson 279/Quiz 73** – Real words/ syllable patterns 1 through 4 – Dictation	X	X				
8	16	82	**Lesson 280** – Nonsense words/ syllable patterns 1 through 4 – Oral Reading			X	X	X	
8	16	82	**Lesson 281** – Nonsense words/syllable patterns 1 through 4 – Identify groups	X	X	X		X	
8	16	82	**Lesson 282** – Real words/ syllable patterns 1 through 4 – Oral Reading			X	X	X	
8	16	82	**Lesson 283/Quiz 74** – Real words/ syllable patterns 1 through 4 – Dictation	X	X				
8	16	83	**Lesson 284** – Nonsense sentences with syllable patterns 1 to 4 – Oral Reading			X	X	X	
8	16	83	**Lesson 285** – Identify teams in nonsense sentences with syllable patterns 1 to 4	X	X	X		X	
8	16	83	**Lesson 286** – Real sentences with syllable patterns 1 to 4 – Oral Reading			X	X	X	
8	16	83	**Lesson 287** – Real sentences with syllable patterns 1 to 4 – Dictation	X	X			X	
8	16	84	**Lesson 288** – Nonsense word story with syllable patterns 1 to 4 – Oral Reading			X	X	X	
8	16	84	**Lesson 289** – Real word story with syllable patterns 1 to 4 – Oral Reading			X	X	X	
9	17	85	**Lesson 290** – Introduction of syllable pattern 5 teams					X	
9	17	86	**Lesson 291** – Nonsense words/syllable pattern 5 teams – Oral Reading			X	X	X	
9	17	86	**Lesson 292** – Nonsense words/ syllable pattern 5 teams – Identify Teams	X	X	X		X	
9	17	86	**Lesson 293** – Real words/ syllable pattern 5 teams – Oral Reading			X	X	X	
9	17	86	**Lesson 294/Quiz 75** – Real words/ syllable pattern 5 teams – Dictation	X	X				
9	17	87	**Lesson 295** – Nonsense words/ syllable pattern 5 teams – Oral Reading			X	X	X	
9	17	87	**Lesson 296** – Nonsense words/ syllable pattern 5 teams – Identify Teams	X	X	X		X	
9	17	87	**Lesson 297** – Real words/ syllable pattern 5 teams – Oral Reading			X	X	X	
9	17	87	**Lesson 298/Quiz 76** – Real words/ syllable pattern 5 teams – Dictation	X	X				
9	17	88	**Lesson 299** – Nonsense sentences with syllable pattern 5 words – Oral Reading			X	X	X	
9	17	88	**Lesson 300**–Identify teams in nonsense sentences with syllable pattern 5 words	X	X	X		X	
9	17	88	**Lesson 301** – Real sentences with syllable pattern 5 words – Oral Reading			X	X	X	
9	17	88	**Lesson 302** – Real sentences with syllable pattern 5 words – Dictation	X	X			X	
9	17	89	**Lesson 303**–Nonsense word story with syllable pattern 5 words–Oral Reading			X	X	X	
9	17	89	**Lesson 304** – Real word story with syllable pattern 5 words – Oral Reading			X	X	X	
9	17	90	**Lesson 305** – Mastery Check 10 – syllable pattern 5 teams – *ar*					X	
9	17	90	**Lesson 306** – Mastery Check 10 – syllable pattern 5 teams – *er* and *ear*					X	
9	17	90	**Lesson 307** – Mastery Check 10 – syllable pattern 5 teams – *ir*					X	
9	17	90	**Lesson 308** – Mastery Check 10 – syllable pattern 5 teams – *ur*					X	
9	17	90	**Lesson 309** – Mastery Check 10 – syllable pattern 5 teams – *or*					X	
9	18	91	**Lesson 310** – Nonsense words/syllable patterns 1 through 5 – Oral Reading			X	X	X	
9	18	91	**Lesson 311** – Nonsense words/syllable patterns 1 through 5 – Identify groups	X	X	X		X	
9	18	91	**Lesson 312** – Real words/ syllable patterns 1 through 5 – Oral Reading			X	X	X	
9	18	91	**Lesson 313/Quiz 77** – Real words/ syllable patterns 1 through 5 – Dictation	X	X				
9	18	92	**Lesson 314** – Nonsense words/ syllable patterns 1 through 5 – Oral Reading			X	X	X	
9	18	92	**Lesson 315** – Nonsense words/syllable patterns 1 through 5 – Identify groups	X	X	X		X	
9	18	92	**Lesson 316** – Real words/ syllable patterns 1 through 5 – Oral Reading			X	X	X	
9	18	92	**Lesson 317/Quiz 78** – Real words/ syllable patterns 1 through 5 – Dictation	X	X				
9	18	93	**Lesson 318** – Nonsense sentences with syllable patterns 1 to 5 – Oral Reading			X	X	X	
9	18	93	**Lesson 319** – Identify teams in nonsense sentences with syllable patterns 1 to 5	X	X	X		X	
9	18	93	**Lesson 320** – Real sentences with syllable patterns 1 to 5 – Oral Reading			X	X	X	
9	18	93	**Lesson 321** – Real sentences with syllable patterns 1 to 5 – Dictation	X	X			X	
9	18	94	**Lesson 322** – Nonsense word story with syllable patterns 1 to 5 – Oral Reading			X	X	X	
9	18	94	**Lesson 323** – Real word story with syllable patterns 1 to 5 – Oral Reading			X	X	X	
10	19	95	**Lesson 324** – Introduction of syllable pattern 6 teams					X	

Student reads words in lesson **Accurately (A)**, **Fluently (F)**, **Spells (S)** and **Marks (M)** each word correctly and scores 80% or higher on **Quiz (Q)**. Check each box when task completed. **Date (D)** each lesson completed.

VHS Video Guide	Video CD Guide	Book Page Guide	Informal Student Assessment Procedure and Chart Student's Name _____	A	F	S	M	Q	D
10	19	96	**Lesson 325** – Nonsense words/syllable pattern 6 teams – Oral Reading			X	X	X	
10	19	96	**Lesson 326** – Nonsense words/ syllable pattern 6 teams – Identify Teams	X	X	X		X	
10	19	96	**Lesson 327** – Real words/ syllable pattern 6 teams – Oral Reading			X	X	X	
10	19	96	**Lesson 328/Quiz 79** – Real words/ syllable pattern 6 teams – Dictation	X	X				
10	19	97	**Lesson 329** – Nonsense words/ syllable pattern 6 teams – Oral Reading			X	X	X	
10	19	97	**Lesson 330** – Nonsense words/ syllable pattern 6 teams – Identify Teams	X	X	X		X	
10	19	97	**Lesson 331** – Real words/ syllable pattern 6 teams – Oral Reading			X	X	X	
10	19	97	**Lesson 332/Quiz 80** – Real words/ syllable pattern 6 teams – Dictation	X	X				
10	19	98	**Lesson 333** – Nonsense words/ syllable pattern 6 teams – Oral Reading			X	X	X	
10	19	98	**Lesson 334** – Nonsense words/ syllable pattern 6 teams – Identify Teams	X	X	X		X	
10	19	98	**Lesson 335** – Real words/ syllable pattern 6 teams – Oral Reading			X	X	X	
10	19	98	**Lesson 336/Quiz 81** – Real words/ syllable pattern 6 teams – Dictation	X	X				
10	19	99	**Lesson 337** – Nonsense sentences with syllable pattern 6 words – Oral Reading			X	X	X	
10	19	99	**Lesson 338**–Identify teams in nonsense sentences with syllable pattern 6 words	X	X	X		X	
10	19	99	**Lesson 339** – Real sentences with syllable pattern 6 words – Oral Reading			X	X	X	
10	19	99	**Lesson 340** – Real sentences with syllable pattern 6 words – Dictation	X	X			X	
10	19	100	**Lesson 341**–Nonsense word story with syllable pattern 6 words–Oral Reading			X	X	X	
10	19	100	**Lesson 342** – Real word story with syllable pattern 6 words – Oral Reading			X	X	X	
10	19	101	**Lesson 343** – Mastery Check 11 – syllable pattern 6 teams – _au_					X	
10	19	101	**Lesson 344** – Mastery Check 11 – syllable pattern 6 teams – _aw_					X	
10	19	101	**Lesson 345** – Mastery Check 11 – syllable pattern 6 teams – _ew_ + 2nd sound _ew_					X	
10	19	101	**Lesson 346** – Mastery Check 11 – syllable pattern 6 teams – _oi_ / _oy_					X	
10	19	101	**Lesson 347** – Mastery Check 11 – syllable pattern 6 teams – _oo_					X	
10	19	101	**Lesson 348** – Mastery Check 11 – syllable pattern 6 teams – 2nd sound of _oo_					X	
10	19	101	**Lesson 349** – Mastery Check 11 – syllable pattern 6 teams – _ou_					X	
10	19	101	**Lesson 350** – Mastery Check 11 – syllable pattern 6 teams – _ow_					X	
10	20	102	**Lesson 351** – Nonsense words/ syllable patterns 1 through 6 – Oral Reading			X	X	X	
10	20	102	**Lesson 352** – Nonsense words/syllable patterns 1 through 6 – Identify groups	X	X	X		X	
10	20	102	**Lesson 353** – Real words/ syllable patterns 1 through 6 – Oral Reading			X	X	X	
10	20	102	**Lesson 354/Quiz 82** – Real words/ syllable patterns 1 to 6 teams – Dictation	X	X				
10	20	103	**Lesson 355** – Nonsense words/ syllable patterns 1 to 6 teams – Oral Reading			X	X	X	
10	20	103	**Lesson 356** – Nonsense words/syllable patterns 1 to 6 teams – Identify groups	X	X	X		X	
10	20	103	**Lesson 357** – Real words/ syllable patterns 1 through 6 teams – Oral Reading			X	X	X	
10	20	103	**Lesson 358/Quiz 83** – Real words/ syllable patterns 1 to 6 teams – Dictation	X	X				
10	20	104	**Lesson 359** – Nonsense sentences with syllable patterns 1 to 6 – Oral Reading			X	X	X	
10	20	104	**Lesson 360** – Identify teams in nonsense sentences with syllable patterns 1 to 6	X	X	X		X	
10	20	104	**Lesson 361** – Real sentences with syllable patterns 1 to 6 – Oral Reading			X	X	X	
10	20	104	**Lesson 362** – Real sentences with syllable patterns 1 to 6 – Dictation	X	X			X	
10	20	105	**Lesson 363** – Nonsense word story with syllable patterns 1 to 6 – Oral Reading			X	X	X	
10	20	105	**Lesson 364** – Real word story with syllable patterns 1 to 6 – Oral Reading			X	X	X	
10	20	106	**Lesson 365** – Review of 6 syllable patterns	X	X	X	X	X	
10	20	107	**Lesson 366** – Review of beginning consonant blends				X	X	
10	20	107	**Lesson 367** – Review of ending consonant blends				X	X	
10	20	107	**Lesson 368** – Review of consonant teams				X	X	
10	20	107	**Lesson 369** – Review of vowel teams				X	X	
11	21	109	**Lesson 370** – Syllable rule 1 – Oral Reading			X	X	X	
11	21	109	**Lesson 371/Quiz 84** – Syllable rule 1 – Dictation	X	X				
11	22	110	**Lesson 372** – Syllable rule 2– Oral Reading			X	X	X	
11	22	110	**Lesson 373/Quiz 85** – Syllable rule 2 – Dictation	X	X				
11	22	110	**Lesson 374** – Syllable rule 2 – Oral Reading			X	X	X	
11	22	110	**Lesson 375/Quiz 86** – Syllable rule 2 – Dictation	X	X				
12	23	111	**Lesson 376** – Review of syllable rules 1 and 2 – Oral Reading			X	X	X	
12	23	111	**Lesson 377/Quiz 87** – Review of syllable rules 1 and 2 – Dictation	X	X				
12	23	111	**Lesson 378** – Review of syllable rules 1 and 2 – Oral Reading			X	X	X	

Student reads words in lesson **Accurately (A)**, **Fluently (F)**, **Spells (S)** and **Marks (M)** each word correctly and scores 80% or higher on **Quiz (Q)**. Check each box when task completed. **Date (D)** each lesson completed.

VHS Video Guide	Video CD Guide	Book Page Guide	**Informal Student Assessment Procedure and Chart** Student's Name _____	A	F	S	M	Q	D
12	24	111	**Lesson 379/Quiz 88** – Review of syllable rules 1 and 2 – Dictation	X	X				
12	24	112	**Lesson 380** – Syllable rules 1 and 2 / blends + teams – Oral Reading			X	X	X	
12	24	112	**Lesson 381/Quiz 89** – Syllable rules 1 and 2 / blends + teams – Dictation	X	X				
12	24	113	**Lesson 382** – Sentences / Syllable rules 1 and 2 – Oral Reading			X	X	X	
12	24	113	**Lesson 383** – Sentences / Syllable rules 1 and 2 – Dictation	X	X			X	
12	24	113	**Lesson 384** – Story / Syllable rules 1 and 2 – Oral Reading			X	X	X	
13	25	114	**Lesson 385** – Syllable pattern 7 – Oral Reading			X	X	X	
13	25	114	**Lesson 386/Quiz 90** – Syllable pattern 7 – Dictation	X	X				
13	25	115	**Lesson 387** – Sentences / Syllable pattern 7 – Oral Reading			X	X	X	
13	25	115	**Lesson 388** – Sentences / Syllable pattern 7 – Dictation	X	X			X	
13	25	115	**Lesson 389** – Story / Syllable pattern 7 – Oral Reading			X	X	X	
13	25	116	**Lesson 390** – Mastery Check 12 – syllable pattern 7 teams – *le*					X	
13	25	116	**Lesson 391** – Mastery Check 12 – syllable pattern 7 teams – *le*					X	
13	25	116	**Lesson 392** – Mastery Check 12 – syllable pattern 7 teams – *ck* followed by *le*					X	
13	25	117	**Lesson 393** – 2 syllable words / syllable pattern 4 teams – Oral Reading			X	X	X	
13	25	117	**Lesson 394/Quiz 91** – 2 syllable words / syllable pattern 4 teams – Dictation	X	X				
13	25	117	**Lesson 395** – 2 syllable words / syllable pattern four teams – Oral Reading			X	X	X	
13	25	117	**Lesson 396/Quiz 92** – 2 syllable words / syllable pattern 4 teams – Dictation	X	X				
13	25	118	**Lesson 397** – 2 syllable words / groups 5 + 6 teams – Oral Reading			X	X	X	
13	25	118	**Lesson 398/Quiz 93**–2 syllable words / syllable patterns 5 + 6 teams – Dictation	X	X				
13	26	118	**Lesson 399** – 2 syllable words / syllable patterns 5 + 6 teams – Oral Reading			X	X	X	
13	26	118	**Lesson 400/Quiz 94** –2 syllable words/ syllable patterns 5 + 6 teams – Dictation	X	X				
13	26	119	**Lesson 401** – Sentences / 2 syllable words – Oral Reading			X	X	X	
13	26	119	**Lesson 402** – Sentences / 2 syllable words – Dictation	X	X			X	
13	26	119	**Lesson 403** – Story / 2 syllable words – Oral Reading			X	X	X	
13	26	120	**Lesson 404** – 2 syllable words / groups 4, 5, 6 teams – Oral Reading			X	X	X	
13	26	120	**Lesson 405/Quiz 95** – 2 syllable words / groups 4, 5, 6 teams – Dictation	X	X				
13	26	120	**Lesson 406** – 2 syllable words / groups 4, 5, 6 teams – Oral Reading			X	X	X	
13	26	120	**Lesson 407/Quiz 96** – 2 syllable words / groups 4, 5, 6 teams – Dictation	X	X				
13	26	121	**Lesson 408** – 2 syllable words / groups 4, 5, 6 teams – Oral Reading			X	X	X	
13	26	121	**Lesson 409/Quiz 97** – 2 syllable words / groups 4, 5, 6 teams – Dictation	X	X				
13	26	121	**Lesson 410** – 2 syllable words / groups 4, 5, 6 teams – Oral Reading			X	X	X	
13	26	121	**Lesson 411/Quiz 98** – 2 syllable words / groups 4, 5, 6 teams – Dictation	X	X				
13	26	122	**Lesson 412** – Sentences / 2 syllable words – Oral Reading			X	X	X	
13	26	122	**Lesson 413** – Sentences / 2 syllable words – Dictation	X	X			X	
13	26	122	**Lesson 414** – Story / 2 syllable words – Oral Reading			X	X	X	
13	26	123	**Lesson 415** – Syllable pattern 8 – Oral Reading			X	X	X	
14	27	123	**Lesson 416/Quiz 99** – Syllable pattern 8 – Dictation	X	X				
14	27	124	**Lesson 417** – Sentences / Syllable pattern 8 – Oral Reading			X	X	X	
14	27	124	**Lesson 418** – Sentences / Syllable pattern 8 – Dictation	X	X			X	
14	27	124	**Lesson 419** – Story / Syllable pattern 8 – Oral Reading			X	X	X	
14	27	125	**Lesson 420** – Mastery Check 13 – extra sound for *a*					X	
14	27	125	**Lesson 421** – Mastery Check 13 – extra sound for *o* and *u*					X	
14	27	126	**Lesson 422** – Review of 8 syllable patterns	X	X	X	X	X	
14	27	127	**Lesson 423** – Exceptions to syllable patterns 1, 2, 3 – Oral Reading			X	X	X	
14	27	127	**Lesson 424/Quiz 100** – Exceptions to syllable patterns 1, 2, 3 – Dictation	X	X				
14	28	128	**Lesson 425** – Letters *ar, er, ir, or, ur* followed by a vowel sound – Oral Reading			X	X	X	
14	28	128	**Lesson 426/Quiz 101** – *ar, er, ir, or, ur* followed by vowel sound – Dictation	X	X				
14	28	129	**Lesson 427** – Cumulative review of 2 syllable words – Oral Reading			X	X	X	
14	28	129	**Lesson 428/Quiz 102** – Cumulative review of 2 syllable words – Dictation	X	X				
14	28	129	**Lesson 429** – Cumulative review of 2 syllable words – Oral Reading			X	X	X	
14	28	129	**Lesson 430/Quiz 103** – Cumulative review of 2 syllable words – Dictation	X	X				
14	28	130	**Lesson 431** – Cumulative review of 2 syllable words – Oral Reading			X	X	X	
14	28	130	**Lesson 432/Quiz 104** – Cumulative review of 2 syllable words – Dictation	X	X				

Student reads words in lesson **Accurately (A)**, **Fluently (F)**, **Spells (S)** and **Marks (M)** each word correctly and scores 80% or higher on **Quiz (Q)**. Check each box when task completed. **Date (D)** each lesson completed.

VHS Video Guide	Video CD Guide	Book Page Guide	Informal Student Assessment Procedure and Chart Student's Name _____	A	F	S	M	Q	D
14	28	130	**Lesson 433** – Cumulative review of 2 syllable words – Oral Reading			X	X	X	
14	28	130	**Lesson 434/Quiz 105** – Cumulative review of 2 syllable words – Dictation	X	X			X	
14	28	131	**Lesson 435** – Sentences / 2 syllable words – Oral Reading			X	X	X	
14	28	131	**Lesson 436** – Sentences / 2 syllable words – Dictation	X	X			X	
14	28	131	**Lesson 437** – Story / 2 syllable words – Oral Reading			X	X	X	
14	28	132–3	**Lesson 438** – 2nd sounds for *c* and *g*, *ce*, *ge*, *dge* / Oral Reading *c* and *ce*			X	X	X	
15	29	133	**Lesson 439/Quiz 106** – 2nd sound for *c* and team *ce* – Dictation	X	X			X	
15	29	133	**Lesson 440** – 2nd sound for *c* and team *ce* – Oral Reading			X	X	X	
15	29	133	**Lesson 441/Quiz 107** – 2nd sound for *c* and team *ce* – Dictation	X	X			X	
15	29	134	**Lesson 442** – Sentences / 2nd sound for *c* and team *ce* – Oral Reading			X	X	X	
15	29	134	**Lesson 443** – Sentences / 2nd sound for *c* and team *ce* – Dictation	X	X			X	
15	29	134	**Lesson 444** – Story / 2nd sound for *c* and team *ce* – Oral Reading			X	X	X	
15	29	135	**Lesson 445** – Mastery Check 14 – 2nd sound for *c*					X	
15	29	135	**Lesson 446** – Mastery Check 14 – consonant team *ce*					X	
15	29	136	**Lesson 447** – 2nd sound for *g* and teams *ge* and *dge* – Oral Reading			X	X	X	
15	29	136	**Lesson 448/Quiz 108** – 2nd sound for *g* and teams *ge* and *dge* – Dictation	X	X			X	
15	29	136	**Lesson 449** – 2nd sound for *g* and teams *ge* and *dge* – Oral Reading			X	X	X	
15	29	136	**Lesson 450/Quiz 109** – 2nd sound for *g* and teams *ge* and *dge* – Dictation	X	X			X	
15	29	137	**Lesson 451** – Sentences / 2nd sound for *g* and teams *ge* and *dge* – Oral Reading			X	X	X	
15	29	137	**Lesson 452** – Sentences / 2nd sound for *g* and teams *ge* and *dge* – Dictation	X	X			X	
15	29	137	**Lesson 453** – Story / 2nd sound for *g* and teams *ge* and *dge* – Oral Reading			X	X	X	
15	29	138	**Lesson 454** – Mastery Check 15 – 2nd sound for *g*					X	
15	29	138	**Lesson 455** – Mastery Check 15 – consonant team *ge*					X	
15	29	138	**Lesson 456** – Mastery Check 15 – consonant team *dge*					X	
15	30	139–40	**Lesson 457** – Introducing the letter *y* as both vowel and consonant					X	
15	30	141	**Lesson 458** – *y* representing the short and long sound of *i* – Oral Reading			X	X	X	
15	30	141	**Lesson 459/Quiz 110** – *y* representing the short and long sound of *i* – Dictation	X	X			X	
15	30	141	**Lesson 460** – *y* representing the long sound of *e* – Oral Reading			X	X	X	
15	30	141	**Lesson 461/Quiz 111** – *y* representing the long sound of *e* – Dictation	X	X			X	
15	30	142	**Lesson 462** – Review of the letter *y* as vowel + consonant – Oral Reading			X	X	X	
15	30	142	**Lesson 463/Quiz 112** – Review of the letter *y* as vowel + consonant – Dictation	X	X			X	
15	30	142	**Lesson 464** – Review of the letter *y* as vowel + consonant – Oral Reading			X	X	X	
15	30	142	**Lesson 465/Quiz 113** – Review of the letter *y* as vowel + consonant – Dictation	X	X			X	
15	30	143	**Lesson 466** – Sentences/Review letter *y* as vowel + consonant – Oral Reading			X	X	X	
15	30	143	**Lesson 467** – Sentences / Review letter *y* as vowel + consonant – Dictation	X	X			X	
15	30	143	**Lesson 468** – Story / Review letter *y* as vowel + consonant – Oral Reading			X	X	X	
15	30	144	**Lesson 469** – Mastery Check 16 – *y* as short *i* sound					X	
15	30	144	**Lesson 470** – Mastery Check 16 – *y* as long *i* sound					X	
15	30	144	**Lesson 471** – Mastery Check 16 – *y* as long *e* sound					X	
15	30	145	**Lesson 472** – Comprehensive review – Oral Reading			X	X	X	
15	30	145	**Lesson 473/Quiz 114** – Comprehensive review – Dictation	X	X			X	
15	30	145	**Lesson 474** – Comprehensive review – Oral Reading			X	X	X	
15	30	145	**Lesson 475/Quiz 115** – Comprehensive review – Dictation	X	X			X	
15	30	146	**Lesson 476** – Comprehensive review – Oral Reading			X	X	X	
15	30	146	**Lesson 477/Quiz 116** – Comprehensive review – Dictation	X	X			X	
15	30	146	**Lesson 478** – Comprehensive review – Oral Reading			X	X	X	
15	30	146	**Lesson 479/Quiz 117** – Comprehensive review – Dictation	X	X			X	
16	31	147	**Lesson 480** – 3 syllable words – Oral Reading			X	X	X	
16	31	147	**Lesson 481/Quiz 118** – 3 syllable words – Dictation	X	X			X	
16	31	147	**Lesson 482** – 3 syllable words – Oral Reading			X	X	X	
16	31	147	**Lesson 483/Quiz 119** – 3 syllable words – Dictation	X	X			X	
16	31	148	**Lesson 484** – 3 syllable words – Oral Reading			X	X	X	
16	31	148	**Lesson 485/Quiz 120** – 3 syllable words – Dictation	X	X			X	
16	31	148	**Lesson 486** – 3 syllable words – Oral Reading			X	X	X	

Student reads words in lesson **Accurately (A)**, **Fluently (F)**, **Spells (S)** and **Marks (M)** each word correctly and scores 80% or higher on **Quiz (Q)**. Check each box when task completed. **Date (D)** each lesson completed.

VHS Video Guide	Video CD Guide	Book Page Guide	Informal Student Assessment Procedure and Chart Student's Name _____	A	F	S	M	Q	D
16	31	148	**Lesson 487/Quiz 121** – 3 syllable words – Dictation	X	X				
16	31	149	**Lesson 488** – Syllable rule 3 – Oral Reading			X	X	X	
16	31	149	**Lesson 489/Quiz 122** – Syllable rule 3 – Dictation	X	X				
16	31	149	**Lesson 490** – Syllable rule 3 – Oral Reading			X	X	X	
16	31	149	**Lesson 491/Quiz 123** – Syllable rule 3 – Dictation	X	X				
16	31	150	**Lesson 492** – Sentences / 3 syllable words – Oral Reading			X	X	X	
16	31	150	**Lesson 493** – Sentences / 3 syllable words – Dictation	X	X			X	
16	31	150	**Lesson 494** – Story / 3 syllable words – Oral Reading			X	X	X	
16	32	151	**Lesson 495** – Introducing consonant teams _ci, si, si, ti, qu, ve, wh, wr_					X	
16	32	152	**Lesson 496** – Consonant teams _ci, si, si, ti, qu, ve, wh, wr_ – Oral Reading			X	X	X	
16	32	152	**Lesson 497/Quiz 124** – Consonant teams _ci, si, si, ti, qu, ve, wh, wr_ – Dictation	X	X				
16	32	152	**Lesson 498** – Consonant teams _ci, si, si, ti, qu, ve, wh, wr_ – Oral Reading			X	X	X	
16	32	152	**Lesson 499/Quiz 125** – Consonant teams _ci, si, si, ti, qu, ve, wh, wr_ – Dictation	X	X				
16	32	153	**Lesson 500** – Consonant teams _ci, si, si, ti, qu, ve, wh, wr_ – Oral Reading			X	X	X	
16	32	153	**Lesson 501/Quiz 126** – Consonant teams _ci, si, si, ti, qu, ve, wh, wr_ – Dictation	X	X				
16	32	153	**Lesson 502** – Consonant teams _ci, si, si, ti, qu, ve, wh, wr_ – Oral Reading			X	X	X	
16	32	153	**Lesson 503/Quiz 127** – Consonant teams _ci, si, si, ti, qu, ve, wh, wr_ – Dictation	X	X				
16	32	154	**Lesson 504** – Sentences / Teams _ci, si, si, ti, qu, ve, wh, wr_ – Oral Reading			X	X	X	
16	32	154	**Lesson 505** – Sentences / Consonant teams _ci, si, si, ti, qu, ve, wh, wr_ – Dictation	X	X			X	
16	32	154	**Lesson 506** – Story / Consonant teams _ci, si, si, ti, qu, ve, wh, wr_ – Oral Reading			X	X	X	
16	32	155	**Lesson 507** – Mastery Check 17 – consonant team _si_					X	
16	32	155	**Lesson 508** – Mastery Check 17 – consonant team _si_ – second sound					X	
16	32	155–6	**Lesson 509** – Mastery Check 17 – consonant team _ti_					X	
16	32	156	**Lesson 510** – Mastery Check 17 – consonant team _ci_					X	
16	32	156	**Lesson 511** – Mastery Check 17 – consonant team _ve_					X	
16	32	156	**Lesson 512** – Mastery Check 17 – consonant team _qu_ – 2nd sound					X	
16	32	156	**Lesson 513** – Mastery Check 17 – consonant teams _wr_ and _wh_ – 2nd sounds					X	
17	33	157	**Lesson 514** – Introducing vowel teams _ei, ey, ie, ue, ue_					X	
17	33	158	**Lesson 515** – Vowel teams _ei, ey, ie, ue, ue_ – Oral Reading			X	X	X	
17	33	158	**Lesson 516/Quiz 128** – Vowel teams _ei, ey, ie, ue, ue_ – Dictation	X	X				
17	33	158	**Lesson 517** – Vowel teams _ei, ey, ie, ue, ue_ – Oral Reading			X	X	X	
17	33	158	**Lesson 518/Quiz 129** – Vowel teams _ei, ey, ie, ue, ue_ – Dictation	X	X				
17	33	159	**Lesson 519** – Vowel teams _ei, ey, ie, ue, ue_ – Oral Reading			X	X	X	
17	33	159	**Lesson 520/Quiz 130** – Vowel teams _ei, ey, ie, ue, ue_ – Dictation	X	X				
17	33	159	**Lesson 521** – Vowel teams _ei, ey, ie, ue, ue_ – Oral Reading			X	X	X	
17	33	159	**Lesson 522/Quiz 131** – Vowel teams _ei, ey, ie, ue, ue_ – Dictation	X	X				
17	33	160	**Lesson 523** – Sentences / Vowel teams _ei, ey, ie, ue, ue_ – Oral Reading			X	X	X	
17	33	160	**Lesson 524** – Sentences / Vowel teams _ei, ey, ie, ue, ue_ – Dictation	X	X			X	
17	33	160	**Lesson 525** – Story / Vowel teams _ei, ey, ie, ue, ue_ – Oral Reading			X	X	X	
17	33	161	**Lesson 526** – Mastery Check 18 – vowel team _ei_					X	
17	33	161	**Lesson 527** – Mastery Check 18 – vowel team _ey_					X	
17	33	161	**Lesson 528** – Mastery Check 18 – vowel team _ie_					X	
17	33	161	**Lesson 529** – Mastery Check 18 – vowel team _ue_					X	
X	X	162–3	**Lesson 530** – Adding Suffixes / Rule 1 – Oral Reading			X	X	X	
X	X	162–3	**Lesson 531/Quiz 132** – Adding Suffixes / Rule 1 – Dictation	X	X				
X	X	162–3	**Lesson 532** – Adding Suffixes / Rule 2 – Oral Reading			X	X	X	
X	X	162–3	**Lesson 533/Quiz 133** – Adding Suffixes / Rule 2 – Dictation	X	X				
X	X	162–3	**Lesson 534** – Adding Suffixes / Rule 3 – Oral Reading			X	X	X	
X	X	162–3	**Lesson 535/Quiz 134** – Adding Suffixes / Rule 3 – Dictation	X	X				
X	X	164	**Lesson 536** – Forming the Plural / Rules 1 and 2 – Oral Reading			X	X	X	
X	X	164	**Lesson 537/Quiz 135** – Forming the Plural / Rules 1 and 2 – Dictation	X	X				
X	X	164	**Lesson 538** – Forming plurals / Rules 3, 4, and 5 – Oral Reading			X	X	X	
X	X	164	**Lesson 539/Quiz 136** – Forming plurals / Rules 3, 4, + 5 – Rule three – Dictation	X	X				
16	31	165	**Lesson 540** – The letter team _ed_ – Oral Reading			X	X	X	

Student reads words in lesson **Accurately (A)**, **Fluently (F)**, **Spells (S)** and **Marks (M)** each word correctly and scores 80% or higher on **Quiz (Q)**. Check each box when task completed. **Date (D)** each lesson completed.

VHS Video Guide	Video CD Guide	Book Page Guide	Informal Student Assessment Procedure and Chart Student's Name _____	A	F	S	M	Q	D
16	31	165	**Lesson 541/Quiz 137** – The letter team *ed* – Dictation	X	X				
16	31	166	**Lesson 542** – Sentences / Words ending in suffixes – Oral Reading			X	X	X	
16	31	166	**Lesson 543** – Sentences / Words ending in suffixes – Dictation	X	X			X	
16	31	166	**Lesson 544** – Story / Words ending in suffixes – Oral Reading			X	X	X	
17	33	167	**Lesson 545** – Introducing vowel teams *augh, eigh, ea, igh, ou, ar, or*					X	
17	33	168	**Lesson 546** – Vowel teams *augh, eigh, ea, igh, ou, ar, or* – Oral Reading			X	X	X	
17	33	168	**Lesson 547/Quiz 138** – Vowel teams *augh, eigh, ea, igh, ou, ar, or* – Dictation	X	X				
17	33	168	**Lesson 548** – Vowel teams *augh, eigh, ea, igh, ou, ar, or* – Oral Reading			X	X	X	
17	33	168	**Lesson 549/Quiz 139** – Vowel teams *augh, eigh, ea, igh, ou, ar, or* – Dictation	X	X				
17	33	169	**Lesson 550** – Vowel teams *augh, eigh, ea, igh, ou, ar, or* – Oral Reading			X	X	X	
17	33	169	**Lesson 551/Quiz 140** – Vowel teams *augh, eigh, ea, igh, ou, ar, or* – Dictation	X	X				
17	33	169	**Lesson 552** – Vowel teams *augh, eigh, ea, igh, ou, ar, or* – Oral Reading			X	X	X	
17	33	169	**Lesson 553/Quiz 141** – Vowel teams *augh, eigh, ea, igh, ou, ar, or* – Dictation	X	X				
17	33	170	**Lesson 554** – Sentences/ Teams *augh, eigh, ea, igh, ou, ar, or* – Oral Reading			X	X	X	
17	33	170	**Lesson 555** – Sentences / Vowel teams *augh, eigh, ea, igh, ou, ar, or* – Dictation	X	X			X	
17	33	170	**Lesson 556** – Story / Vowel teams *augh, eigh, ea, igh, ou, ar, or* – Oral Reading			X	X	X	
17	33	171	**Lesson 557** – Mastery Check 19 – vowel 6 teams *augh* and *eigh*					X	
17	33	171	**Lesson 558** – Mastery Check 19 – vowel 6 team *ea*					X	
17	33	171	**Lesson 559** – Mastery Check 19 – vowel 4 team *igh*					X	
17	33	171	**Lesson 560** – Mastery Check 19 – vowel 6 team *ou* – 2nd sound					X	
17	33	171	**Lesson 561** – Mastery Check 19 – vowel 6 teams *ar* and *or* – 2nd sound					X	
17	34	172	**Lesson 562** – Introducing consonant teams *ch, ch, gh, gn, gu, kn, rh, sc*					X	
17	34	173	**Lesson 563** – Consonant teams *ch, ch, gh, gn, gu, kn, rh, sc* – Oral Reading			X	X	X	
17	34	173	**Lesson 564/Quiz 142** – Consonant teams *ch, ch, gh, gn, gu, kn, rh, sc* – Dictation	X	X				
17	34	173	**Lesson 565** – Consonant teams *ch, ch, gh, gn, gu, kn, rh, sc* – Oral Reading			X	X	X	
17	34	173	**Lesson 566/Quiz 143** – Consonant teams *ch, ch, gh, gn, gu, kn, rh, sc* – Dictation	X	X				
17	34	174	**Lesson 567** – Consonant teams *ch, ch, gh, gn, gu, kn, rh, sc* – Oral Reading			X	X	X	
17	34	174	**Lesson 568/Quiz 144** – Consonant teams *ch, ch, gh, gn, gu, kn, rh, sc* – Dictation	X	X				
17	34	174	**Lesson 569** – Consonant teams *ch, ch, gh, gn, gu, kn, rh, sc* – Oral Reading			X	X	X	
17	34	174	**Lesson 570/Quiz 145** – Consonant teams *ch, ch, gh, gn, gu, kn, rh, sc* – Dictation	X	X				
17	34	175	**Lesson 571** – Sentences / Teams *ch, ch, gh, gn, gu, kn, rh, sc* – Oral Reading			X	X	X	
17	34	175	**Lesson 572** – Sentences / Teams *ch, ch, gh, gn, gu, kn, rh, sc* – Dictation	X	X			X	
17	34	175	**Lesson 573** – Story / Teams *ch, ch, gh, gn, gu, kn, rh, sc* – Oral Reading			X	X	X	
17	34	176	**Lesson 574** – Mastery Check 20 – consonant team *ch* – 2nd sound					X	
17	34	176	**Lesson 575** – Mastery Check 20 – consonant team *ch* – 3rd sound					X	
17	34	176	**Lesson 576** – Mastery Check 20 – consonant teams *gh* and *gn*					X	
17	34	176	**Lesson 577**– Mastery Check 20 – consonant team *gu*					X	
17	34	176	**Lesson 578** – Mastery Check 20 – consonant team *kn* and *rh*					X	
17	34	176	**Lesson 579** – Mastery Check 20 – consonant team *sc*					X	
18	35	177	**Lesson 580** – 4 syllable words – Oral Reading			X	X	X	
18	35	177	**Lesson 581/Quiz 146** – 4 syllable words – Dictation	X	X				
18	35	177	**Lesson 582** – 4 syllable words – Oral Reading			X	X	X	
18	35	177	**Lesson 583/Quiz 147** – 4 syllable words – Dictation	X	X				
18	35	178	**Lesson 584** – 4 syllable words – Oral Reading			X	X	X	
18	35	178	**Lesson 585/Quiz 148** – 4 syllable words – Dictation	X	X				
18	35	178	**Lesson 586** – 4 syllable words – Oral Reading			X	X	X	
18	35	178	**Lesson 587/Quiz 149** – 4 syllable words – Dictation	X	X				
18	35	179	**Lesson 588** – Sentences / 4 syllable words – Oral Reading			X	X	X	
18	35	179	**Lesson 589** – Sentences / 4 syllable words – Dictation	X	X			X	
18	35	179	**Lesson 590** – Story / 4 syllable words – Oral Reading			X	X	X	
18	35	180	**Lesson 591** – Introducing vowel teams *ou, ou, our, ough*					X	
18	35	181	**Lesson 592** – Vowel teams *ou, ou, our, ough* – Oral Reading			X	X	X	
18	35	181	**Lesson 593/Quiz 150** – Vowel teams *ou, ou, our, ough* – Dictation	X	X				
18	35	181	**Lesson 594** – Vowel teams *ou, ou, our, ough* – Oral Reading			X	X	X	

Student reads words in lesson **Accurately (A)**, **Fluently (F)**, **Spells (S)** and **Marks (M)** each word correctly and scores 80% or higher on **Quiz (Q)**. Check each box when task completed. **Date (D)** each lesson completed.

VHS Video Guide	Video CD Guide	Book Page Guide	Informal Student Assessment Procedure and Chart Student's Name _____	A	F	S	M	Q	D
18	35	181	**Lesson 595/Quiz 151** – Vowel teams _ou, ou, our, ough_ – Dictation	X	X				
18	35	182	**Lesson 596** – Sentences / Vowel teams _ou, ou, our, ough_ – Oral Reading			X	X	X	
18	35	182	**Lesson 597** – Sentences / Vowel teams _ou, ou, our, ough_ – Dictation	X	X			X	
18	35	182	**Lesson 598** – Story / Vowel teams _ou, ou, our, ough_ – Oral Reading			X	X	X	
18	35	183	**Lesson 599** – Mastery Check 21 – vowel 4 team _ou_					X	
18	35	183	**Lesson 600** – Mastery Check 21 – vowel 6 team _ou_					X	
18	35	183	**Lesson 601** – Mastery Check 21 – vowel 5 team _our_					X	
18	35	183	**Lesson 602** – Mastery Check 21 – vowel 4 and 6 team _ough_					X	
18	36	184	**Lesson 603** – 4, 5, and 6 syllable words – Oral Reading			X	X	X	
18	36	184	**Lesson 604/Quiz 152** – 4, 5, and 6 syllable words – Dictation	X	X			X	
18	36	184	**Lesson 605** – 4, 5, and 6 syllable words – Oral Reading			X	X	X	
18	36	184	**Lesson 606/Quiz 153** – 4, 5, and 6 syllable words – Dictation	X	X			X	
18	36	185	**Lesson 607** – 4, 5, and 6 syllable words – Oral Reading			X	X	X	
18	36	185	**Lesson 608/Quiz 154** – 4, 5, and 6 syllable words – Dictation	X	X			X	
18	36	185	**Lesson 609** – 4, 5, and 6 syllable words – Oral Reading			X	X	X	
18	36	185	**Lesson 610/Quiz 155** – 4, 5, and 6 syllable words – Dictation	X	X			X	
18	36	186	**Lesson 611** – Sentences / 4, 5, and 6 syllable words – Oral Reading			X	X	X	
18	36	186	**Lesson 612** – Sentences / 4, 5, and 6 syllable words – Dictation	X	X			X	
18	36	186	**Lesson 613** – Story / 4, 5, and 6 syllable words – Oral Reading			X	X	X	
18	36	191	**Lesson 614** – Review of single consonant letters					X	
18	36	191	**Lesson 615** – Review of consonant teams					X	
18	36	193	**Lesson 616** – Review of vowel sounds					X	
18	36	193	**Lesson 617** – Review of syllable pattern four teams					X	
18	36	193	**Lesson 618** – Review of syllable pattern five teams					X	
18	36	193	**Lesson 619** – Review of syllable pattern six teams					X	
18	36	193	**Lesson 620** – Review of syllable pattern 7 team _le_ and sounds of _y_ as a vowel					X	
19	37	195	**Lesson 621** – Review of English letters and common letter teams					X	
19	37	198	**Lesson 622** – Review of consonant sounds and letters that represent them					X	
19	37	200	**Lesson 623** – Review of vowel sounds and letters that represent them					X	
19	37	202	**Lesson 624** – Review of the forty–two sounds of the English language					X	
19	38	214	**Lesson 625** – Spelling – Word List _A_ – Words 1–25	X	X			X	
19	38	214	**Lesson 626/Quiz 156** – Spelling – Word List _A_ – Words 26–50	X	X				
19	38	215	**Lesson 627** – Spelling – Word List _A_ – Words 51–75	X	X			X	
20	39	215	**Lesson 628/Quiz 157** – Spelling – Word List _A_ – Words 76–100	X	X				
20	39	216	**Lesson 629** – Spelling – Word List _A_ – Words 101–125	X	X			X	
20	39	216	**Lesson 630/Quiz 158** – Spelling – Word List _A_ – Words 126–150	X	X				
20	39	217	**Lesson 631** – Spelling – Word List _A_ – Words 151–175	X	X			X	
20	40	217	**Lesson 632/Quiz 159** – Spelling – Word List _A_ – Words 176–200	X	X				
20	40	218	**Lesson 633** – Spelling – Word List _A_ – Words 201–225	X	X			X	
20	40	218	**Lesson 634/Quiz 160** – Spelling – Word List _A_ – Words 226–250	X	X				
20	40	219	**Lesson 635** – Spelling – Word List _A_ – Words 251–275	X	X			X	
20	40	219	**Lesson 636/Quiz 161** – Spelling – Word List _A_ – Words 276–300	X	X				
21	41	220	**Lesson 637** – Spelling – Word List _A_ – Words 301–325	X	X			X	
21	41	220	**Lesson 638/Quiz 162** – Spelling – Word List _A_ – Words 326–350	X	X				
21	41	221	**Lesson 639** – Spelling – Word List _A_ – Words 351–375	X	X			X	
21	41	221	**Lesson 640/Quiz 163** – Spelling – Word List _A_ – Words 376–400	X	X				
21	42	222	**Lesson 641** – Spelling – Word List _A_ – Words 401–425	X	X			X	
21	42	222	**Lesson 642/Quiz 164** – Spelling – Word List _A_ – Words 426–450	X	X				
21	42	223	**Lesson 643** – Spelling – Word List _A_ – Words 451–475	X	X			X	
21	42	223	**Lesson 644/Quiz 165** – Spelling – Word List _A_ – Words 476–500	X	X				
X	X	224	**Lesson 645** – Spelling – Word List _A_ – Words 501–525	X	X			X	
X	X	224	**Lesson 646/Quiz 166** – Spelling – Word List _A_ – Words 526–550	X	X				
X	X	225	**Lesson 647** – Spelling – Word List _A_ – Words 551–575	X	X			X	
X	X	225	**Lesson 648/Quiz 167** – Spelling – Word List _A_ – Words 576–600	X	X				

Student reads words in lesson **Accurately** (**A**), **Fluently** (**F**), **Spells** (**S**) and **Marks** (**M**) each word correctly and scores 80% or higher on **Quiz** (**Q**). Check each box when task completed. **Date** (**D**) each lesson completed.

VHS Video Guide	Video CD Guide	Book Page Guide	Informal Student Assessment Procedure and Chart Student's Name _____	A	F	S	M	Q	D
X	X	226	**Lesson 649** – Spelling – Word List *A* – Words 601–625	X	X			X	
X	X	226	**Lesson 650/Quiz 168** – Spelling – Word List *A* – Words 626–650	X	X				
X	X	227	**Lesson 651** – Spelling – Word List *A* – Words 651–675	X	X			X	
X	X	227	**Lesson 652/Quiz 169** – Spelling – Word List *A* – Words 676–700	X	X				
X	X	228	**Lesson 653** – Spelling – Word List *A* – Words 701–725	X	X			X	
X	X	228	**Lesson 654/Quiz 170** – Spelling – Word List *A* – Words 726–750	X	X				
X	X	229	**Lesson 655** – Spelling – Word List *A* – Words 751–775	X	X			X	
X	X	229	**Lesson 656/Quiz 171** – Spelling – Word List *A* – Words 776–800	X	X				
X	X	230	**Lesson 657** – Spelling – Word List *B* – Words 1–25	X	X			X	
X	X	230	**Lesson 658/Quiz 172** – Spelling – Word List *B* – Words 26–50	X	X				
X	X	231	**Lesson 659** – Spelling – Word List *B* – Words 51–75	X	X			X	
X	X	231	**Lesson 660/Quiz 173** – Spelling – Word List *B* – Words 75–100	X	X				
X	X	232	**Lesson 661** – Spelling – Word List *B* – Words 101–125	X	X			X	
X	X	232	**Lesson 662/Quiz 174** – Spelling – Word List *B* – Words 126–150	X	X				
X	X	233	**Lesson 663**– Spelling – Word List *B* – Words 151–175	X	X			X	
X	X	233	**Lesson 664/Quiz 175** – Spelling – Word List *B* – Words 176–200	X	X				
X	X	234	**Lesson 665** – Spelling – Word List *B* – Words 201–225	X	X			X	
X	X	234	**Lesson 666/Quiz 176** – Spelling – Word List *B* – Words 226–250	X	X				
X	X	235	**Lesson 667** – Spelling – Word List *B* – Words 251–275	X	X			X	
X	X	235	**Lesson 668/Quiz 177** – Spelling – Word List *B* – Words 276–300	X	X				
X	X	236	**Lesson 669** – Spelling – Word List *B* – Words 301–325	X	X			X	
X	X	236	**Lesson 670/Quiz 178** – Spelling – Word List *B* – Words 326–350	X	X				
X	X	237	**Lesson 671** – Spelling – Word List *B* – Words 351–375	X	X			X	
X	X	237	**Lesson 672/Quiz 179** – Spelling – Word List *B* – Words 376–400	X	X				
X	X	238	**Lesson 673** – Spelling – Word List *B* – Words 401–425	X	X			X	
X	X	238	**Lesson 674/Quiz 180** – Spelling – Word List *B* – Words 426–450	X	X				
X	X	239	**Lesson 675** – Spelling – Word List *B* – Words 451–475	X	X			X	
X	X	239	**Lesson 676/Quiz 181** – Spelling – Word List *B* – Words 476–500	X	X				
X	X	240	**Lesson 677** – Spelling – Word List *B* – Words 501–525	X	X			X	
X	X	240	**Lesson 678/Quiz 182** – Spelling – Word List *B* – Words 526–550	X	X				
X	X	241	**Lesson 679** – Spelling – Word List *B* – Words 551–575	X	X			X	
X	X	241	**Lesson 680/Quiz 183** – Spelling – Word List *B* – Words 576–600	X	X				
X	X	242	**Lesson 681** – Spelling – Word List *B* – Words 601–625	X	X			X	
X	X	242	**Lesson 682/Quiz 184** – Spelling – Word List *B* – Words 626–650	X	X				
X	X	243	**Lesson 683** – Spelling – Word List *B* – Words 651–675	X	X			X	
X	X	243	**Lesson 684/Quiz 185** – Spelling – Word List *B* – Words 676–700	X	X				
X	X	244	**Lesson 685** – Spelling – Word List *B* – Words 701–725	X	X			X	
X	X	244	**Lesson 686/Quiz 186** – Spelling – Word List *B* – Words 726–750	X	X				
X	X	245	**Lesson 687** – Spelling – Word List *B* – Words 751–775	X	X			X	
X	X	245	**Lesson 688/Quiz 187** – Spelling – Word List *B* – Words 776–800	X	X				
X	X	246	**Lesson 689** – Spelling – Word List *C* – Words 1–25	X	X			X	
X	X	246	**Lesson 690/Quiz 188** – Spelling – Word List *C* – Words 26–50	X	X				
X	X	247	**Lesson 691** – Spelling – Word List *C* – Words 51–75	X	X			X	
X	X	247	**Lesson 692/Quiz 189** – Spelling – Word List *C* – Words 75–100	X	X				
X	X	248	**Lesson 693** – Spelling – Word List *C* – Words 101–125	X	X			X	
X	X	248	**Lesson 694/Quiz 190** – Spelling – Word List *C* – Words 126–150	X	X				
X	X	249	**Lesson 695** – Spelling – Word List *C* – Words 151–175	X	X			X	
X	X	249	**Lesson 696/Quiz 191** – Spelling – Word List *C* – Words 176–200	X	X				
X	X	250	**Lesson 697** – Spelling – Word List *C* – Words 201–225	X	X			X	
X	X	250	**Lesson 698/Quiz 192** – Spelling – Word List *C* – Words 226–250	X	X				
X	X	251	**Lesson 699** – Spelling – Word List *C* – Words 251–275	X	X			X	
X	X	251	**Lesson 700/Quiz 193** – Spelling – Word List *C* – Words 276–300	X	X				
X	X	252	**Lesson 701** – Spelling – Word List *C* – Words 301–325	X	X			X	
X	X	252	**Lesson 702/Quiz 194** – Spelling – Word List *C* – Words 326–350	X	X				

Student reads words in lesson **Accurately (A)**, **Fluently (F)**, **Spells (S)** and **Marks (M)** each word correctly and scores 80% or higher on **Quiz (Q)**. Check each box when task completed. **Date (D)** each lesson completed.

VHS Video Guide	Video CD Guide	Book Page Guide	Informal Student Assessment Procedure and Chart Student's Name _____	A	F	S	M	Q	D
X	X	253	**Lesson 703** – Spelling – Word List *C* – Words 351–375	X	X			X	
X	X	253	**Lesson 704/Quiz 195** – Spelling – Word List *C* – Words 376–400	X	X				
X	X	254	**Lesson 705** – Spelling – Word List *C* – Words 401–425	X	X			X	
X	X	254	**Lesson 706/Quiz 196** – Spelling – Word List *C* – Words 426–450	X	X				
X	X	255	**Lesson 707** – Spelling – Word List *C* – Words 451–475	X	X			X	
X	X	255	**Lesson 708/Quiz 197** – Spelling – Word List *C* – Words 476–500	X	X				
X	X	256	**Lesson 709** – Spelling – Word List *C* – Words 501–525	X	X			X	
X	X	256	**Lesson 710/Quiz 198** – Spelling – Word List *C* – Words 526–550	X	X				
X	X	257	**Lesson 711** – Spelling – Word List *C* – Words 551–575	X	X			X	
X	X	257	**Lesson 712/Quiz 199** – Spelling – Word List *C* – Words 576–600	X	X				
X	X	258	**Lesson 713** – Spelling – Word List *C* – Words 601–625	X	X			X	
X	X	258	**Lesson 714/Quiz 200** – Spelling – Word List *C* – Words 626–650	X	X				
X	X	259	**Lesson 715** – Spelling – Word List *C* – Words 651–675	X	X			X	
X	X	259	**Lesson 716/Quiz 201** – Spelling – Word List *C* – Words 676–700	X	X				
X	X	260	**Lesson 717** – Spelling – Word List *C* – Words 701–725	X	X			X	
X	X	260	**Lesson 718/Quiz 202** – Spelling – Word List *C* – Words 726–750	X	X				
X	X	261	**Lesson 719** – Spelling – Word List *C* – Words 751–775	X	X			X	
X	X	261	**Lesson 720/Quiz 203** – Spelling – Word List *C* – Words 776–800	X	X				

Go to http://www.weallcanread.com/downloads.html to print additional copies of this chart.

Answer Key for Spelling Quizzes

Quiz 1
Lesson 3 / Page 2
1. g
2. m
3. t
4. v
5. j
6. y
7. x
8. n
9. l
10. c, k, <u>ck</u>

Quiz 2
Lesson 5 / Page 3
1. ag
2. ax
3. a<u>ck</u>
4. a<u>s</u>
5. av
6. an
7. ab
8. at
9. ap
10. an

Quiz 3
Lesson 7 / Page 3
1. af
2. az
3. am
4. ax
5. ap
6. at
7. av
8. a<u>s</u>
9. an
10. ab

Quiz 4
Lesson 9 / Page 4
1. lan
2. fa<u>s</u>
3. rav
4. va<u>ck</u>
5. pag
6. zam
7. vav
8. lat
9. naz
10. zaz

Quiz 5
Lesson 11 / Page 4
1. yam
2. pad
3. sap
4. rag
5. dad
6. wag
7. dab
8. sad
9. jam
10. van

Quiz 6
Lesson 13 / Page 5
1. em
2. e<u>s</u>
3. et
4. e<u>ck</u>
5. ex
6. el
7. ez
8. ef
9. ep
10. ev

Quiz 7
Lesson 15/ Page 5
1. e<u>ck</u>
2. el
3. ax
4. ef
5. ag
6. ef
7. ap
8. eb
9. am
10. en

Quiz 8
Lesson 17 / Page 6
1. heg
2. tef
3. se<u>s</u>
4. pem
5. zeg
6. vev
7. jen
8. ded
9. mem
10. fet

Quiz 9
Lesson 19 / Page 6
1. let
2. web
3. pen
4. pep
5. wed
6. ne<u>ck</u>
7. ten
8. bet
9. hem
10. fed

Quiz 10
Lesson 21 / Page 7
1. vaz
2. zet
3. tes
4. hab
5. sep
6. jav
7. res
8. nas
9. yav
10. teb

Quiz 11
Lesson 23 / Page 7
1. hem
2. man
3. leg
4. pal
5. fed
6. ba<u>ck</u>
7. hen
8. ran
9. gas
10. bed

Quiz 12
Lesson 31 / Page 10
1. op
2. os
3. ot
4. ov
5. oz
6. ob
7. od
8. og
9. o<u>s</u>
10. ol

Answer Key for Spelling Quizzes

Quiz 13
Lesson 33 / Page 10
1. ot
2. av
3. em
4. ol
5. a<u>ck</u>
6. af
7. eb
8. os
9. ab
10. el

Quiz 14
Lesson 35 / Page 11
1. nom
2. sof
3. zob
4. gop
5. jof
6. bon
7. <u>qu</u>op
8. sot
9. fov
10. vo<u>ck</u>

Quiz 15
Lesson 37 / Page 11
1. bog
2. tot
3. gob
4. ox
5. cot
6. top
7. bob
8. cog
9. fog
10. Tom

Quiz 16
Lesson 39 / Page 12
1. vav
2. tog
3. zes
4. <u>qu</u>og
5. za<u>s</u>
6. tem
7. hof
8. zax
9. pav
10. nen

Quiz 17
Lesson 41 / Page 12
1. Sam
2. hop
3. sod
4. tan
5. met
6. lab
7. net
8. job
9. cap
10. let

Quiz 18
Lesson 49 / Page 15
1. uv
2. uz
3. ub
4. u<u>ck</u>
5. uf
6. ul
7. ud
8. um
9. uv
10. un

Quiz 19
Lesson 51 / Page 15
1. ab
2. e<u>ck</u>
3. av
4. ot
5. el
6. ux
7. um
8. ob
9. ud
10. en

Quiz 20
Lesson 53 / Page 16
1. tu<u>s</u>
2. <u>gu</u><u>ck</u>
3. bup
4. duf
5. vut
6. tup
7. lut
8. wup
9. nux
10. hud

Quiz 21
Lesson 55 / Page 16
1. run
2. lug
3. fun
4. tub
5. sun
6. bum
7. dug
8. gum
9. cup
10. pup

Quiz 22
Lesson 57 / Page 17
1. zus
2. taz
3. feg
4. wot
5. vun
6. mav
7. tep
8. nug
9. de<u>s</u>
10. lom

Quiz 23
Lesson 59 / Page 17
1. get
2. log
3. du<u>ck</u>
4. rap
5. fed
6. hut
7. ten
8. nut
9. lab
10. den

Quiz 24
Lesson 67 / Page 20
1. id
2. im
3. in
4. ip
5. ig
6. ix
7. iz
8. is
9. iv
10. <u>ick</u>

Answer Key for Spelling Quizzes

Quiz 25
Lesson 69 / Page 20
1. un
2. af
3. op
4. i<u>ck</u>
5. es
6. ag
7. uz
8. iz
9. el
10. ap

Quiz 26
Lesson 71 / Page 21
1. tif
2. mim
3. pib
4. tid
5. riv
6. zi<u>ck</u>
7. nin
8. fis
9. rin
10. bix

Quiz 27
Lesson 73 / Page 21
1. dig
2. pit
3. sis
4. fig
5. bib
6. wig
7. jig
8. fit
9. hid
10. rig

Quiz 28
Lesson 75 / Page 22
1. hob
2. fim
3. duv
4. yad
5. zed
6. sug
7. bav
8. se<u>ck</u>
9. tol
10. vif

Quiz 29
Lesson 77 / Page 22
1. pet
2. dot
3. dad
4. lot
5. mo<u>ck</u>
6. bid
7. vet
8. bun
9. ti<u>ck</u>
10. rag

Quiz 30
Lesson 79 / Page 23
1. vob
2. mim
3. dup
4. yan
5. res
6. mun
7. sa<u>z</u>
8. e<u>ck</u>
9. roz
10. wup

Quiz 31
Lesson 81 / Page 23
1. set
2. pot
3. ba<u>ck</u>
4. fox
5. ro<u>ck</u>
6. hi<u>s</u>
7. yet
8. pep
9. li<u>ck</u>
10. Hal

Quiz 32
Lesson 89 / Page 26
1. teff
2. vill
3. sess
4. daff
5. kess
6. ness
7. lill
8. jass
9. boll
10. duss

Quiz 33
Lesson 91 / Page 26
1. Jill
2. sell
3. Jeff
4. lass
5. <u>qu</u>ill
6. kiss
7. puff
8. bass
9. dell
10. muss

Quiz 34
Lesson 93 / Page 27
1. kex
2. coss
3. cov
4. kiv
5. cax
6. caz
7. cu<u>ck</u>
8. kib
9. coz
10. kell

Quiz 35
Lesson 95 / Page 27
1. cuff
2. kin
3. cap
4. kill
5. cot
6. kid
7. cup
8. cat
9. keg
10. cub

Quiz 36
Lesson 103 / Page 31
1. blav
2. troz
3. blop
4. snill
5. plon
6. snat
7. crav
8. slux
9. scun
10. blet

Answer Key for Spelling Quizzes

Quiz 37
Lesson 105 / Page 31
1. fled
2. smell
3. gruff
4. swam
5. spot
6. stun
7. plus
8. swell
9. stop
10. press

Quiz 38
Lesson 107 / Page 32
1. skiv
2. flom
3. dreff
4. snun
5. smaz
6. plov
7. clet
8. spreff
9. glat
10. snuss

Quiz 39
Lesson 109 / Page 32
1. tri<u>ck</u>
2. span
3. scrub
4. bled
5. prop
6. slap
7. stru<u>ck</u>
8. split
9. dress
10. clot

Quiz 40
Lesson 123 / Page 37
1. olk
2. usk
3. ilf
4. olm
5. ips
6. ulk
7. esk
8. uft
9. ilm
10. ops

Quiz 41
Lesson 125 / Page 37
1. unt
2. ild
3. ent
4. act
5. apt
6. ump
7. esk
8. ind
9. aft
10. und

Quiz 42
Lesson 127 / Page 38
1. zint
2. tolp
3. rulb
4. semp
5. pilm
6. lect
7. mund
8. leps
9. dask
10. woft

Quiz 43
Lesson 129 / Page 38
1. fast
2. limp
3. belt
4. fend
5. tent
6. tilt
7. bunt
8. golf
9. rest
10. fist

Quiz 44
Lesson 141 / Page 42
1. drulf
2. slunt
3. squolp
4. sprilb
5. glulm
6. snasp
7. greft
8. pluf
9. strint
10. twoft

Quiz 45
Lesson 143 / Page 42
1. stunt
2. drift
3. blast
4. slump
5. frost
6. scalp
7. slept
8. crust
9. swift
10. trust

Quiz 46
Lesson 145 / Page 43
1. clelt
2. swulp
3. glolt
4. skist
5. slulb
6. prasp
7. sprips
8. trund
9. frild
10. croft

Quiz 47
Lesson 147 / Page 43
1. plump
2. dwelt
3. script
4. frisk
5. stand
6. swept
7. draft
8. spend
9. slant
10. glint

Quiz 48
Lesson 160 / Page 48
1. <u>ch</u>az
2. <u>sh</u>eck
3. <u>wh</u>off
4. <u>th</u>ung
5. <u>qu</u>eff
6. <u>th</u>o<u>tch</u>
7. <u>ch</u>ez
8. peng
9. <u>th</u>ix
10. <u>wh</u>u<u>tch</u>

120

Answer Key for Spelling Quizzes

Quiz 49
Lesson 162 / Page 48
1. thin
2. quit
3. chat
4. fetch
5. shut
6. pang
7. thrill
8. sham
9. pick
10. this

Quiz 50
Lesson 164 / Page 49
1. chotch
2. thom
3. queff
4. phon
5. chuth
6. sheck
7. photch
8. thung
9. thim
10. whiv

Quiz 51
Lesson 166 / Page 49
1. botch
2. pitch
3. chum
4. tang
5. ash
6. quiz
7. peck
8. ding
9. dash
10. shed

Quiz 52
Lesson 174 / Page 52
1. teng
2. zunk
3. bink
4. zang
5. lunk
6. ving
7. nunk
8. fong
9. vung
10. senk

Quiz 53
Lesson 176 / Page 52
1. lung
2. rink
3. dank
4. bunk
5. wing
6. sang
7. long
8. sung
9. link
10. rank

Quiz 54
Lesson 186 / Page 55
1. queps
2. shand
3. tholf
4. crung
5. shisp
6. shapt
7. phend
8. shrup
9. steck
10. thruld

Quiz 55
Lesson 188 / Page 55
1. shrink
2. whisk
3. smack
4. cling
5. quench
6. sting
7. thump
8. thrush
9. clench
10. shred

Quiz 56
Lesson 190 / Page 56
1. scrong
2. tritch
3. shupt
4. phent
5. grack
6. tholm
7. whuft
8. quosk
9. splick
10. bretch

Quiz 57
Lesson 192 / Page 56
1. brick
2. slosh
3. stock
4. bench
5. splash
6. shrimp
7. theft
8. snack
9. hunch
10. crush

Quiz 58
Lesson 213 / Page 62
1. bla-2
2. blaft-1
3. fli-2
4. flim-1
5. bre-2
6. brelt-1
7. cha-2
8. chasp-1
9. cle-2
10. clelb-1

Quiz 59
Lesson 215 / Page 62
1. cri-2
2. crimp-1
3. sla-2
4. slang-1
5. twi-2
6. twitch-1
7. spe-2
8. spend-1
9. spla-2
10. splash-1

Quiz 60
Lesson 217 / Page 63
1. whi-2
2. whiv-1
3. sca-2
4. scand-1
5. gle-2
6. glenk-1
7. shro-2
8. shrop-1
9. phi-2
10. phitch-1

Answer Key for Spelling Quizzes

Quiz 61
Lesson 219 / Page 63
1. te-2
2. tempt-1
3. che-2
4. chest-1
5. chi-2
6. chill-1
7. bla-2
8. blast-1
9. hi-2
10. hitch-1

Quiz 62
Lesson 221 / Page 64
1. gop-1
2. gope-3
3. slin-1
4. sline-3
5. prat-1
6. prate-3
7. hin-1
8. hine-3
9. lel-1
10. lele-3

Quiz 63
Lessson 223 / Page 64
1. fill-1
2. file-3
3. glad-1
4. glade-3
5. stock-1
6. stoke-3
7. slop
8. slope-3
9. pick-1
10. pike-3

Quiz 64
Lesson 225 / Page 65
1. maf-1
2. mafe-3
3. dod-1
4. dode-3
5. veb-1
6. vebe-3
7. fid-1
8. fide-3
9. chack-1
10. chake-3

Quiz 65
Lesson 227 / Page 65
1. whiff-1
2. wife-3
3. sack-1
4. sake-3
5. rob-1
6. robe-3
7. Tim-1
8. time-3
9. fad-1
10. fade-3

Quiz 66
Lesson 229 / Page 66
1. fuse-3
2. dude-3
3. use-3
4. rule-3
5. cube-3
6. brute-3
7. dune-3
8. mute-3
9. lube-3
10. pure-3

Quiz 67
Lesson 241 / Page 70
1. shast-1
2. chilp-1
3. bo-2
4. jeme-3
5. chome-3
6. ti-2
7. bape-3
8. cax-1
9. coze-3
10. plip-1

Quiz 68
Lesson 243 / Page 70
1. crank-1
2. white-3
3. hi-2
4. swell-1
5. quote-3
6. file-3
7. shut-1
8. trip-1
9. eve-3
10. shade-3

Quiz 69
Lesson 245 Page 71
1. chand–1
2. otch–1
3. stre–2
4. shope–3
5. theln-1
6. prack-1
7. bebe–3
8. flusp–1
9. sle–2
10. whilst–1

Quiz 70
Lesson 247 / Page 71
1. shelf-1
2. drape-3
3. clench-1
4. hose-3
5. spend-1
6. shrink-1
7. she-2
8. bathe-3
9. rule-3
10. thank-1

Quiz 71
Lesson 258 / Page 75
1. heat-4
2. gloat-4
3. bowl-4
4. beach-4
5. spray-4
6. blue-4
7. pray-4
8. fruit-4
9. sheet-4
10. leaf-4

Quiz 72
Lesson 262 / Page 76
1. throat-4
2. wheat-4
3. oath-4
4. speech-4
5. hoax-4
6. cheek-4
7. growth-4
8. preach-4
9. key-4
10. cue-4

Answer Key for Spelling Quizzes

Quiz 73
Lesson 279 / Page 81
1. trot-1
2. swipe-3
3. speed-4
4. slide-3
5. blend-1
6. fresh-1
7. dude-3
8. no-2
9. cheap-4
10. bride-3

Quiz 74
Lesson 283 / Page 82
1. brisk-1
2. chose-3
3. duke-3
4. those-3
5. blond-1
6. munch-1
7. me-2
8. bruise-4
9. depth-1
10. she-2

Quiz 75
Lesson 294 / Page 86
1. cart-5
2. thorn-5
3. first-5
4. burst-5
5. earth-5
6. fork-5
7. learn-5
8. dark-5
9. dirt-5
10. verb-5

Quiz 76
Lesson 298 / Page 87
1. cork-5
2. marsh-5
3. chirp-5
4. yearn-5
5. surf-5
6. church-5
7. squirt-5
8. horn-5
9. heard-5
10. harsh-5

Quiz 77
Lesson 313 / Page 91
1. charm-5
2. fresh-1
3. birch-5
4. stove-3
5. farm-5
6. green-4
7. splint-1
8. shell-1
9. burst-5
10. hi-2

Quiz 78
Lesson 317 / Page 92
1. vote-3
2. phrase-3
3. length-1
4. perch-5
5. cruise-4
6. crust-1
7. tube-3
8. pose-3
9. throw-4
10. sprain-4

Quiz 79
Lesson 328 / Page 96
1. stood-6
2. moon-6
3. hoof-6
4. launch-6
5. shook-6
6. crawl-6
7. booth-6
8. book-6
9. broil-6
10. smooth-6

Quiz 80
Lesson 332 / Page 97
1. pound-6
2. growl-6
3. trout-6
4. cloud-6
5. clown-6
6. owl-6
7. grouch-6
8. wow-6
9. scout-6
10. proud-6

Quiz 81
Lesson 336 / Page 98
1. sound-6
2. new-6
3. join-6
4. mouth-6
5. oink-6
6. spoil-6
7. hood-6
8. hawk-6
9. gown-6
10. hook-6

Quiz 82
Lesson 354/Page 102
1. say-4
2. split-1
3. boil-6
4. hard-5
5. seal-4
6. prompt-1
7. fume-3
8. couch-6
9. blow-4
10. burst-5

Quiz 83
Lesson 358/Page 103
1. trust-1
2. trail-4
3. charm-5
4. cook-6
5. hoist-6
6. squint-1
7. blast-1
8. skirt-5
9. sheep-4
10. strike-3

Quiz 84
Lesson 371/Page 109
1. re-1-sent
    2   1
2. fo-1-cus
    2   1
3. a-1-dult
    2   1
4. sea-1-son
    4   1
5. to-1-ken
    2   1

6. re-1-fund
   2   1

7. de-1-t<u>er</u>
   2   5

8. st<u>u</u>-1-dent
   2   1

9. no-1-mad
   2   1

10. re-1-<u>s</u>ult
   2   1

Quiz 85
Lesson 373/Page 110

1. ton-2-sil
   1   1

2. bas-2-ket
   1   1

3. con-2-tact
   1   1

4. les-2-son
   1   1

5. sel-2-dom
   1   1

6. sub-2-ject
   1   1

7. af-2-f<u>or</u>d
   1   5

8. pub-2-li<u>sh</u>
   1   1

9. dis-2-trict
   1   1

10. ten-2-nis
   1   1

Quiz 86
Lesson 375/Page 110

1. bet-2-t<u>er</u>
   1   5

2. d<u>ow</u>n-2-t<u>ow</u>n
   6   6

3. nap-2-kin
   1   1

4. pub-2-lic
   1   1

5. wil-2-li<u>ng</u>
   1   1

6. un-2-pa<u>ck</u>
   1   1

7. snap-2-p<u>er</u>
   1   5

8. at-2-tempt
   1   1

9. muf-2-fin
   1   1

10. buz-2-z<u>ard</u>
   1   5

Quiz 87
Lesson 377 /Page 111

1. gus-2-to
   1   2

2. splin-2-t<u>er</u>
   1   5

3. vi-1-p<u>er</u>
   2   5

4. vo-1-t<u>er</u>
   2   5

5. dol-2-<u>ph</u>in
   1   1

6. <u>wh</u>im-2-p<u>er</u>
   1   5

7. de-1-fend
   2   1

8. b<u>ar</u>-1-b<u>er</u>
   5   5

9. <u>Au</u>-1-gust
   6   1

10. in-2-clin<u>e</u>
   1   3

Quiz 88
Lesson 379 /Page 111

1. t<u>ee</u>-1-p<u>ee</u>
   4   4

2. f<u>ur</u>-1-ni<u>sh</u>
   5   1

3. flus-2-t<u>er</u>
   1   5

4. a-1-w<u>ai</u>t
   2   4

5. pol-2-len
   1   1

6. fe-1-mal<u>e</u>
   2   3

7. f<u>oo</u>t-2-print
   6   1

8. ig-2-nit<u>e</u>
   1   3

9. mo-1-tel
   2   1

10. el-2-b<u>ow</u>
   1   4

Quiz 89
Lesson 381 /Page 112

1. be-1-tr<u>ay</u>
   2 ˘4

2. re-1-tr<u>ea</u>t
   2 ˘4

3. ma-1-trix
   2 ˘1

4. <u>or</u>-1-<u>ph</u>an
   5   1

5. ran-2-<u>ch</u>er
   1   5

6. ne-1-glect
   2 ˘1

7. pl<u>ay</u>-1-gr<u>ou</u>nd
   4 ˘6

8. spend-2-<u>thr</u>ift
   1 ˘ 1

9. se-1-cret
   2 ˘1

10. de-1-str<u>oy</u>
   2 ˘6

Quiz 90
Lesson 386/ Page 114

1. cra<u>ck</u>-<u>1</u>-l<u>e</u>
   1   7

2. bu<u>ck</u>-<u>1</u>-l<u>e</u>
   1   7

3. sim-2-p<u>le</u>
   1   7

4. wig-2-g<u>le</u>
   1   7

5. fid-2-d<u>le</u>
   1   7

6. ta<u>ck</u>-<u>1</u>-l<u>e</u>
   1   7

7. tw<u>in</u>-2-k<u>le</u>
   1   7

8. rid-2-d<u>le</u>
   1   7

9. hag-2-g<u>le</u>
   1   7

10. lit-2-t<u>le</u>
   1   7

Answer Key for Spelling Quizzes

Quiz 91
Lesson 394 /Page 117

1. ab-2-b<u>ey</u>
   1   4
2. can-2-t<u>ee</u>n
   1   4
3. Ya<u>n</u>-2-k<u>ee</u>
   1   4
4. b<u>ea</u>-1-ten
   4   1
5. com-2-pl<u>ai</u>nt
   1   4
6. up-2-k<u>ee</u>p
   1   4
7. tr<u>ea</u>-1-<u>s</u>on
   4   1
8. <u>ch</u>im-2-n<u>ey</u>
   1   4
9. ap-2-pr<u>oa</u><u>ch</u>
   1   4
10. r<u>ai</u>-1-ling
   4   1

Quiz 92
Lesson 396/Page 117

1. fif-2-t<u>ee</u>n
   1   4
2. dis-2-pl<u>ay</u>
   1   4
3. r<u>ai</u>-1-<u>s</u>in
   4   1
4. pl<u>ay</u>-1-pen
   4   1
5. p<u>ea</u>-1-co<u>ck</u>
   4   1
6. dis-2-cr<u>ee</u>t
   1   4
7. b<u>ow</u>-1-ling
   4   1
8. mis-2-tak<u>e</u>
   1   3
9. p<u>ay</u>-1-ment
   4   1
10. res-2-c<u>ue</u>
   1   4

Quiz 93
Lesson 398 /Page 118

1. f<u>oo</u>-1-li<u>sh</u>
   6   1

2. <u>th</u><u>ou</u>-1-<u>s</u>and
   6   1
3. <u>ou</u>t-2-wit
   6   1
4. m<u>ar</u>-1-ket
   5   1
5. en-2-j<u>oy</u>
   1   6
6. bal-2-l<u>oo</u>n
   1   6
7. f<u>or</u>-1-get
   5   1
8. es-2-c<u>or</u>t
   1   5
9. <u>ar</u>-1-tist
   5   1
10. c<u>ar</u>-1-pet
   5   1

Quiz 94
Lesson 400 /Page 118

1. <u>au</u>-1-to
   6   2
2. fas-2-t<u>er</u>
   1   5
3. rac-2-c<u>oo</u>n
   1   6
4. g<u>ar</u>-1-den
   5   1
5. in-2-s<u>er</u>t
   1   5
6. h<u>or</u>-1-net
   5   1
7. soft-2-war<u>e</u>
   1˘   3
8. mu<u>sh</u>-2-r<u>oo</u>m
   1   6
9. ban-2-n<u>er</u>
   1   5
10. plat-2-f<u>or</u>m
   1   5

Quiz 95
Lesson 405 /Page 120

1. ha-1-lo
   2   2
2. po-1-lite
   2   3
3. a-1-h<u>oy</u>
   2   6

4. ti-1-g<u>er</u>
   2   5
5. de-1-f<u>ea</u>t
   2   4
6. pro-1-mote
     2   3
7. ra-1-d<u>ar</u>
   2   5
8. t<u>u</u>-1-mor
   2   5
9. re-1-late
   2   3
10. re-1-f<u>er</u>
   2   5

Quiz 96
Lesson 407 /Page 120

1. <u>ch</u><u>ow</u>-1-d<u>er</u>
     6   5
2. tr<u>ea</u>t-2-ment
   4   1
3. wa-1-f<u>er</u>
   2   5
4. a-1-go
   2   2
5. de-1-v<u>our</u>
   2   6
6. spi-1-d<u>er</u>
   2   5
7. t<u>ur</u>-1-nip
   5   1
8. so-1-lo
   2   2
9. de-1-c<u>ay</u>
   2   4
10. re-1-g<u>ai</u>n
   2   4

Quiz 97
Lesson 409 /Page 121

1. cloud-2-b<u>ur</u>st
   6   5
2. sp<u>ea</u>-1-k<u>er</u>
   4   5
3. b<u>oy</u>-1-h<u>oo</u>d
   6   6
4. l<u>au</u>n-2-d<u>er</u>
   6   5
5. c<u>ar</u>-1-t<u>oo</u>n
   5   6

Answer Key for Spelling Quizzes

6. c<u>oo</u>-1-l<u>er</u>
    6   5

7. sc<u>oo</u>-1-t<u>er</u>
    6   5

8. fl<u>ou</u>n-2-der
    6   5

9. s<u>ai</u>l-2-b<u>oa</u>t
    4   4

10. <u>ow</u>-1-ner
    4   5

Quiz 98
Lesson 411 /Page 121

1. r<u>ai</u>l-2-r<u>o</u>ad
    4   4

2. lob-2-st<u>er</u>
    1   5

3. c<u>or</u>-1-n<u>er</u>
    5   5

4. side-1-w<u>ays</u>
    3   4

5. c<u>ar</u>-1-l<u>oa</u>d
    5   4

6. grap<u>e</u>-1-vin<u>e</u>
    3   3

7. f<u>or</u>-1-gav<u>e</u>
    5   3

8. m<u>ea</u>n-2-<u>while</u>
    4   3

9. r<u>oa</u>d-2-sid<u>e</u>
    4   3

10. r<u>oo</u>m-mat<u>e</u>
    6   3

Quiz 99
Lesson 416 / Page 123

1. halt
    8

2. am-2-bu<u>sh</u>
    1   8

3. do
    8

4. full
    8

5. small
    8

6. h<u>ar</u>m-2-ful
    5   8

7. wall
    8

8. j<u>oy</u>-1-ful
    6   8

9. fal-2-len
    8   1

10. bu<u>sh</u>
    8

Quiz 100
Lesson 424 /Page 127

1. mold
    <u>1</u>

2. de-1-cad<u>e</u>
    <u>2</u>   3

3. di-1-vin<u>e</u>
    <u>2</u>   3

4. scold
    <u>1</u>

5. bin-2-d<u>er</u>
    <u>1</u>   5

6. kind
    <u>1</u>

7. <u>ch</u>am-2-ber
    <u>1</u>   5

8. de-1-vil
    <u>2</u>   1

9. poll
    <u>1</u>

10. cli-1-mat<u>e</u>
    2   <u>3</u>

Quiz 101
Lesson 426/Page 128

1. s<u>ur</u>-1-r<u>o</u>und
    5   6

2. he-1-ro
    2   2

3. h<u>or</u>-1-r<u>or</u>
    5   5

4. e-1-rod<u>e</u>
    2   3

5. far<u>e</u>-1-well
    3   1

6. du-1-ri<u>ng</u>
    2   1

7. si-1-ren
    2   1

8. bar-2-rel
    1   1

9. bor<u>e</u>-1-dom
    3   1

10. mir-2-r<u>or</u>
    1   5

Quiz 102
Lesson 428/Page 129

1. s<u>ir</u>-1-l<u>oi</u>n
    5   6

2. <u>sh</u>ar-1-pen
    5   1

3. <u>sh</u>el-2-t<u>er</u>
    1   5

4. ex-2-po<u>se</u>
    1   3

5. li-1-mit
    <u>2</u>   1

6. m<u>oo</u>n-beam
    6   4

7. ruf-f<u>le</u>
    1   7

8. do-1-nat<u>e</u>
    2   3

9. ad-2-dress
    1   1

10. m<u>er</u>-1-m<u>ai</u>d
    5   4

Quiz 103
Lesson 430/Page 129

1. stam-2-ped<u>e</u>
    1   3

2. traf-2-fic
    1   1

3. o-1-pen
    2   1

4. ma-1-j<u>or</u>
    2   5

5. snug-2-g<u>le</u>
    1   7

6. wal-2-nut
    8   1

7. <u>sh</u>am-2-b<u>le</u>
    1   7

8. ti-1-mid
    <u>2</u>   1

9. m<u>ar</u>-1-<u>ch</u>ing
    5   1

10. mu-1-<u>s</u>ic
    2   1

Quiz 104
Lesson 432/Page 130
1. s<u>e</u>r-1-pent
  5   1
2. m<u>ai</u>n-2-t<u>ai</u>n
  4   4
3. wal-2-rus
  8   1
4. os-2-tri<u>ch</u>
  1   1
5. wit-2-ness
  1   1
6. tat-2-t<u>oo</u>
  1   6
7. tram-2-p<u>le</u>
  1   7
8. <u>ei</u>-1-<u>ther</u>
  4   5
9. tic<u>k</u>-2-li<u>sh</u>
  1   1
10. p<u>oi</u>-1-<u>s</u>on
  6   1

Quiz 105
Lesson 434/Page 130
1. wel-2-com<u>e</u>
  1   <u>3</u>
2. <u>wh</u>is-2-p<u>er</u>
  1   5
3. <u>or</u>-1-d<u>er</u>
  5   5
4. lo-1-<u>ser</u>
  8   5
5. e-1-ject
  2   1
6. m<u>ea</u>-1-<u>ger</u>
  4   5
7. la-1-bel
  2   1
8. <u>ch</u>ap-2-t<u>er</u>
  1   5
9. fi-1-ni<u>sh</u>
  <u>2</u>   1
10. t<u>u</u>r-1-k<u>ey</u>
  5   4

Quiz 106
Lesson 439/Page 133
1. spi<u>ce</u>
  3

2. <u>ou</u>nce
  6
3. bi-1-<u>ce</u>ps
  2   1
4. suc-2-<u>ce</u>ed
  1   4
5. ac-2-<u>ce</u>nt
  1   1
6. con-2-<u>ce</u>rt
  1   5
7. <u>for ce</u>
  5
8. of-2-fi<u>ce</u>
  1   1
9. con-2-<u>ce</u>rn
  1   5
10. <u>ci</u>-1-<u>gar</u>
  <u>2</u>   5

Quiz 107
Lesson 441 / Page 133
1. i-1-<u>ci</u>ng
  2   1
2. glan<u>ce</u>
  1
3. b<u>ou</u>n<u>ce</u>
  6
4. a-1-<u>ci</u>d
  <u>2</u>   1
5. de-1-<u>ci</u>de
  2   3
6. <u>ch oi ce</u>
  6
7. re-1-j<u>oi ce</u>
  2   6
8. di-1-v<u>or ce</u>
  <u>2</u>   5
9. s<u>au ce</u>
  6
10. pen-2-<u>ci</u>l
  1   1

Quiz 108
Lesson 448 / Page 136
1. slu<u>dge</u>
  1
2. sta-1-gin<u>g</u>
  2   1
3. he<u>dge</u>
  1

4. l<u>oun ge</u>
  6
5. <u>u</u>r-1-gent
  5   1
6. man-2-<u>ger</u>
  <u>1</u>   5
7. strange
  3
8. wa-1-<u>ger</u>
  2   5
9. ba<u>dge</u>
  1
10. e-1-m<u>er ge</u>
  2   5

Quiz 109
Lesson 450 / Page 136
1. dis-2-<u>ch ar ge</u>
  1   5
2. <u>ou</u>t-2-ra<u>ge</u>
  6   3
3. b<u>ar ge</u>
  5
4. a-1-<u>g</u>ing
  2   1
5. col-2-le<u>ge</u>
  1   1
6. lo<u>dge</u>
  1
7. hu<u>ge</u>
  3
8. ran-2-<u>ger</u>
  <u>1</u>   5
9. ple<u>dge</u>
  1
10. g<u>ou ge</u>
  6

Quiz 110
Lesson 459 / Page 141
1. sky
  2
2. typ<u>e</u>
  3
3. sys-2-tem
  1   1
4. py-1-<u>th</u>on
  2   1
5. de-1-fy
  2   2

127

6. c͟y-1-clon͟e
   1 ˘˘3

7. pry
   2

8. crys-2-tal
   1   8

9. vi-1-nyl
   2 1

10. c͟y-1-cl͟e
    2   7

Quiz 111
Lesson 461 / Page 141

1. a͟n-2-gr͟y
   1   2

2. mu͟r-1-k͟y
   5   2

3. mar-2-r͟y
   1   2

4. mo͟o-1-d͟y
   6   2

5. gent-2-l͟y
   1˘   2

6. hu͟r-1-r͟y
   5   2

7. ru͟-1-by
   2   2

8. co-1-z͟y
   2   2

9. bre͟e-1-z͟y
    4   2

10. e͟ar-1-l͟y
    5   2

Quiz 112
Lesson 463 / Page 142

1. fan-2-c͟y
   1   2

2. yet
   1

3. lou͟-1-s͟y
   6   2

4. a͟r-1-m͟y
   5   2

5. bo-1-d͟y
   2   2

6. bo-1-n͟y
   2   2

7. c͟i-1-ty
   2   2

8. typ͟e
   3

9. gym
   1

10. gra-1-v͟y
   2   2

Quiz 113
Lesson 465 / Page 142

1. bel-2-l͟y
   1   2

2. c͟hil-2-l͟y
   1   2

3. s͟hy
   2

4. ba-1-by
   2   2

5. re-1-ply
   2 ˘˘2

6. w͟hy
   2

7. y͟ard
   5

8. me͟r-1-c͟y
   5   2

9. fau͟l-2-t͟y
   6   2

10. lynx
   1

Quiz 114
Lesson 473/ Page 145

1. ne͟ed-2-ful
   4   8

2. co-1-p͟y
   2   2

3. mu͟r-1-der
   5   5

4. ta-1-bl͟e
   2   7

5. su͟r-1-pris͟e
   5 ˘˘3

6. le-1-gend
   2   1

7. go͟r͟ge
   5

8. gro-1-ce͟r
   2   5

9. de-1-c͟ent
   2   1

10. in-2-san͟e
   1   3

Quiz 115
Lesson 475/ Page 145

1. bot-2-tl͟e
   1   7

2. re͟al-2-l͟y
   4   2

3. su͟r-1-viv͟e
   5   3

4. brac͟e-1-let
   3   1

5. re-1-c͟ess
   2   1

6. ty-1-rant
   2   1

7. ro͟o-1-ster
   6 ˘˘5

8. c͟ir-1-cl͟e
   5   7

9. c͟h͟ar-1-co͟al
   5   4

10. c͟ham-2-be͟r
   1   5

Quiz 116
Lesson 477/ Page 146

1. no-1-bl͟e
   2   7

2. E͟n-2-gli͟sh
   2   1

3. ma-1-g͟ic
   2   1

4. mo-1-ment
   2   1

5. trai-1-to͟r
   4   5

6. crum-2-bl͟e
   1   7

7. pen-2-ny
   1   2

8. cler-1-g͟y
   5   2

9. blis-2-te͟r
   1   5

10. ac-2-c͟ept
   1   1

Quiz 117
Lesson 479/ Page 146

1. fif-2-ty
   1   2

2. a-1-cross
  2 ˘˘1

3. let-2-tuce
  1   1

4. Chi-1-nese
   2   3

5. bad-2-ger
   1   5

6. u-1-nit
  2 1

7. de-1-nounce
   2   6

8. ce-1-ment
  2   1

9. lo-1-gic
  2 1

10. clou-1-dy
    6   2

Quiz 118
Lesson 481/ Page 147

1. in-2-dus-2-try
  1   1   2

2. in-2-ci-1dent
  1   2 1

3. dis-2-co-1-ver
   1   2   5

4. ad-2-ver-1-tise
   1   5   3

5. un-2-com-2-mon
   1   1   1

6. com-2-pen-2-sate
   1   1   3

7. re-1-tire-1-ment
   2   3   1

8. O-1-lym-2-pics
   2   1   1

9. con-2-so-1-nant
   1   2   1

10. bal-2-co-1-ny
    1   2   2

Quiz 119
Lesson 483/ Page 147

1. de-1-ter-1-gent
   2   5   1

2. syl-2-la-1-ble
   1   2   7

3. mer-1-chan-2-dise
   5   1   3

4. pro-1-jec-2-tor
   2   1   5

5. in-2-no-1-cent
  1   2   1

6. al-2-pha-1-bet
  1   2   1

7. cur-1-ren-2-cy
   5   1   2

8. ab-2-nor-1-mal
  1   5   8

9. of-2-fi-1-cer
  1   2   5

10. fur-1-ni-1-ture
   5   2   3

Quiz 120
Lesson 485/ Page 148

1. Oc-2-to-1-ber
   1   2   5

2. sub-2-sti-1-tute
   1   2   3

3. com-2-pu-1-ter
   1   2   5

4. to-1-ma-1-to
  2   2   2

5. in-2-ter-1-cept
  1   2   1

6. im-2-po-1-lite
   1   2   3

7. pas-2-sen-2-ger
   1   1   5

8. u-1-ni-1-verse
  2   2   5

9. tur-1-bu-1-lent
   5   2   1

10. ex-2-cite-1-ment
   1   3   1

Quiz 121
Lesson 487/ Page 148

1. ob-2-so-1-lete
   1   2   3

2. e-1-ner-1-gy
  2   5   2

3. bul-2-le-1-tin
   1   2   1

4. tor-1-pe-1-do
   5   2   2

5. a-1-muse-1-ment
  2   3   1

6. ap-2-pen-2-dix
   1   1   1

7. con-2-su-1-mer
   1   2   5

8. lum-ber-jack
   1   5 1

9. ac-2-com-2-plish
   1   1   1

10. en-2-ter-1-tain
   1   5   4

Quiz 122
Lesson 489/ Page 149

1. tow-3-el
   6   1

2. cre-3-ate
   2   3

3. o-3-a-1-sis
  2   2 1

4. or-3-ange
   5   1

5. roy-3-al
   6   8

6. glor-3-y
   5   2

7. mow-3-er
    4   5

8. hy-3-e-na
   2   2 8

9. ro-1-de-3-o
  2   2   2

10. vi-3-o-1-lent
   2   2   1

Quiz 123
Lesson 491/ Page 149

1. vi-3-o-1-let
  2   2   1

2. ne-3-on
  2   1

3. ru-3-in
  2   1

4. tri-3-an-2-gle
   2   1   7

5. his-2-tor-3-y
   1   5   2

6. cr<u>ay</u>-3-on
    <u>4</u>   <u>1</u>

7. g<u>i</u>-3-ant
   <u>2</u> <u>1</u>

8. o-1-p<u>er</u>-3-ate
   <u>2</u>   <u>5</u>   <u>3</u>

9. di-3-et
   <u>2</u> <u>1</u>

10. pr<u>ay</u>-3-<u>er</u>
      <u>4</u>   <u>5</u>

Quiz 124
Lesson 497/ Page 152

1. con-2-fes-2-<u>sion</u>
   <u>1</u>   <u>1</u>   <u>1</u>

2. <u>wr</u>ap
  <u>1</u>

3. in-2-vo<u>lve</u>
   <u>1</u>   <u>1</u>

4. men-2-<u>ti</u>on
   <u>1</u>   <u>1</u>

5. <u>wr</u>eck
   <u>1</u>

6. frac-2-<u>ti</u>on
   <u>1</u>   <u>1</u>

7. <u>wh</u>ole
   <u>3</u>

8. con-2-clu-1-<u>sion</u>
   <u>1</u>   <u>2</u>   <u>1</u>

9. col-2-lec-2-<u>ti</u>on
   <u>1</u>   <u>1</u>   <u>1</u>

10. po-1-<u>si</u>-1-<u>ti</u>on
    <u>2</u> <u>2</u>   <u>1</u>

Quiz 125
Lesson 499/ Page 152

1. <u>wh</u>om
   <u>8</u>

2. man-2-<u>sion</u>
   <u>1</u>   <u>1</u>

3. tax-<u>1</u>-a-1-<u>ti</u>on
   <u>1</u>   <u>2</u> <u>1</u>

4. ex-2-plo-1-<u>sion</u>
   <u>1</u>   <u>2</u>   <u>1</u>

5. <u>wr</u>ap-2-p<u>er</u>
   <u>1</u>   <u>5</u>

6. re-1-vo<u>lve</u>
   <u>2</u>   <u>1</u>

7. ex-2-ten-2-si<u>ve</u>
   <u>1</u>   <u>1</u>   <u>1</u>

8. <u>wr</u>eath
   <u>4</u>

9. de-1-<u>ser</u>-1-<u>ti</u>on
   <u>2</u>   <u>5</u>   <u>1</u>

10. ad-2-he-1-si<u>ve</u>
    <u>1</u>   <u>2</u> <u>1</u>

Quiz 126
Lesson 501/ Page 153

1. <u>wr</u>i-1-t<u>er</u>
   <u>2</u>   <u>5</u>

2. n<u>er</u><u>ve</u>
   <u>5</u>

3. di-1-vi-1-<u>sion</u>
   <u>2</u> <u>2</u>   <u>1</u>

4. <u>wr</u>ig-2-<u>gle</u>
   <u>1</u>   <u>7</u>

5. ten-2-<u>sion</u>
   <u>1</u>   <u>1</u>

6. <u>qu</u>o-1-ta-1-<u>ti</u>on
   <u>2</u>   <u>2</u> <u>1</u>

7. cre-3-a-1-<u>ti</u>on
   <u>2</u>   <u>2</u> <u>1</u>

8. <u>wr</u>in-2-<u>kle</u>
   <u>1</u>   <u>7</u>

9. p<u>er</u>-1-fec-2-<u>ti</u>on
   <u>5</u>   <u>1</u>   <u>1</u>

10. ig-2-ni-1-<u>ti</u>on
    <u>1</u>   <u>2</u> <u>1</u>

Quiz 127
Lesson 503/ Page 153

1. <u>wr</u>ath
   <u>1</u>

2. vi-1-<u>sion</u>
   <u>2</u>   <u>1</u>

3. pro-1-mo-1-<u>ti</u>on
   <u>2</u>   <u>2</u> <u>1</u>

4. <u>au</u>c-2-<u>ti</u>on
   <u>6</u>   <u>1</u>

5. spe-1-<u>ci</u>al
   <u>2</u>   <u>8</u>

6. <u>wr</u>ong
   <u>1</u>

7. con-2-fu-1-<u>sion</u>
   <u>1</u>   <u>2</u>   <u>1</u>

8. e-1-rup-2-<u>ti</u>on
   <u>2</u>   <u>1</u>   <u>1</u>

9. pro-1-fes-2-<u>sion</u>
   <u>2</u>   <u>1</u>   <u>1</u>

10. pre-1-<u>ci</u>-1-<u>sion</u>
    <u>2</u> <u>2</u>   <u>1</u>

Quiz 128
Lesson 516/ Page 158

1. <u>sh</u>ield
   <u>6</u>

2. pul-2-l<u>ey</u>
   <u>1</u>   <u>4</u>

3. be-1-l<u>ie</u>f
   <u>2</u>   <u>6</u>

4. yield
   <u>6</u>

5. re-1-<u>cei</u><u>ve</u>
   <u>2</u>   <u>4</u>

6. <u>cei</u>-1-ling
   <u>4</u>   <u>1</u>

7. v<u>ir</u>-1-t<u>ue</u>
   <u>5</u>   <u>4</u>

8. col-2-l<u>ie</u>
   <u>1</u>   <u>6</u>

9. bl<u>ue</u>-1-b<u>ir</u>d
    <u>4</u>   <u>5</u>

10. ge-1-n<u>ie</u>
    <u>2</u>   <u>6</u>

Quiz 129
Lesson 518/ Page 158

1. val-2-l<u>ey</u>
   <u>1</u>   <u>4</u>

2. <u>th</u>ief
   <u>6</u>

3. d<u>ue</u>
   <u>4</u>

4. don-2-k<u>ey</u>
   <u>1</u>   <u>4</u>

5. <u>ch</u>ief
   <u>6</u>

6. re-1-l<u>ie</u>f
   <u>2</u>   <u>6</u>

7. tr<u>ue</u>
   <u>4</u>

8. <u>shr</u>i<u>e</u>k
   <u>6</u>

9. be-1-l<u>ie</u>f
   <u>2</u>   <u>6</u>

10. <u>th</u>eir
   <u>6</u>

Answer Key for Spelling Quizzes

Quiz 130
Lesson 520/ Page 159

1. br<u>ow</u>-1-n<u>ie</u>
    6   6

2. las-2-s<u>ie</u>
    1   6

3. con-2-ti-1-n<u>ue</u>
    1   <u>2</u>   4

4. kid-2-n<u>ey</u>
    1   4

5. ho<u>ck</u>-<u>1</u>-<u>ey</u>
    1   4

6. bl<u>ue</u>
    4

7. dis-2-be-1-l<u>ie</u>f
    1   2   6

8. mo-1-n<u>ey</u>
   <u>2</u>   4

9. b<u>ar</u>-1-be-1-c<u>ue</u>
    5   <u>2</u>   4

10. w<u>ei</u>rd
    4

Quiz 131
Lesson 522/ Page 159

1. re-1-l<u>ie</u><u>ve</u>
    2   6

2. j<u>er</u>-1-<u>sey</u>
    5   4

3. p<u>ie</u><u>ce</u>
    6

4. br<u>ui</u><u>se</u>
    4

5. p<u>ur</u>-1-s<u>ue</u>
    5   4

6. gl<u>ue</u>
    4

7. s<u>ie</u><u>ge</u>
    6

8. t<u>ur</u>-1-k<u>ey</u>
    5   4

9. n<u>ei</u>-1-<u>ther</u>
    4   5

10. re-1-ve-1-n<u>ue</u>
   <u>2</u> <u>2</u>   4

Quiz 132
Lesson 531/ Page 163

1. j<u>oy</u>
    6

2. j<u>oy</u>-3-<u>ous</u>
    6   6

3. de-1-fy
    2   2

4. de-1-fi-3-ant
    2   2   1

5. a<u>n</u>-2-gr<u>y</u>
    1   2

6. a<u>n</u>-2-gri-3-<u>er</u>
    1   <u>2</u>   5

7. car-2-r<u>y</u>
    1   2

8. car-2-r<u>y</u>-3-i<u>ng</u>
    1   2   1

9. pen-2-n<u>y</u>
    1   2

10. pen-2-n<u>ies</u>
    1   6

Quiz 133
Lesson 533/ Page 163

1. wast<u>e</u>
    3

2. wast<u>e</u>-1-ful
    3   8

3. fil<u>e</u>
    3

4. fi-1-li<u>ng</u>
    2   1

5. spok<u>e</u>
    3

6. spo-1-ken
    2   1

7. tid<u>e</u>
    3

8. ti-1-di<u>ngs</u>
    2   1

9. haz<u>e</u>
    3

10. ha-1-z<u>y</u>
    2   2

Quiz 134
Lesson 535/ Page 163

1. drip
    1

2. drip-2-pi<u>ng</u>
    1   1

3. man
    1

4. man-2-l<u>y</u>
    1   2

5. tra-1-vel
   <u>2</u>   1

6. tra-1-ve-1-li<u>ng</u>
   <u>2</u> <u>2</u>   1

7. spli<u>n</u>-2-t<u>er</u>
    1   5

8. spli<u>n</u>-2-t<u>er</u>-3-i<u>ng</u>
    1   5   1

9. cram
    1

10. cram-2-mi<u>ng</u>
    1   1

Quiz 135
Lesson 537/ Page 164

1. bel-2-l<u>y</u>
    1   2

2. bel-2-l<u>ies</u>
    1   6

3. so<u>ng</u>
    1

4. so<u>ngs</u>
    1

5. can-2-d<u>le</u>
    1   7

6. can-2-d<u>les</u>
    1   7

7. r<u>u</u>-1-b<u>y</u>
    2   2

8. r<u>u</u>-1-b<u>ies</u>
    2   6

9. r<u>ai</u>-1-<u>s</u>in
    4   1

10. r<u>ai</u>-1-<u>s</u>in<u>s</u>
    4   1

Quiz 136
Lesson 539/ Page 164

1. elf
    1

2. elve<u>s</u>
    1

3. tor<u>ch</u>
    5

4. tor-1-<u>ches</u>
    5   1

5. to-1-ma-1-to
    2   2   2

6. to-1-ma-1-t<u>oe</u>s
   2   2   4

7. fox
   1

8. fox-<u>1</u>-e<u>s</u>
   1   1

9. pe<u>a</u>ch
   4

10. pea-1-ch<u>es</u>
    4   1

Quiz 137
Lesson 541/ Page 165

1. sh<u>ou</u>-1-t<u>ed</u>
   6   1

2. s<u>ee</u>m<u>ed</u>
   4

3. rak<u>ed</u>
   3

4. stopp<u>ed</u>
   1

5. t<u>oa</u>-1-st<u>ed</u> / t<u>oa</u>s-2-t<u>ed</u>
   4 ~1   4   1

6. nod-2-d<u>ed</u>
   1   1

7. bak<u>ed</u>
   3

8. hop<u>ed</u>
   3

9. pl<u>ea</u>-1-d<u>ed</u>
   4

10. lif-2-t<u>ed</u>
   1   1

Quiz 138
Lesson 547/ Page 168

1. re-1-w<u>ar</u>d
   2   5

2. l<u>ea</u>-1-<u>th</u>er
   6   5

3. fr<u>igh</u>t
   4

4. y<u>oung</u>-2-ster
   6   5

5. t<u>augh</u>t
   6

6. h<u>ea</u>l-2-<u>thy</u>
   6   2

7. w<u>ea</u>-1-pon
   6   1

8. w<u>ar</u>
   5

9. fa-1-m<u>ous</u>
   2   6

10. n<u>eigh</u>-1-b<u>or</u>
   6   5

Quiz 139
Lesson 549/ Page 168

1. c<u>ou</u>-1-p<u>le</u>
   6   7

2. <u>eigh</u>t
   6

3. w<u>ea</u>lth
   6

4. br<u>ea</u>d
   6

5. qu<u>ar</u>t
   5

6. c<u>ou</u>n-2-try
   6   2

7. d<u>ou</u>-1-b<u>le</u>
   6   7

8. w<u>or</u>ld
   5

9. <u>th</u>r<u>ea</u>t
   6

10. n<u>igh</u>t
   4

Quiz 140
Lesson 551/ Page 169

1. c<u>augh</u>t
   6

2. w<u>or</u>d
   5

3. in-2-st<u>ea</u>d
   1   6

4. tr<u>ea</u>-1-<u>ch</u>er-3-y
   6   5   2

5. <u>eigh</u>-1-teen
   6   4

6. <u>air</u>-2-t<u>igh</u>t
   4   4

7. dan-2-g<u>er</u>-3-<u>ous</u>
   1   5   6

8. br<u>ea</u>k-2-fast
   6   1

9. <u>wh</u>arf
   5

10. d<u>augh</u>-1-t<u>er</u>
    6   5

Quiz 141
Lesson 553/ Page 169

1. sl<u>igh</u>t
   4

2. e-1-nor-1-m<u>ous</u>
   2   5   6

3. de-1-l<u>igh</u>t
   2   4

4. a-1-h<u>ea</u>d
   2   6

5. <u>eigh</u>-1-ty
   6   2

6. h<u>ea</u>-1-vy
   6   2

7. w<u>ar</u>-1-den
   5   1

8. fa-1-bu-1-l<u>ous</u>
   2   2   6

9. w<u>or</u>st
   5

10. y<u>oung</u>
    6

Quiz 142
Lesson 564/ Page 173

1. <u>gh</u>ost
   <u>1</u>

2. <u>sc</u>i-3-en<u>ce</u>
   2   1

3. <u>kn</u>ack
   1

4. a<u>ch</u>e
   3

5. <u>gu</u>i-1-t<u>ar</u>
   2   5

6. <u>kn</u>eel
   4

7. <u>ch</u>e-1-mist
   2   1

8. as-2-si<u>gn</u>
   1   <u>1</u>

9. bro-1-<u>ch</u><u>ure</u>
   2   3

10. a<u>n</u>-2-<u>ch</u>or
   1   5

Answer Key for Spelling Quizzes

Quiz 143
Lesson 566/ Page 173

1. lea gu e
    4

2. knob
    1

3. sto-1-ma ch
    2   1

4. sche-1-dule
    2   3

5. knife
    3

6. sign
    1

7. or-1-ches-2-tra
    5 1   8

8. scis-2-sors
    1   5

9. che-1-mis-2-try
    2 1   2

10. chef
    1

Quiz 144
Lesson 568/ Page 174

1. e-1-cho
    2   2

2. knives
    3

3. knock
    1

4. rhythm
    1

5. sci-3-en-2-tist
    2 1   1

6. scheme
    3

7. van-2-gu ard
    1   5

8. sce-1-ner-3-y
    2 5 2

9. cham-2-pagn e
    1   3

10. gui-1-dan ce
    2   1

Quiz 145
Lesson 570/ Page 174

1. cha-3-os
    2 1

2. kn ight
    4

3. dis-2-gui se
    1   3

4. de-1-scent
    2   1

5. sce-1-nic
    2   1

6. rhine-1-stone
    3   ~3

7. con-2-sign
    1   1

8. chor-3-us
    5 1

9. kn ee
    4

10. de-1-scend
    2 1

Quiz 146
Lesson 581/ Page 177

1. ex-2-pla-1-na-1-tion
    1   2 2   1

2. au-1-th or-3-i-1-ty
    6   5 2 2

3. se-1-cre-1-ta-1-ry
    2 ~2 2   2

4. con-2-tri-1-bu-1-ted
    1   2 2   1

5. in-2-ter-1-sec-2-tion
    1 5   1   1

6. ad-2-di-1-tion-1-al
    1   2   1   8

7. Ja-1-nu-3-a-1-ry
    2   2 2   2

8. ma-1-jor-3-i-1-ty
    2   5 2   2

9. ex-2-pe-1-di-1-tion
    1   2   2   1

10. au-1-to-1-ma-1-tic
    6   2   2   1

Quiz 147
Lesson 583/ Page 177

1. al-2-to-1-ge-1-ther
    8   8   2   5

2. A-1-me-1-ri-1-can
    2   2 2 1

3. un-1-ex-2-pec-2-ted
    1   1   1   1

4. un-2-der-1-wa-1-ter
    1   5   8   5

5. e-1-mo-1-tion-1-al
    2   2   1   8

6. de-1-ve-1-lop-1-ment
    2   2   1   1

7. o-1-per-3-a-1-tion
    2   5   2   1

8. in-2-ter-3-es-2-ting
    1   5   1   1

9. con-2-ti-1-nen-2-tal
    1   2   1   8

10. lo-1-co-1-mo-1-tiv e
    2   2   2   1

Quiz 148
Lesson 585/ Page 178

1. com-2-for-1-ta-1-b le
    1   5   2   7

2. val-1-u-3-a-1-b le
    1   2   2   7

3. in-2-de-1-ci-1-siv e
    1   2   2   1

4. dis-2-ho-1-nes-2-ty
    1 ~2 1   2

5. de-3-o-1-dor-3-ant
    2   2 5   1

6. com-2-pre-1-hen-2-sion
    1   2   1   1

7. te-1-ri-1-tor-3-y
    2   2   5   2

8. fa-1-vor-3-a-1-b le
    2   5   2   7

9. ac-2-tu-3-al-2-ly
    1   2   8   2

10. di-3-a-1-me-1-ter
    2   2   2   5

Quiz 149
Lesson 587/ Page 178

1. ge-1-ner-3-a-1-tion
    2   5   2   1

2. pho-1-to-1-gra-1-phy
    2   2   2   2

3. ir-2-re-1-gu-1-lar
    1   2   2   5

4. cal-2-cu-1-la-1-ting
    1   2   2   1

5. u-1-ni-1-ver-1-sal
    2   2   5   8

6. ex-2-pe-1-ri-3-en<u>ce</u>
  1   2   2   1

7. dif-2-fi-1-cul-2-ty
  1   2   1   2

8. ne-1-<u>c</u>es-2-sa-1-r<u>y</u>
  2   1   2   2

9. vi-3-o-1-li-1-nist
  2   2   2   1

10. im-2-pos-2-si-1-b<u>le</u>
  1   1   2   7

Quiz 150
Lesson 593/ Page 181

1. s<u>ou</u>l
  4

2. t<u>ou</u>gh
  6

3. jour-1-n<u>ey</u>
  5   4

4. gr<u>ou</u>p
  6

5. d<u>ough</u>-1-nut
  4   1

6. c<u>ou</u>r-3-age
  5   3

7. sh<u>ou</u>l-2-der
  4   5

8. c<u>ough</u>
  6

9. b<u>ou</u>-1-le-1-v<u>ar</u>d
  6   2   5

10. y<u>ou</u>th
  6

Quiz 151
Lesson 595/ Page 181

1. c<u>ou</u>r-1-te-1-s<u>y</u>
  5   2   2

2. y<u>ou</u>
  6

3. re-1-s<u>our</u>ce
  2   4

4. c<u>ou</u>-1-g<u>ar</u>
  6   5

5. e-1-n<u>ough</u>
  2   6

6. r<u>ou</u>-1-tine
  6   x

7. c<u>ou</u>-1-pon
  6   1

8. thr<u>ough</u>
  6

9. <u>th</u> <u>ough</u>
  4

10. dr<u>ough</u>t
  6

Quiz 152
Lesson 604/ Page 184

1. pre-1-pos-2-t<u>er</u>-3-<u>ous</u>
  2   1   5   6

2. s<u>u</u>-1-p<u>er</u>-1-sti-1-<u>tious</u>
  2   5   ˘2   6

3. ir-2-re-1-spon-2-si-1-b<u>le</u>
  1   2 ˘1   2   7

4. com-2-mu-1-ni-1-ca-1-<u>ti</u>on
  1   2   2   1

5. <u>c</u>i-1-vi-1-li-1-za-1-<u>ti</u>on
  2   2   2   1

6. in-2-di-1-vi-1-du-3-al
  1   2   2   8

7. as-2-so-1-<u>c</u>i-3-a-1-<u>ti</u>on
  1   2   2   1

8. s<u>u</u>-1-pe-1-ri-3-<u>or</u>-3-i-ty
  2   2   2   5 22

9. con-2-gra-1-tu-1-la-1-<u>tions</u>
  1   2   2   1

10. de-1-<u>s</u>i-1-ra-1-b<u>le</u>
  2   2   2   7

Quiz 153
Lesson 606/ Page 184

1. in-2-tel-2-lec-2-tu-3-al
  1   1   1   2   8

2. c<u>or</u>-1-re-1-spon-2-dent
  5   2 ˘1   1

3. pro-1-fes-2-<u>si</u>on-<u>1</u>-al
  2   1   1   8

4. re-1-ha-1-bi-1-li-1-ta-1-<u>ti</u>on
  2   2   2   2   1

5. t<u>u</u>-1-b<u>er</u>-1-cu-1-lo-1-sis
  2   5   2   1

6. re-3-in-2-f<u>or</u>ce-2-ment
  2 1   5   1

7. ton-2-sil-2-lec-2-to-1-m<u>y</u>
  1   1   1   2   2

8. dis-<u>1</u>-ap-2-p<u>ea</u>-1-ran<u>ce</u>
  1   1   4   1

9. flex-<u>1</u>-i-1-bi-1-li-1-t<u>y</u>
  1   2   2   2

10. con-2-si-1-d<u>er</u>-3-a-1-<u>ti</u>on
  1   2   5   2   1

Quiz 154
Lesson 608/ Page 185

1. <u>q</u>ues-2-<u>ti</u>on-<u>1</u>-a-1-b<u>le</u>
  1   1   2   7

2. de-1-p<u>er</u>-1-so-1-na-1-liz<u>e</u>
  2   5   2   2   3

3. un-2-pre-1-<u>c</u>e-1-den-2-t<u>ed</u>
  1   2   2   1   1

4. li-1-<u>q</u>ui-1-da-1-tion
  2   2   2   1

5. pre-3-oc-2-cu-1-py
  2   1   2   2

6. v<u>ir</u>-1-tu-3-o-1-si-1-ty
  5   2   2   2   2

7. bi-3-o-1-gra-1-<u>phi</u>-1-cal
  2   2 ˘2   2   8

8. <u>glor</u>-3-i-1-fi-1-ca-1-<u>ti</u>on
  5   2   2   1

9. pan-2-de-1-mo-1-ni-3-um
  1   2   2   1

10. <u>chor</u>-3-e-3-o-1-graph
  5   2   2   1

Quiz 155
Lesson 610/ Page 185

1. e-1-lec-2-tri-1-<u>c</u>i-1-ty
  2   1   2   2   2

2. un-2-s<u>ea</u>-1-son-<u>1</u>-a-1-b<u>le</u>
  1   4   1   2   7

3. ir-2-re-1-spon-2-si-1-b<u>le</u>
  1   2 ˘1   2   7

4. se-1-mi-3-an-2-nu-3-al
  2   2   1   2   8

5. ex-2-tra-3-<u>or</u>-1-di-1-na-1-r<u>y</u>
  1   8   5   2   2   2

6. pre-1-de-1-<u>c</u>es-2-s<u>or</u>
  2   2   1   5

7. dan-2-de-1-li-3-on
  1   2   2   1

8. un-2-s<u>er</u>-1-vi<u>ce</u>-<u>1</u>-a-1-b<u>le</u>
  1   5   1   2   7

9. ste-1-re-3-o-1-typ<u>e</u>
  2   2   2   3

10. tri-3-an-2-gu-1-l<u>ar</u>
  2   1   2   5

Quiz 156
Lesson 626 / Page 214

1. <u>ch</u> <u>air</u>
  4

134

2. la-1-d<u>y</u>
      2   2

3. ac-2-<u>c</u>ept
      1   1

4. en-2-t<u>er</u>
      1   5

5. ex-<u>1</u>-am-2-p<u>le</u>
     1 1   7

6. dif-2-f<u>er</u>-3-en<u>ce</u>
      1 5 1

7. m<u>ou th</u>
      6

8. sil-2-v<u>er</u>
      1   5

9. <u>th ou</u>-1-<u>s</u>and
      6   1

10. <u>ar</u>-1-ti-1-c<u>le</u>
      5 <u>2</u> 7

Quiz 157
Lesson 628 / Page 215

1. stra<u>igh</u>t
      4

2. tr<u>ie</u>d
      4

3. de-1-str<u>oy</u>
      2   6

4. pro-1-d<u>u</u>-1-<u>c</u>er
      2 2 5

5. ex-2-<u>c</u>ept
      1   1

6. be-1-tw<u>ee</u>n
      2   4

7. sta-1-<u>ti</u>on
      2   1

8. bat-2-t<u>le</u>
      1   7

9. co-1-l<u>or</u>
      <u>2</u> 5

10. <u>c</u>i-1-t<u>y</u>
      <u>2</u> 2

Quiz 158
Lesson 630 / Page 216

1. con-2-ti-1-n<u>ue</u>
     1 <u>2</u> 4

2. at-2-ten-2-<u>ti</u>on
     1 1 1

3. m<u>or</u>-1-ning
      5   1

4. c<u>ir</u>-1-c<u>le</u>
      5   7

5. lis-2-ten
      1 ~1

6. st<u>or</u>-3-<u>y</u>
      5   2

7. l<u>ea ve</u>
      4

8. sug-2-<u>g</u>est
      1   1

9. ex-2-press
      1   1

10. sup-2-ply
      1   2

Quiz 159
Lesson 632/ Page 217

1. de-1-<u>c</u>i<u>de</u>
      2   3

2. dis-2-tan<u>ce</u>
      1   1

3. can-2-not
      1   1

4. in-2-t<u>er</u>-3-est
      1 5 1

5. pos-2-si-1-b<u>le</u>
      1 <u>2</u> 7

6. be-1-gan
      2   1

7. <u>kn igh</u>t
      4

8. pl<u>ea</u>-1-<u>s</u>ant
      6   1

9. to-1-ge-1-<u>ther</u>
      8 <u>2</u> 5

10. in-2-cl<u>u</u>de
      1   3

Quiz 160
Lesson 634 / Page 218

1. clo<u>se</u>
      3

2. be-1-ca<u>use</u>
      2   6

3. <u>ear</u>-1-l<u>y</u>
      5   2

4. co-1-ming
      <u>2</u> 1

5. <u>though</u>
      4

6. fi-1-<u>shing</u>
      <u>2</u> 1

7. mo<u>ve</u>
      8

8. bl<u>ue</u>
      4

9. ne-1-<u>c</u>es-2-sa-1-ry
      <u>2</u> 1 <u>2</u> 2

10. im-2-p<u>or</u>-1-tant
      1 5 1

Quiz 161
Lesson 636 / Page 219

1. <u>ea ch</u>
      4

2. mo-1-<u>ther</u>
      <u>2</u> 5

3. let-2-t<u>er</u>
      1   5

4. t<u>ea</u>-1-<u>ch</u> er
      4   5

5. num-2-b<u>er</u>
      1   5

6. clo<u>the</u><u>s</u>
      3

7. a-1-r<u>ou</u>nd
      2   6

8. twen-2-t<u>y</u>
      1   2

9. be-1-came
      2   3

10. g<u>oo</u>d
      6

Quiz 162
Lesson 638/ Page 220

1. fa-1-m<u>ou</u>s
      2   6

2. c<u>or</u>-1-n<u>er</u>
      5   5

3. in-2-dus-2-try
      1 1 2

4. pro-1-p<u>er</u>
      <u>2</u> 5

5. go-3-ing
      2   1

6. <u>threw</u>
      6

7. sim-2-p<u>le</u>
      1   7

8. re-1-<u>c</u>ei <u>v</u>e
   2   4

9. a-1-ni-1-mal
  <u>2</u>   2   8

10. mo-1-ment
     2   1

Quiz 163
Lesson 640/ Page 221

1. <u>ch</u>il-2-dren
   1   1

2. fur-1-<u>ther</u>
   5   5

3. ga-1-<u>ther</u>
  <u>2</u>   5

4. <u>ou</u>t-2-side
   6   3

5. go-1-v<u>er</u>n-2-ment
  <u>2</u>   5   1

6. wa<u>tch</u>
   8

7. n<u>or</u>-1-mal
   5   8

8. w<u>er</u> e
   5

9. cap-2-t<u>ai</u>n
   1   4

10. stu-1-d<u>y</u>
  <u>2</u>   2

Quiz 164
Lesson 642/ Page 222

1. si-1-len<u>ce</u>
   2   1

2. af-2-t<u>er</u>-1-n<u>oo</u>n
   1   5   6

3. sold
  <u>1</u>

4. gr<u>ou</u>nd
   6

5. ne-1-v<u>er</u>
  <u>2</u>   5

6. a-1-fr<u>ai</u>d
  2 ⌣4

7. of-2-fi<u>ce</u>
   1   1

8. dan<u>ce</u>
   1

9. roll
  <u>1</u>

10. u<u>n</u>-2-cle
   1   7

Quiz 165
Lesson 644/ Page 223

1. fi-1-ni<u>shed</u>
  <u>2</u>   1

2. dis-2-co-1-v<u>er</u>
   1   <u>2</u> 5

3. col-2-lege
   1   1

4. br<u>ea</u>k
    x

5. be-1-come
   2   <u>3</u>

6. ex-<u>1</u>-er-1-<u>ci</u>se
   1   5   <u>3</u>

7. re-1-<u>qui</u>re
   2   3

8. l<u>ea</u>-1-d<u>er</u>
   4   5

9. fa-1-<u>ther</u>
   8   5

10. a-1-no-1-<u>ther</u>
   2   <u>2</u> 5

Quiz 166
Lesson 646/ Page 224

1. som<u>e</u>-1-time<u>s</u>
  <u>3</u>   3

2. b<u>ea</u>-3-u-1-t<u>y</u>
   4   2   2

3. con-2-t<u>ai</u>n
   1   4

4. con-2-trol
   1   <u>1</u>

5. fif-2-t<u>y</u>
   1   2

6. r<u>ai</u><u>se</u>
   4

7. fi-1-ni<u>sh</u>
  <u>2</u>   1

8. <u>wh</u>ere
   <u>3</u>

9. sup-2-po<u>se</u>
   1   3

10. a-1-bo<u>ve</u>
   2   1

Quiz 167
Lesson 648/ Page 225

1. mo-1-d<u>er</u>n
  <u>2</u>   5

2. tru<u>th</u>
  <u>1</u>

3. of-2-fi-1-<u>c</u>er
   1   <u>2</u> 5

4. <u>quar</u>-1-t<u>er</u>
   5   5

5. ar-2-ri<u>v</u>e
   1   3

6. ex-2-pe-1-ri-3-en<u>ce</u>
   1   2   <u>2</u> 1

7. <u>gu</u> <u>ar</u>d
    5

8. re-1-p<u>or</u>t
   2   5

9. <u>low</u>-3-<u>er</u>
   4   5

10. <u>their</u>
    6

Quiz 168
Lesson 650/ Page 226

1. my-1-self
   2   1

2. p<u>ur</u>-1-pose
   5   <u>3</u>

3. tra-1-vel<u>ed</u>
  <u>2</u>   1

4. u-1-pon
  <u>2</u>   1

5. spe-1-<u>c</u>ial
   <u>2</u>   8

6. dif-2-f<u>er</u>-3-ent
   1   5   1

7. doc-2-t<u>or</u>
   1   5

8. sur-1-pri<u>se</u>
   5 ⌣3

9. be-1-n<u>ea</u> <u>th</u>
   2   4

10. al-2-r<u>ea</u>-1-d<u>y</u>
   8   6   2

Quiz 169
Lesson 652/ Page 227

1. suc-2-<u>c</u>ess
   1   1

2. val-2-l<u>ey</u>
   1   4

3. pas-2-sage
   1   3

4. e-1-le-1-phant
   <u>2</u>   <u>2</u>   1

5. n<u>ei</u>-1-<u>ther</u>
   4   5

6. ap-2-p<u>ear</u>
   1   4

7. s<u>ch</u>o<u>ol</u>
     6

8. hu<u>s</u>-2-band
   1   1

9. dan-2-<u>g</u>er
   <u>1</u>   5

10. <u>through</u>
     6

Quiz 170
Lesson 654/ Page 228

1. at-2-tempt
   1   1

2. vil-2-la<u>ge</u>
   1   3

3. re-1-<u>g</u>ard
   2   5

4. ob-2-ject
   1   1

5. c<u>ou</u>n-2-tr<u>y</u>
    6   2

6. <u>whose</u>
     8

7. pro-1-d<u>uce</u>
    2   3

8. re-1-<u>s</u>ult
   2   1

9. ob-2-t<u>ai</u>n
   1   4

10. <u>guide</u>
     3

Quiz 171
Lesson 656/ Page 229

1. m<u>ou</u>n-2-t<u>ai</u>n
    6   4

2. s<u>er</u>-1-vi<u>ce</u>
   5   1

3. in-2-cr<u>ea</u>se
   1   4

4. al-2-w<u>ay</u><u>s</u>
   8   4

5. va-1-ri-3-<u>ous</u>
   <u>2</u>   <u>2</u>   6

6. fl<u>ow</u>-3-<u>er</u>
    6   5

7. re-1-mo<u>ve</u>
   2   8

8. win-2-d<u>ow</u>
   1   4

9. la-b<u>or</u>
   2   5

10. <u>whe</u>-1-<u>ther</u>
   <u>2</u>   5

Quiz 172
Lesson 658/ Page 230

1. con-2-fi-1-den<u>ce</u>
   1   <u>2</u>   1

2. in-2-fl<u>u</u>-3-en<u>ce</u>
   1   2   1

3. rep-2-re-1-<u>s</u>ent
   1   2   1

4. f<u>ou</u>n-2-da-1-<u>ti</u>on
   6   2   1

5. <u>au</u>-1-<u>th</u> <u>or</u>-3-i-1-t<u>y</u>
   6   5   <u>2</u>   2

6. a<u>n</u>-2-ger
   1   5

7. di-1-rect-2-ly
   2   1˘˘   2

8. ac-2-tu-3-al
   1   2   8

9. vic-2-t<u>or</u>-3-<u>y</u>
   1   5   2

10. <u>au</u>-1-<u>th</u> <u>or</u>
   6   5

Quiz 173
Lesson 660/ Page 231

1. com-2-mu-1-ni-1-t<u>y</u>
   1   2   <u>2</u>   2

2. e-1-le-1-ment
   <u>2</u>   <u>2</u>   1

3. n<u>u</u>-1-mer-3-<u>ous</u>
   2   5   6

4. an-2-<u>c</u>ient
   <u>1</u>   1

5. li-1-b<u>er</u>-1-t<u>y</u>
   <u>2</u>   5   2

6. suf-2-fi-1-<u>c</u>ient
   1   <u>2</u>   1

7. sec-2-<u>ti</u>on
   1   1

8. pos-2-<u>s</u>ess
   <u>1</u>~   1

9. s<u>ai</u>-1-l<u>or</u>
   4   5

10. po-1-<u>si</u>-1-<u>ti</u>on
    2   <u>2</u>   1

Quiz 174
Lesson 662/ Page 232

1. splen-2-did
    1   1

2. pi-1-t<u>y</u>
    2   2

3. at-2-ti-1-t<u>ude</u>
   1   <u>2</u>   3

4. <u>wrong</u>
    1

5. mar-1-r<u>ied</u>
    1   6

6. p<u>or</u>-1-<u>ti</u>on
    5   1

7. fan-2-<u>c</u> y
    1   2

8. ad-2-ven-2-t<u>ure</u>
   1   1   3

9. fac-2-t<u>or</u>-3-<u>y</u>
   1   5   2

10. p<u>er</u>-1-so-1-nal
   5   2   8

Quiz 175
Lesson 664/ Page 233

1. pro-1-p<u>er</u>-1-t<u>y</u>
   <u>2</u>   5   2

2. ex-1-a-1-mine
   1   <u>2</u>   <u>3</u>

3. hu<u>n</u>-2-gr<u>y</u>
   1   2

4. im-2-pos-2-si-1-b<u>le</u>
   1   1   <u>2</u>   7

5. <u>through</u>-3-<u>out</u>
    6   6

6. con-2-cl<u>ude</u>
   1   3

7. fr<u>ee</u>-1-dom
   4   1

8. re-1-l<u>ief</u>
   2   6

9. ac-2-ti<u>ve</u>
      1   1

10. ter-2-ri-1-b<u>le</u>
      1   <u>2</u>   7

Quiz 176
Lesson 666/ Page 234

1. ki<u>ng</u>-2-dom
     1   1

2. <u>c</u>i-1-ti-1-zen
     <u>2</u> <u>2</u> 1

3. li-3-on
     2 1

4. si-1-tu-3-a-1-<u>ti</u>on
     <u>2</u> 2 2 1

5. scat-2-ter
     1   5

6. hos-2-pi-1-tal
     1   <u>2</u> 8

7. <u>sci</u>-3-en<u>ce</u>
     2   1

8. po-1-pu-1-la-1-<u>ti</u>on
     <u>2</u> 2 <u>2</u> 1

9. co-1-py
     <u>2</u> 2

10. val-<u>1</u>-u-3-a-1-b<u>le</u>
     1 2 2 7

Quiz 177
Lesson 668/ Page 235

1. <u>ea</u>-1-<u>s</u>i-1-ly
     4 <u>2</u> 2

2. go-1-v<u>er</u>-1-n<u>or</u>
     <u>2</u> 5 5

3. <u>p</u>er-1-f<u>or</u>m
     5   5

4. c<u>ou</u>-1-<u>s</u>in
     6 1

5. <u>threa</u>-1-ten
      6 1

6. as-2-s<u>ume</u>
     1   3

7. be-1-ne-1-fit
     <u>2</u> <u>2</u> 1

8. tri-3-al
     2 8

9. tra-1-ve-1-l<u>er</u>
     <u>2</u> <u>2</u> 5

10. dif-2-fi-1-cult
     1 <u>2</u> 1

Quiz 178
Lesson 670/ Page 236

1. si-1-mi-1-l<u>ar</u>
     <u>2</u> <u>2</u> 5

2. e-1-vi-1-den<u>ce</u>
     <u>2</u> <u>2</u> 1

3. de-1-mo-1-cra-1-tic
     <u>2</u> <u>2</u> ⌣<u>2</u> 1

4. de-1-fen<u>se</u>
     2 <u>3</u>

5. o-1-<u>ther</u>-1-wi<u>se</u>
     <u>2</u> 5 3

6. pre-1-<u>cious</u>
     <u>2</u>   6

7. im-2-me-1-di-3-a<u>te</u>
     1   2   <u>2</u> <u>3</u>

8. some-1-<u>where</u>
     <u>3</u>   <u>3</u>

9. c<u>our</u>-3-a<u>ge</u>
     5   3

10. <u>the</u>-3-<u>or</u>-3-y
     2   5   2

Quiz 179
Lesson 672/ Page 237

1. ac-2-com-2-pli<u>sh</u>
     1   1   1

2. s<u>ou</u>-1-<u>thern</u>
     6   5

3. con-2-ven-2-<u>ti</u>on
     1   1   1

4. ba-1-lan<u>ce</u>
     <u>2</u> 1

5. <u>or</u>-3-i-1-<u>g</u>i-1-nal
     5 <u>2</u> <u>2</u> 8

6. prin-2-<u>c</u>i-1-p<u>le</u>
     1   <u>2</u>   7

7. re-1-cog-2-ni<u>ze</u>
     <u>2</u>   1   3

8. a-1-v<u>er</u>-3-age
     <u>2</u> 5 3

9. po-3-et
     2 1

10. jus-2-ti-1-fy
     1   <u>2</u> 2

Quiz 180
Lesson 674/ Page 238

1. tr<u>ea</u>-1-ty
     4   2

2. ex-2-<u>change</u>
     1   3

3. jus-2-ti<u>ce</u>
     1   1

4. ter-2-ri-1-t<u>or</u>-3-y
     1 <u>2</u> 5 2

5. <u>or</u>-3-an<u>ge</u>
     5   1

6. no-1-bo-1-dy
     2   2   2

7. <u>ar</u>-1-tist
     5   1

8. <u>quan</u>-2-ti-1-ty
      8   <u>2</u> 2

9. gl<u>or</u>-3-y
      5 2

10. set-2-t<u>le</u>-1-ment
     1   7   1

Quiz 181
Lesson 676/ Page 239

1. un-2-<u>kn</u> <u>own</u>
     1   4

2. mi-1-nis-2-t<u>er</u>
     <u>2</u> 1   5

3. di-1-<u>sease</u>
     <u>2</u>   4

4. <u>sha</u>-1-d<u>ow</u>
      <u>2</u> 4

5. <u>cir</u>-1-cum-2-stan<u>ce</u>
     5   1   1

6. pr<u>ay</u>-3-<u>er</u>
      4   5

7. pre-1-<u>ser</u> ve
     2   5

8. op-2-po-1-site
     1   2   <u>3</u>

9. w<u>or</u>-1-<u>sh</u>ip
     5   1

10. ly-3-ing
     2 1

Quiz 182
Lesson 678/ Page 240

1. u-1-ni-1-v<u>er</u>-1-si-1-ty
     2 <u>2</u> 5 <u>2</u> 2

2. f<u>or</u>-3-e-1-v<u>er</u>
     5   <u>2</u> 5

3. br<u>ea</u>k-2-fast
      6   1

4. di-1-vi-1-<u>si</u>on
   <u>2</u>   <u>2</u>   1

5. r<u>u</u>-3-in
   2   1   ·

6. **g**i-3-ant
   2   1

7. ap-2-p<u>oi</u>nt
   1   6

8. a-1-n<u>y</u>-1-w<u>ay</u>
   <u>2</u>   <u>2</u>   4

9. ac-2-ti-1-vi-1-t<u>y</u>
   1   <u>2</u>   <u>2</u>   2

10. op-2-p<u>or</u>-1-t<u>u</u>-1-ni-1-t<u>y</u>
   1   5   2   <u>2</u>   2

Quiz 183
Lesson 680/ Page 241

1. ap-2-ply
   1   2

2. won-2-d<u>er</u>-1-ful
   1   5   8

3. <u>ch</u>ick-1-en
   1   1

4. stran-2-**g**er
   <u>1</u>   5

5. ne-1-v<u>er</u>-1-<u>the</u>-1-less
   <u>2</u>   5   2   1

6. pas-2-sen-2-**g**er
   1   1   5

7. in-2-t<u>er</u>-3-es-2-tin<u>g</u>
   1   5   1   1

8. in-2-tro-1-du<u>ce</u>
   1   2   3

9. se-1-p<u>ar</u>-3-at<u>e</u>
   <u>2</u>   5   3

10. m<u>u</u>r-1-m<u>u</u>r
   5   5

Quiz 184
Lesson 682/ Page 242

1. pa-1-<u>ti</u>ent
   2   1

2. h<u>ar</u>d-2-l<u>y</u>
   5   2

3. ran<u>ge</u>
   3

4. con-2-si-1-d<u>er</u>-3-a-1-b<u>le</u>
   1   <u>2</u>   5   2   7

5. w<u>or</u>-1-ry
   5   2

6. <u>wr</u>it-2-ten
   1   1

7. mer<u>e</u>-1-l<u>y</u>
   3   2

8. <u>au</u>-1-to-1-mo-1-bil<u>e</u>
   6   2   2   <u>3</u>

9. ap-2-p<u>ea</u>l
   1   4

10. h<u>ar</u>-1-b<u>or</u>
   5   5

Quiz 185
Lesson 684/ Page 243

1. dis-2-co-1-v<u>er</u>-3-<u>y</u>
   1   <u>2</u>   5   2

2. oc-2-ca-1-<u>si</u>on
   1   2   1

3. pro-1-gress
   <u>2</u> ˘1

4. s<u>ur</u>-1-r<u>ound</u>
   5   6

5. hap-2-pi-1-ness
   1   <u>2</u>   1

6. oc-2-cu-1-py
   1   2   2

7. ap-2-p<u>ea</u>-1-ran<u>ce</u>
   1   4   1

8. en-2-**g**in<u>e</u>
   1   <u>3</u>

9. <u>c</u>en-2-tral
   1   8

10. com-2-mis-2-<u>si</u>on
   1   1   1

Quiz 186
Lesson 686/ Page 244

1. sub-2-stan<u>ce</u>
   1   1

2. com-2-mer<u>ce</u>
   1   5

3. in-2-de-1-pen-2-dent
   1   2   1   1

4. s<u>u</u>-1-pe-1-ri-3-<u>or</u>
   2   2   <u>2</u>   5

5. a-1-v<u>oi</u>d
   2   6

6. con-2-v<u>er</u>-1-sa-1-<u>ti</u>on
   1   5   2   1

7. f<u>or</u>-1-got-2-ten
   5   1   1

Quiz 187
Lesson 688/ Page 245

1. vol-<u>1</u>-ume
   1   3

2. con-2-<u>c</u>ern
   1   5

3. de-1-t<u>er</u>-1-mine
   2   5   <u>3</u>

4. ex-2-pe-1-ri-1-ment
   1   <u>2</u>   <u>2</u>   1

5. cr<u>ea</u>-1-tur<u>e</u>
   4   3

6. m<u>ea</u>-1-nin<u>g</u>
   4   1

7. re-1-<u>ser</u>ve
   2   5

8. sel-2-dom
   1   1

9. mo-1-t<u>or</u>
   2   5

10. di-3-a-1-mond
   2   2   1

Quiz 188
Lesson 690/ Page 246

1. a-1-ban-2-don
   2   1

2. fe-1-d<u>er</u>-3-al
   <u>2</u>   5   8

3. ex-2-<u>c</u>ep-2-<u>ti</u>on
   1   1   1

4. e-1-ner-1-**g**y
   <u>2</u>   5   2

5. h<u>ea</u>-1-vi-1-l<u>y</u>
   6   <u>2</u>   2

6. con-2-demn
   1   1 ~

7. ho-1-n<u>or</u>-3-a-1-b<u>le</u>
  ~<u>2</u>   5   2   7

8. re-1-<u>s</u>olve
   2   1

9. a-1-bi-1-li-1-t<u>y</u>
   2   2   <u>2</u>   2

Answer Key for Spelling Quizzes

10. ha<u>r</u>-1-vest
     5   1

Quiz 189
Lesson 692/ Page 247

1. un-<u>1</u>-u-1-<u>s</u>u-3-al
    1   2   2   8

2. pro-1-tec-2-<u>ti</u>on
     2   1   1

3. con-2-cl<u>u</u>-1-<u>si</u>on
    1   2   1

4. con-2-tri-1-but<u>e</u>
    1   <u>2</u>   3

5. in-2-no-1-<u>c</u>ent
    1   2   1

6. ter-2-r<u>or</u>
    1   5

7. pa-1-<u>ti</u>enc<u>e</u>
    2   1

8. re-1-pub-2-lic
    2   1   1

9. cri-1-mi-1-nal
    <u>2</u>   <u>2</u>   8

10. <u>g</u>ent-2-l<u>y</u>
    1ˇ   2

Quiz 190
Lesson 694/ Page 248

1. cus-2-to-1-m<u>er</u>
    1   2   5

2. ob-2-s<u>er</u>-1-va-1-<u>ti</u>on
    1   5   2   1

3. con-2-se-1-<u>quence</u>
    1   2   1

4. en-2-dur<u>e</u>
    1   3

5. es-2-ti-1-mat<u>e</u>
    1   <u>2</u>   3

6. as-2-sist
    1   1

7. o-1-p<u>er</u>-3-a
    <u>2</u>   5   8

8. <u>g</u>e-1-n<u>er</u>-3-<u>ous</u>
    <u>2</u>   5   6

9. de-1-<u>ser</u> v<u>e</u>
    2   5

10. un-2-hap-2-p<u>y</u>
    1   1   2

Quiz 191
Lesson 696/ Page 249

1. fr<u>igh</u>-1-ten
    4   1

2. sun-2-l<u>igh</u>t
    1   4

3. sym-2-pa-1-<u>thy</u>
    1   <u>2</u>   2

4. cap-2-tur<u>e</u>
    1   3

5. re-1-n<u>ew</u>
    2   6

6. fi-1-nan-2-<u>c</u>ial
    2   1   8

7. em-2-p<u>er</u>-3-<u>or</u>
    1   5   5

8. pla-1-net
    <u>2</u>   1

9. as-2-sem-2-bl<u>y</u>
    1   1   2

10. <u>sh</u>ield
    6

Quiz 192
Lesson 698/ Page 250

1. re-1-m<u>ar</u>-1-ka-1-b<u>le</u>
    2   5   2   7

2. col-2-l<u>ar</u>
    1   5

3. re-1-me-1-d<u>y</u>
    <u>2</u>   <u>2</u>   2

4. ca-1-pa-1-b<u>le</u>
    2   2   7

5. a-1-<u>shamed</u>
    2   3

6. es-2-sen-2-<u>ti</u>al
    1   1   8

7. com-2-mit
    1   1

8. <u>ph</u>o-1-to-1-graph
    2   2   ˇ1

9. fu-1-n<u>er</u>-3-al
    2   5   8

10. <u>or</u>-1-ga-1-niz<u>e</u>
    5   <u>2</u>   3

Quiz 193
Lesson 700/ Page 251

1. com-2-man-2-d<u>er</u>
    1   1   5

2. <u>ph</u>y-1-<u>s</u>i-1-cal
    <u>2</u>   <u>2</u>   8

3. de-1-<u>c</u>i-1-<u>si</u>on
    2   2   1

4. im-2-pro<u>ve</u>-2-ment
    1   8   1

5. be-1-gin-2-ni<u>ng</u>
    2   1   1

6. func-2-<u>ti</u>on
    1ˇ   1

7. mo-1-nu-1-ment
    <u>2</u>   2   1

8. far<u>e</u>-1-well
    3   1

9. dig-2-ni-1-t<u>y</u>
    1   <u>2</u>   2

10. e-1-le-1-ven
    2   <u>2</u>   1

Quiz 194
Lesson 702/ Page 252

1. de-1-<u>c</u>ei v<u>e</u>
    2   4

2. en-2-c<u>our</u>-3-age
    1   5   1

3. <u>ph</u>i-1-lo-1-so-1-<u>phy</u>
    <u>2</u>   <u>2</u>   <u>2</u>   2

4. per-1-ma-1-nent
    5   2   1

5. pro-1-fes-2-<u>si</u>on-<u>1</u>-al
    2   1   1   8

6. em-2-brac<u>e</u>
    1   3

7. mix-2-tur<u>e</u>
    1   3

8. tri-3-um<u>ph</u>
    2   1

9. <u>grie</u> v<u>e</u>
    6

10. im-2-pres-2-<u>si</u>on
    1   1   1

Quiz 195
Lesson 704/ Page 253

1. <u>au</u>-1-di-3-enc<u>e</u>
    6   <u>2</u>   1

2. go-1-v<u>er</u>n
    <u>2</u>   5

3. pri-1-vi-1-leg<u>e</u>
    <u>2</u>   <u>2</u>   1

Answer Key for Spelling Quizzes

4. col-2-lec-2-<u>ti</u>on
    1   1   1

5. mis-2-tress
    1   1

6. in-2-vi-1-ta-1-<u>ti</u>on
    1   <u>2</u>   2   1

7. f<u>oo</u>-1-li<u>sh</u>
    6   1

8. se-1-ven-2-t<u>y</u>
   <u>2</u>   1   2

9. in-2-tro-1-duc-2-<u>ti</u>on
    1   2   1   1

10. con-2-ve-1-ni-3-ent
    1   2   <u>2</u>   1

Quiz 196
Lesson 706/ Page 254

1. e-1-<u>q</u>uip-2-ment
   2   1   1

2. di-1-rec-2-t<u>or</u>
   2   1   5

3. dis-2-t<u>ur</u>b
   1   5

4. fr<u>eigh</u>t
   6

5. in-2-su-1-ran<u>c</u>e
   1   2   1

6. prin-2-<u>c</u>ess
   1   1

7. ar-2-ran<u>ge</u>-1-ment
   1   3   1

8. ex-2-<u>c</u>ite
   1   3

9. se-1-cu-1-ri-1-t<u>y</u>
  <u>2</u>   2   2 <u>2</u>

10. mir-2-r<u>or</u>
   1   5

Quiz 197
Lesson 708/ Page 255

1. il-2-lu-1-strat<u>e</u>
  1 <u>2</u> 3

2. oc-2-cu-1-pa-1-<u>ti</u>on
  1   2   2   1

3. de-1-po-1-<u>s</u>it
  2 <u>2</u> 1

4. n<u>er</u>-1-v<u>ous</u>
   5   6

5. <u>j</u>e<u>w</u>-3-el
   6   1

6. <u>ar</u>-1-gu-1-ment
   5   2   1

7. fac-2-t<u>or</u>
   1   5

8. ac-2-<u>q</u>uire
   1   3

9. da-1-ma<u>ge</u>
  <u>2</u>   3

10. pre-1-vi-3-<u>ous</u>
   2 <u>2</u> 6

Quiz 198
Lesson 710/ Page 256

1. f<u>oun</u>-2-t<u>ai</u>n
   6   4

2. sad-2-d<u>le</u>
   1   7

3. sug-2-<u>g</u>es-2-<u>ti</u>on
   1   1   1

4. <u>ar</u>-1-g<u>ue</u>
   5   4

5. cr<u>u</u>-3-el
   2   1

6. o-1-pe-1-ni<u>ng</u>
   2 <u>2</u> 1

7. fi<u>erc</u>e
   6

8. ab-2-so-1-l<u>u</u>te
   1   2   3

9. ex-2-tra
   1   8

10. pi-1-<u>g</u>eon
  <u>2</u>   1

Quiz 199
Lesson 712/ Page 257

1. bo-1-<u>ther</u>
  <u>2</u>   5

2. <u>or</u>-1-na-1-ment
  5   2   1

3. re-1-mind
  2 <u>1</u>

4. m<u>ar</u>-1-ve-1-l<u>ous</u>
   5 <u>2</u> 6

5. f<u>or</u>-1-m<u>er</u>-1-ly
   5   5   2

6. dis-2-put<u>e</u>
   1   3

7. mes-2-sen-2-<u>g</u>er
   1   1   5

8. re-1-la-1-ti<u>ve</u>
  <u>2</u> <u>2</u> 1

9. ca-1-pa-1-<u>c</u>i-1-ty
  <u>2</u> <u>2</u> 2 2

10. cle-1-v<u>er</u>
   <u>2</u>   5

Quiz 200
Lesson 714/ Page 258

1. p<u>ur</u>-1-s<u>ue</u>
   5   4

2. g<u>oo</u>d-2-ness
   6   1

3. fol-2-<u>low</u>-3-<u>er</u>
   1   4   5

4. hu<u>n</u>-2-<u>ger</u>
   1   5

5. po-1-li-1-tics
   <u>2</u> <u>2</u> 1

6. ap-2-pli-1-ca-1-<u>ti</u>on
   1   <u>2</u>   2   1

7. p<u>ur</u>-1-p<u>le</u>
   5   7

8. <u>ch</u>im-2-ney
   1   2

9. con-2-s<u>ciou</u>s
   1 ~ 6

10. en-2-c<u>oun</u>-2-t<u>er</u>
   1   6   5

Quiz 201
Lesson 716/ Page 259

1 con-2-nec-2-<u>ti</u>on
    1   1   1

2. a-1-<u>c</u>id
   2   1

3. <u>eigh</u>-1-t<u>ee</u>n
   6   4

4. a-1-p<u>ar</u>t-2-ment
   2   5   1

5. <u>sc</u>i-3-en-2-ti-1-fic
   2 1 <u>2</u> 1

6. gl<u>or</u>-3-i-3-<u>ous</u>
   5 <u>2</u> 6

7. con-2-nec-2-<u>ti</u>on
   1   1   1

8. reck-2-less
   1   1

9. fi-1-nan<u>c</u>e
   2   1

10. ab-2-sen<u>ce</u>
    1   1

Quiz 202
Lesson 718/ Page 260

1. so-1-l<u>u</u>-1-<u>ti</u>on
    2   2   1
2. he-1-<u>s</u>i-1-tat<u>e</u>
    <u>2</u>   <u>2</u>   3
3. me-1-di-1-cal
    <u>2</u>   <u>2</u>   8
4. lon<u>e</u>-1-l<u>y</u>
    3   2
5. mag-2-ni-1-fi-1-<u>c</u>ent
    1   <u>2</u>   <u>2</u>   1
6. an-2-<u>g</u>el
    <u>1</u>   1
7. in-2-t<u>er</u>-1-val
    1   5   8
8. puz-2-z<u>le</u>
    1   7
9. in-2-sti-1-t<u>u</u>-1-<u>ti</u>on
    1   <u>2</u>   2   1
10. pos-2-si-1-bi-1-li-1-ty
    1   <u>2</u>   <u>2</u>   <u>2</u>   2

Quiz 203
Lesson 720/ Page 261

1. a-1-gr<u>ee</u>-1-ment
    2   4   1
2. mu-1-<u>s</u>e-3-um
    2   2   1
3. en-2-gi-1-n<u>ee</u>r
    1   <u>2</u>   4
4. tr<u>u</u>-1-l<u>y</u>
   2 2
5. m<u>ea</u>n-2-<u>while</u>
    4   3
6. n<u>ee</u>-1-d<u>le</u>
    4   7
7. w<u>ea</u>-1-r<u>y</u>
    4   2
8. pu-1-ni<u>sh</u>-2-ment
    <u>2</u>   1   1
9. in-2-ven-2-<u>ti</u>on
    1   1   1
10. <u>law</u>-1-y<u>er</u>
    4   5

Sequence of Lessons to Introduce to Students Beyond Fifth Grade

Nonsense words (words that have no meaning) are essential to use in teaching phonics to older students and adults. Older students may know thousands of words by sight. Often the only way to insist that these students rely upon their knowledge of phonics to sound out words is to present them with words they have never seen before. The same principle is equally true when dictating words for spelling. Some students have memorized the spelling of hundreds or even thousands of words regardless of whether or not they understand the relationship of letters within a word and the sounds those letters represent. When students are asked to read or spell a nonsense word, they must rely exclusively upon their knowledge of phonics; there is no other way to be able to read or spell a nonsense word.

Most pages of Sections One and Two are divided into two parts: real words and nonsense words. Many students have memorized hundreds or even thousands of words and yet have little or no knowledge of phonics. No purpose is served by having them call out or spell words they have long ago memorized; in fact, **older students who are asked to read and spell one-syllable words they already know will often prematurely conclude that this phonics program is too easy for them. For this reason it is strongly recommended that teachers use only the nonsense words from each lesson in Sections One and Two of the book to teach students in sixth grade through high school and also for adults no longer in school.**

The two exceptions to this recommendation for students in sixth grade and beyond would be in the instance where students in these grades read and spell less than eighty percent of the real words from any given lesson correctly or in the instance where students are learning English as a second language.

Sequence of Lessons to Follow for Third Grade to Fifth Grade
Students in third grade through fifth grade should proceed through all lessons in the *We All Can Read* **program in exact numerical order. No lessons are to be skipped.**

Sequence of Lessons to Follow for Sixth Grade and Up
Students in sixth grade and above should work in only the following lessons and in this exact order:
Print Lessons 1, 2, 3, 4, 5, 8, 9, 12, 13, 14, 15, 16, 17, 20, 21, 24, 25, 28, 30, 31, 32, 33, 34, 35, 38, 39, 42, 43, 46, 48, 49, 50, 51, 52, 53, 56, 57, 60, 61, 64, 66, 67, 68, 69, 70, 71, 74, 75, 78, 79, 82, 83, 86, 88, 89, 92, 93, 101, 102, 103, 106, 107, 110, 111, 114, 121, 122, 123, 126, 127, 130, 131, 134, 140, 141, 144, 145, 148, 149, 152, 158, 159, 160, 163, 164, 167, 168, 171, 173, 174, 182, 183, 184, 185, 186, 189, 190, 193, 194, 197, 212, 213, 216, 217, 220, 221, 224, 225, 228, 229, 230, 231, 234, 240, 241, 244, 245, 248, 249, 252, 254, 255, 256, 259, 260, 263, 264, 267, 269, 270, 271, 272, 273, 274, 275, 276, 277, 280, 281, 284, 285, 288, 290, 291, 292, 295, 296, 299, 300, 303, 305, 306, 307, 308, 309, 310, 311, 314, 315, 318, 319, 322, 324, 325, 326, 329, 330, 333, 334, 337, 338, 341, 343, 344, 345, 346, 347, 348, 349, 350, 351, 352, 355, 356, 359, 360, 363, 365, 366, 367, 368, 369.

Students of all ages work in all of the remaining lessons in the book after Lesson 369; it is critical that students follow the numerical order of lessons as they proceed through this program. Do not skip lessons, and do not jump ahead in lessons. **Follow the exact numerical sequence indicated in this list.**

We All Can Read: Video Edition Table of Contents *Correlation Guide between Video Lessons and Pages in Blue Book*	Page Guide	Begin Time	End Time
Video One			
Lesson 1/Quiz 1 The Consonant Letters	1-2	0:33	28:32
Lesson 2/Quiz 2 Short *a* followed by a consonant	3	28:33	39:44
Lesson 3/Quiz 3 Nonsense words with short *a*	4	39:45	52:32
Lesson 4/Quiz 4 Real words with short *a*	4	52:33	58:07
Lesson 4/Quiz 4 Real words with short *a* (continues)	4	58:15	1:04:35
Lesson 5/Quiz 5 Short *e* followed by a consonant	5	1:04:36	1:11:47
Lesson 6/Quiz 6 Short *a* and *e* followed by a consonant	5	1:11:48	1:21:29
Lesson 7/Quiz 7 Nonsense words with short *e*	6	1:21:30	1:31:19
Lesson 8/Quiz 8 Real words with short *e*	6	1:31:20	1:39:40
Lesson 9/Quiz 9 Nonsense word with short *a* and *e*	7-9	1:39:41	1:51:52
Video Two			
Lesson 10/Quiz 10 Real words with short *a* and *e*	7-9	0:36	11:07
Oral Reading Exercise with short *a* / *e*	7-9	11:08	25:28
Nonsense sentence dictation exercise short *a* / *e*	8	25:29	30:52
Real sentence dictation exercise short *a*/*e*	8	30:53	35:52
Lesson 11/Quiz 11 Short *o* followed by a consonant	10	35:53	42:48
Lesson 12/Quiz 12 Review of short *a*, *e*, and *o*	10	42:49	50:08
Lesson 13/Quiz 13 Nonsense words with short *o*	11	50:09	55:27
Lesson 13/Quiz 13 Nonsense words with short *o* (continues)	11	55:30	1:01:17
Lesson 14/Quiz 14 Real words with short *o*	11	1:01:18	1:11:23
Lesson 15/Quiz 15 Nonsense words with short *a*, *e*, and *o*	12-14	1:11:24	1:29:10
Lesson 16/Quiz 16 Real words containing *a*, *e*, and *o*	12-14	1:29:11	1:42:57
Lesson 17/Quiz 17 Short *u* followed by a consonant	15	1:42:58	1:49:36
Video Three			
Lesson 18/Quiz 18 Review of short *a*, *e*, *o*, and *u*	15	0:28	8:32
Lesson 19/Quiz 19 Nonsense words with short *u*	16	8:33	20:14
Lesson 20/Quiz 20 Real words with short *u*	16	20:15	29:49
Lesson 21/Quiz 21 Nonsense words with short *a*, *e*, *o*, *u*	17-19	29:50	48:50
Lesson 22/Quiz 22 Real words with *a*, *e*, *o*, and *u*	17-19	48:51	57:52
Lesson 22/Quiz 22 Real words with *a*, *e*, *o*, and *u* (continues)	17-19	58:01	1:04:45
Lesson 23/Quiz 23 Short *i* followed by a consonant	20	1:04:46	1:12:08
Lesson 24/Quiz 24 Review of short *a*, *e*, *i*, *o*, and *u*	20	1:12:09	1:20:01
Lesson 25/Quiz 25 Nonsense words with short *i*	21	1:20:02	1:31:05
Lesson 26/Quiz 26 Real words with short *i*	21	1:31:06	1:41:22
Lesson 27/Quiz 27 Nonsense words with short *a*, *e*, *i*, *o*, *u*	22-25	1:41:23	1:54:27
Video Four			
Lesson 28/Quiz 28 Nonsense sentences with vowels *a*, *e*, *i* *o*, *u*	24	0:27	7:51
Lesson 29/Quiz 29 Real words with vowels *a*, *e*, *i*, *o*, and *u*	22-25	7:52	19:36
Lesson 30/Quiz 30 Real Sentences with vowels *a*, *e*, *i*, *o*, and *u*	24	19:37	25:59
Lesson 31/Quiz 31 Nonsense words ending in *ff*, *ll*, *ss*	26	26:00	37:22
Lesson 32/Quiz 32 Real words ending in *ff*, *ll*, *ss*	26	37:23	45:12

We All Can Read: Video Edition Table of Contents Correlation Guide between Video Lessons and Pages in Blue Book		Page Guide	Begin Time	End Time
Lesson 33/Quiz 33	Nonsense words beginning with *c* or *k*	27	45:13	59:58
Lesson 34/Quiz 34	Real words beginning with *c* or *k*	27	1:00:09	1:08:37
Lesson 35/Quiz 35	Nonsense words with beginning consonant blends	30-34	1:08:38	1:34:22
Lesson 36/Quiz 36	Real words with beginning consonant blends	30-35	1:34:23	1:52:47
Lesson 37/Quiz 37	Ending consonant blends	36-41	1:52:48	1:55:52
Video Five				
Lesson 37/Quiz 37	Ending consonant blends (continues)	36-41	0:28	6:50
Lesson 38/Quiz 38	Nonsense words with ending consonant blends	36-40	6:51	25:16
Lesson 39/Quiz 39	Real words with ending consonant blends	36-41	25:17	44:27
Lesson 40/Quiz 40	Nonsense words with beginning and ending blends	42-45	44:28	59:49
Lesson 40/Quiz 40	Nonsense words with beginning and ending blends (continues)	42-45	1:01:01	1:08:13
Lesson 41/Quiz 41	Real words with beginning and ending blends	42-46	1:08:14	1:26:09
Lesson 42/Quiz 42	Nonsense words and consonant teams	47-51	1:26:10	1:57:58
Video Six				
Lesson 42/Quiz 42	Nonsense words and consonant teams (continues)	47-51	0:28	14:52
Lesson 43/Quiz 43	Real words with consonant teams	47-51	14:53	37:33
Lesson 44/Quiz 44	The second sound for the letter *n* in nonsense words	52	37:34	51:11
Lesson 45/Quiz 45	The second sound for the letter *n* in real words	52	51:12	57:19
Lesson 45/Quiz 45	The second sound for the letter *n* in real words (continues)	52	57:24	1:01:52
Lesson 46/Quiz 46	Nonsense words with consonant teams and blends	54-58	1:01:53	1:21:08
Lesson 47/Quiz 47	Real words with consonant teams and blends	54-59	1:21:09	1:41:19
Lesson 48/Quiz 48	Syllable patterns one and two	62-63	1:41:20	1:55:43
Video Seven				
Lesson 48/Quiz 48	Syllable patterns one and two (continues)	62-63	0:30	19:47
Lesson 49/Quiz 49	Real words with syllable patterns one and two	62-63	19:48	41:11
Lesson 50/Quiz 50	Nonsense words with syllable patterns one and three	64-73	41:12	58:45

We All Can Read: Video Edition Table of Contents Correlation Guide between Video Lessons and Pages in Blue Book		Page Guide	Begin Time	End Time
Lesson 50/Quiz 50	Nonsense words with syllable patterns one and three (continues)	64-73	58:58	1:20:09
Lesson 51/Quiz 51	Marking nonsense words/syllable patterns one, two, and three	70-72	1:20:10	1:34:15
Lesson 52/Quiz 52	Real words with syllable patterns one and three	64-73	1:34:16	1:54:51
Video Eight				
Lesson 52/Quiz 52	Real words with syllable patterns one and three (continues)	64-73	0:31	9:28
Lesson 53/Quiz 53	Marking real words syllable patterns one, two, and three	70-72	9:29	20:38
Lesson 54/Quiz 54	The long sounds of the vowel *u*	66	20:39	45:49
Lesson 55/Quiz 55	Dictation of nonsense words / syllable patterns one, two, and three	64-72	45:50	58:06
Lesson 56/Quiz 56	Dictation of real words / syllable patterns one, two, and three	64-72	58:30	1:15:13
Lesson 57/Quiz 57	Syllable pattern four	74-80	1:15:14	1:52:40
Lesson 58/Quiz 58	Review of syllable patterns one, two, three, and four	81-84	1:52:41	1:57:25
Video Nine				
Lesson 58/Quiz 58	Review of syllable patterns one, two, three, and four (continues)	81-84	0:27	18:52
Lesson 59/Quiz 59	Marking words / syllable patterns one, two, three and four	81-83	18:53	34:53
Lesson 60/Quiz 60	Syllable pattern five	85-90	34:54	58:28
Lesson 60/Quiz 60	Syllable pattern five (continues)	85-90	58:34	1:06:13
Lesson 61/Quiz 61	Review of syllable patterns one, two, three, four, and five	91-94	1:06:14	1:40:28
Lesson 62/Quiz 62	Marking words / syllable patterns one, two, three, four, and five	91-94	1:40:29	1:56
Video Ten				
Lesson 63/Quiz 63	Syllable pattern six	95-101	0:32	42:36
Lesson 64/Quiz 64	Review of syllable patterns one, two, three, four, five, and six	102-105	42:37	58:04
Lesson 64/Quiz 64	Review of syllable patterns one, two, three, four, five, and six (continues)	102-105	58:12	1:00:28
Lesson 65/Quiz 65	Marking words / syllable patterns one, two, three, four, five, and six	102-104	1:00:29	1:15:42
Lesson 66 (There is no Quiz 66.)	Oral reading exercise / syllable patterns one, two, three, four, five, and six	102-105	1:15:43	1:56:38
Video Eleven				
Lesson 67/Quiz 67	Comprehensive Review	106-107	0:32	19:38
Lesson 68/Quiz 68	Syllable rule one	109	19:39	52:17
Lesson 69	Syllable rule one / marking words	109	52:18	59:27
Lesson 69	Syllable rule one / marking words (continues)	109	59:31	1:19:57

We All Can Read: Video Edition Table of Contents *Correlation Guide between Video Lessons and Pages in Blue Book*	Page Guide	Begin Time	End Time
Lesson 70/Quiz 69 Syllable rule two	110	1:19:58	1:45:02
Lesson 71 Marking syllable rule two words	110	1:45:03	1:58
Video Twelve			
Lesson 71 Marking syllable rule two words (continues)	110	0:29	4:28
Lesson 72/Quiz 70 Review of syllable rules one and two	111-113	4:29	23:10
Lesson 73/Quiz 71 Marking words / syllables rules one and two	111-113	23:11	50:08
Lesson 74 Oral reading /syllable rules one and two	111-113	50:09	59:10
Lesson 74 Oral reading / syllable rules one and two (continues)	111-113	59:16	1:03:03
Lesson 75 Syllable rules one and two and consonant blends	112	1:03:04	1:15:09
Lesson 76 Marking words / syllable rules one and two and consonant blends	112	1:15:10	1:37:05
Lesson 77/Quiz 72 Syllable pattern seven	114-116	1:37:06	1:52:25
Lesson 78/Quiz 73 Marking words / syllable pattern seven	114-115	1:52:26	1:57:52
Video Thirteen			
Lesson 78/Quiz 73 Marking words / syllable pattern seven (continues)	114-115	0:33	18:24
Lesson 79 Syllable pattern seven / oral reading	114-116	18:25	22:21
Lesson 80/Quiz 74 Cumulative spelling review / two syllable words / syllable pattern four	117	22:22	33:38
Lesson 81 Cumulative marking review / two syllable words / syllable pattern four	117	33:39	48:35
Lesson 82/Quiz 75 Cumulative spelling review / two syllable words / syllable patterns five and six	118	48:36	59:25
Lesson 83 Cumulative marking review / two syllable words / syllable patterns five and six	118	59:29	1:15:16
Lesson 84/Quiz 76 Cumulative spelling review / two syllable words / syllable patterns four, five, and six	119-122	1:15:17	1:26:22
Lesson 85 Cumulative marking review / two syllable words / syllable patterns four, five, and six	119-122	1:26:23	1:41:45
Lesson 86 Syllable pattern eight	123-125	1:41:46	1:56:42
Video Fourteen			
Lesson 86 Syllable pattern eight (continues)	123-125	0:35	9:14
Lesson 87/Quiz 77 Syllable pattern eight / marking words	123-124	9:15	35:50
Lesson 88 Exceptions to syllable patterns one, two, and three / dictation	127	35:51	52:58
Lesson 89 Exceptions to syllable patterns one, two, and three/ marking words	127	52:59	59:02
Lesson 89 Exceptions to syllable patterns one, two, and three/ marking words (continues)	127	59:05	1:11:05
Lesson 90 When a vowel plus the letter *r* do not form a team / dictation	128	1:11:06	1:26:01

		Page Guide	Begin Time	End Time
We All Can Read: Video Edition Table of Contents *Correlation Guide between Video Lessons and Pages in Blue Book*				
Lesson 91	When a vowel plus the letter *r* do not form a team / marking words	128	1:26:02	1:47:01
Lesson 92/Quiz 78	The second sound of the letter *c* / dictation	132-135	1:47:02	1:58:14
Video Fifteen				
Lesson 92/Quiz 78	The second sound of the letter *c* / dictation (continues)	132-134	0:35	16:49
Lesson 93/Quiz 79	The second sound of the letter *c* / marking words	132-134	16:50	37:23
Lesson 94/Quiz 80	The second sound of the letter *g* / dictation	136-138	37:28	59:16
Lesson 95/Quiz 81	The second sound of the letter *g* / marking words	136-137	59:20	1:15:09
Lesson 96/Quiz 82	The letter *y* as a vowel / dictation	139-144	1:15:10	1:37:25
Lesson 97/Quiz 83	The letter *y* as a vowel / marking words	139-143	1:37:26	1:57:55
Video Sixteen				
Lesson 98/Quiz 84	The letter team *ed* / dictation	165	0:35	21:30
Lesson 99/Quiz 85	The letter team *ed* / marking words	165	21:31	40:59
Lesson 100/Quiz 86	Three syllable words and syllable rule three / dictation	147-150	41:00	58:39
Lesson 101	Three syllable words and syllable rule three / marking words	147-150	58:47	1:11:48
Lesson 102/Quiz 87	New consonant teams / dictation	151-156	1:11:49	1:46:49
Lesson 103/Quiz 88	New consonant teams / marking words	151-154	1:46:50	1:56:54
Video Seventeen				
Lesson 104/Quiz 89	New vowel teams / dictation	157-161	0:35	21:32
Lesson 105/Quiz 90	New vowel teams / marking words	157-160	21:33	38:01
Lesson 106/Quiz 91	New vowel teams / dictation	167-171	38:02	58:24
Lesson 107/Quiz 92	New vowel teams / marking words	167-170	58:31	1:14:08
Lesson 108/Quiz 93	New consonant teams / dictation	172-176	1:14:09	1:39:51
Lesson 109/Quiz 94	New consonant teams / marking words	172-175	1:39:52	1:57:38
Video Eighteen				
Lesson 110/Quiz 95	Four syllable words / dictation	177-179	0:35	16:38
Lesson 111/Quiz 96	Four syllable words / marking words	177-179	16:37	34:01
Lesson 112/Quiz 97	New vowel teams / dictation	180-183	34:02	59:24
Lesson 113/Quiz 98	New vowel teams / marking words	180-182	59:30	1:21:59
Lesson 114/Quiz 99	Four, five, and six syllable words / dictation	184-186	1:22	1:31:51
Lesson 115/Quiz 100	Four, five, and six syllable words / marking words	184-186	1:31:52	1:57:47
Video Nineteen				
Lesson 116/Quiz 101	Review of the eighty major letters and letter teams	195-197	0:35	58:05

We All Can Read: Video Edition Table of Contents Correlation Guide between Video Lessons and Pages in Blue Book	Page Guide	Begin Time	End Time
Intensive Spelling Program / Introduction	205-212	58:10	1:00:53
Lesson 117 Word List A / Words 1-25	214	1:00:54	1:27:37
Lesson 118/Quiz 102 Word List A / Words 26-50	214	1:27:38	1:44:07
Lesson 119 Word List A / Words 51-75	215	1:44:08	1:56:56
Video Twenty			
Lesson 120/Quiz 103 Word List A / Words 76-100	215	0:33	16:51
Lesson 121 Word List A / Words 101-125	216	16:52	29:00
Lesson 122/Quiz 104 Word List A / Words 126-150	216	29:01	44:57
Lesson 123 Word List A / Words 151-175	217	44:58	58:26
Lesson 124/Quiz 105 Word List A / Words 176-200	217	58:35	1:12:28
Lesson 125 Word List A / Words 201-225	218	1:12:29	1:24:49
Lesson 126/Quiz 106 Word List A / Words 226-250	218	1:24:50	1:37:58
Lesson 127 Word List A / Words 251-275	219	1:37:59	1:49:22
Lesson 128/Quiz 107 Word List A / Words 276-300	219	1:49:23	1:58:11
Video Twenty-One			
Lesson 128/Quiz 107 Word List A / Words 276-300 (continues)	219	0:32	7:49
Lesson 129 Word List A / Words 301-325	220	7:50	20:26
Lesson 130/Quiz 108 Word List A / Words 326-350	220	20:27	35:28
Lesson 131 Word List A / Words 351-375	221	35:29	47:56
Lesson 132/Quiz 109 Word List A / Words 376-400	221	47:57	1:00:51
Lesson 132/Quiz 109 Word List A / Words 376-400 (continues)	221	1:01:01	1:03:01
Lesson 133 Word List A / Words 401-425	222	1:03:02	1:15:21
Lesson 134/Quiz 110 Word List A / Words 426-450	222	1:15:22	1:29:16
Lesson 135 Word List A / Words 451-475	223	1:29:17	1:41:41
Lesson 136/Quiz 111 Word List A / Words 476-500	223	1:41:42	1:55:33
A Final Note		1:55:34	1:57:57

We All Can Read: Video CD Edition Table of Contents *Correlation Guide between Video CD Lessons and Pages in Blue Book*		Page Guide	Begin Time	End Time
Video CD One				
Lesson 1/Quiz 1	The Consonant Letters	1-2	0:33	28:32
Lesson 2/Quiz 2	Short *a* followed by a consonant	3	28:33	39:44
Lesson 3/Quiz 3	Nonsense words with short *a*	4	39:45	52:32
Lesson 4/Quiz 4	Real words with short *a*	4	52:33	58:07
Video CD Two				
Lesson 4/Quiz 4	Real words with short *a* (continues)	4	0:33	6:55
Lesson 5/Quiz 5	Short *e* followed by a consonant	5	6:56	14:06
Lesson 6/Quiz 6	Short *a* and *e* followed by a consonant	5	14:07	23:50
Lesson 7/Quiz 7	Nonsense words with short *e*	6	23:51	33:40
Lesson 8/Quiz 8	Real words with short *e*	6	33:41	42:02
Lesson 9/Quiz 9	Nonsense word with short *a* and *e*	7-9	42:03	54:12
Video CD Three				
Lesson 10/Quiz 10	Real words with short *a* and *e*	7-9	0:36	11:07
	Oral Reading Exercise with short *a* and *e*	7-9	11:08	25:28
	Nonsense sentence dictation exercise short *a*/*e*	8	25:29	30:52
	Real sentence dictation exercise short *a* / *e*	8	30:53	35:52
Lesson 11/Quiz 11	Short *o* followed by a consonant	10	35:53	42:48
Lesson 12/Quiz 12	Review of short *a*, *e*, and *o*	10	42:49	50:08
Lesson 13/Quiz 13	Nonsense words with short *o*	11	50:09	55:27
Video CD Four				
Lesson 13/Quiz 13	Nonsense words with short *o* (continues)	11	0:27	6:23
Lesson 14/Quiz 14	Real words with short *o*	11	6:24	16:30
Lesson 15/Quiz 15	Nonsense words with short *a*, *e*, and *o*	12-14	16:31	34:19
Lesson 16/Quiz 16	Real words containing *a*, *e*, and *o*	12-14	34:20	48:07
Lesson 17/Quiz 17	Short *u* followed by a consonant	15	48:08	54:46
Video CD Five				
Lesson 18/Quiz 18	Review of short *a*, *e*, *o*, and *u*	15	0:28	8:32
Lesson 19/Quiz 19	Nonsense words with short *u*	16	8:33	20:14
Lesson 20/Quiz 20	Real words with short *u*	16	20:15	29:49
Lesson 21/Quiz 21	Nonsense words with short *a*, *e*, *o*, and *u*	17-19	29:50	48:50
Lesson 22/Quiz 22	Real words with *a*, *e*, *o*, and *u*	17-19	48:51	57:52
Video CD Six				
Lesson 22/Quiz 22	Real words with *a*, *e*, *o*, and *u* (continues)	17-19	0:29	7:12
Lesson 23/Quiz 23	Short *i* followed by a consonant	20	7:13	14:35
Lesson 24/Quiz 24	Review of short *a*, *e*, *i*, *o*, and *u*	20	14:36	22:28
Lesson 25/Quiz 25	Nonsense words with short *i*	21	22:29	33:33
Lesson 26/Quiz 26	Real words with short *i*	21	33:34	43:50
Lesson 27/Quiz 27	Nonsense words with short *a*, *e*, *i*, *o*, and *u*	22-25	43:51	56:56
Video CD Seven				
Lesson 28/Quiz 28	Nonsense sentences with vowels *a*, *e*, *i o*, *u*	24	0:27	7:51
Lesson 29/Quiz 29	Real words with vowels *a*, *e*, *i*, *o*, and *u*	22-25	7:52	19:36
Lesson 30/Quiz 30	Real Sentences with vowels *a*, *e*, *i*, *o*, and *u*	24	19:37	25:59
Lesson 31/Quiz 31	Nonsense words ending in *ff*, *ll*, *ss*	26	26:00	37:22
Lesson 32/Quiz 32	Real words ending in *ff*, *ll*, *ss*	26	37:23	45:12

We All Can Read: Video CD Edition Table of Contents *Correlation Guide between Video CD Lessons and Pages in Blue Book*		Page Guide	Begin Time	End Time
Lesson 51/Quiz 51	Marking nonsense words/syllable patterns one, two, and three	70-72	21:51	35:56
Lesson 52/Quiz 52	Real words with syllable patterns one and three	64-73	35:57	56:34
Video CD Fifteen				
Lesson 52/Quiz 52	Real words with syllable patterns one and three (continues)	64-73	0:31	9:28
Lesson 53/Quiz 53	Marking real words syllable patterns one, two, and three	70-72	9:29	20:38
Lesson 54/Quiz 54	Real words/the long sounds of the vowel *u*	66	20:39	45:49
Lesson 55/Quiz 55	Real words/dictation of nonsense words / syllable patterns one, two, and three	64-72	45:50	58:06
Video CD Sixteen				
Lesson 56/Quiz 56	Dictation of real words / syllable patterns one, two, and three	64-72	0:35	17:19
Lesson 57/Quiz 57	Syllable pattern four	74-80	17:20	54:46
Lesson 58/Quiz 58	Review of syllable patterns one, two, three, and four	81-84	54:55	59:33
Video CD Seventeen				
Lesson 58/Quiz 58	Review of syllable patterns one, two, three, and four (continues)	81-84	0:27	18:52
Lesson 59/Quiz 59	Marking words / syllable patterns one, two, three and four	81-83	18:53	34:53
Lesson 60/Quiz 60	Syllable pattern five	85-90	34:54	58:28
Video CD Eighteen				
Lesson 60/Quiz 60	Syllable pattern five (continues)	85-90	0:33	8:14
Lesson 61/Quiz 61	Review of syllable patterns one, two, three, four, and five	91-94	8:15	42:29
Lesson 62/Quiz 62	Marking words / syllable patterns one, two, three, four, and five	91-94	42:30	58:06
Video CD Nineteen				
Lesson 63/Quiz 63	Syllable pattern six	95-101	0:32	42:36
Lesson 64/Quiz 64	Review of syllable patterns one, two, three, four, five, and six	102-105	42:37	58:04
Video CD Twenty				
Lesson 64/Quiz 64	Review of syllable patterns one, two, three, four, five, and six (continues)	102-105	0:27	02:43
Lesson 65/Quiz 65	Marking words / syllable patterns one, two, three, four, five, and six	102-104	02:44	17:54
Lesson 66 (There is no Quiz 66.)	Oral reading exercise / syllable patterns one, two, three, four, five, and six	102-105	17:55	58:56
Video CD Twenty-One				
Lesson 67/Quiz 67	Comprehensive Review	106-107	0:32	19:38
Lesson 68/Quiz 68	Syllable rule one	109	19:39	52:17
Lesson 69	Syllable rule one / marking words	109	52:18	59:27

We All Can Read: Video CD Edition Table of Contents Correlation Guide between Video CD Lessons and Pages in Blue Book		Page Guide	Begin Time	End Time
Video CD Twenty-Two				
Lesson 69	Syllable rule one / marking words (continues)	109	0:33	20:54
Lesson 70/Quiz 69	Syllable rule two	110	20:55	46:07
Lesson 71	Marking syllable rule two words	110	46:08	59:05
Video CD Twenty-Three				
Lesson 71	Marking syllable rule two words (continues)	110	0:29	4:28
Lesson 72/Quiz 70	Review of syllable rules one and two	111-113	4:29	23:10
Lesson 73/Quiz 71	Marking words / syllables rules one and two	111-113	23:11	50:08
Lesson 74	Oral reading / syllable rules one and two	111-113	50:09	59:10
Video CD Twenty-Four				
Lesson 74	Oral reading / syllable rules one and two (continues)	111-113	0:33	4:15
Lesson 75	Syllable rules one and two and consonant blends	112	4:16	16:22
Lesson 76	Marking words / syllable rules one and two and consonant blends	112	16:23	38:19
Lesson 77/Quiz 72	Syllable pattern seven	114-116	38:20	53:39
Lesson 78/Quiz 73	Marking words / syllable pattern seven	114-115	53:40	59:08
Video CD Twenty-Five				
Lesson 78/Quiz 73	Marking words / syllable pattern seven (continues)	114-115	0:33	18:24
Lesson 79	Syllable pattern seven / oral reading	114-116	18:25	22:21
Lesson 80/Quiz 74	Cumulative spelling review / two syllable words / syllable pattern four	117	22:22	33:38
Lesson 81	Cumulative marking review / two syllable words / syllable pattern four	117	33:39	48:35
Lesson 82/Quiz 75	Cumulative spelling review / two syllable words / syllable patterns five and six	118	48:36	59:25
Video CD Twenty-Six				
Lesson 83	Cumulative marking review / two syllable words / syllable patterns five and six	118	0:33	16:22
Lesson 84/Quiz 76	Cumulative spelling review / two syllable words / syllable patterns four, five, and six	119-122	16:23	27:28
Lesson 85	Cumulative marking review / two syllable words / syllable patterns four, five, and six	119-122	27:29	42:52
Lesson 86	Syllable pattern eight	123-125	42:53	57:50
Video CD Twenty-Seven				
Lesson 86	Syllable pattern eight (continues)	123-125	0:35	9:14
Lesson 87/Quiz 77	Syllable pattern eight / marking words	123-124	9:15	35:50
Lesson 88	Exceptions to syllable patterns one, two, and three / dictation	127	35:51	52:58
Lesson 89	Exceptions to syllable patterns one, two, and three/ marking words	127	52:59	59:02
Video CD Twenty-Eight				
Lesson 89	Exceptions to syllable patterns one, two, and three / marking words (continues)	127	0:36	12:46

We All Can Read: Video CD Edition Table of Contents Correlation Guide between Video CD Lessons and Pages in Blue Book	Page Guide	Begin Time	End Time
Video CD Thirty-Eight			
Intensive Spelling Program / Introduction	205-212	0:33	3:15
Lesson 117 Word List A / Words 1-25	214	3:16	30:00
Lesson 118/Quiz 102 Word List A / Words 26-50	214	30:01	46:30
Lesson 119 Word List A / Words 51-75	215	46:31	59:25
Video CD Thirty-Nine			
Lesson 120/Quiz 103 Word List A / Words 76-100	215	0:33	16:51
Lesson 121 Word List A / Words 101-125	216	16:52	29:00
Lesson 122/Quiz 104 Word List A / Words 126-150	216	29:01	44:57
Lesson 123 Word List A / Words 151-175	217	44:58	58:26
Video CD Forty			
Lesson 124/Quiz 105 Word List A / Words 176-200	217	0:33	14:26
Lesson 125 Word List A / Words 201-225	218	14:27	26:48
Lesson 126/Quiz 106 Word List A / Words 226-250	218	26:49	39:56
Lesson 127 Word List A / Words 251-275	219	39:57	51:21
Lesson 128/Quiz 107 Word List A / Words 276-300	219	51:22	1:00:14
Video CD Forty-One			
Lesson 128/Quiz 107 Word List A / Words 276-300 (continues)	219	0:32	7:49
Lesson 129 Word List A / Words 301-325	220	7:50	20:26
Lesson 130/Quiz 108 Word List A / Words 326-350	220	20:27	35:28
Lesson 131 Word List A / Words 351-375	221	35:29	47:56
Lesson 132/Quiz 109 Word List A / Words 376-400	221	47:57	1:00:51
Video CD Forty-Two			
Lesson 132/Quiz 109 Word List A / Words 376-400 (continues)	221	0:33	2:35
Lesson 133 Word List A / Words 401-425	222	2:36	14:56
Lesson 134/Quiz 110 Word List A / Words 426-450	222	14:57	28:49
Lesson 135 Word List A / Words 451-475	223	28:50	41:17
Lesson 136/Quiz 111 Word List A / Words 476-500	223	41:18	55:10
A Final Note		55:11	57:35